Microsoft

SharePoint Bible

A Comprehensive Handbook for Seamless Navigation, Enhanced Collaboration, Unrivaled Business Intelligence and Innovative Workflows

Jenny Pattyn

Copyright © 2024 **Jenny Pattyn**

All Rights Reserved

This book or parts thereof may not be reproduced in any form, stored in any retrieval system, or transmitted in any form by any means—electronic, mechanical, photocopy, recording, or otherwise—without prior written permission of the publisher, except as provided by United States of America copyright law and fair use.

Disclaimer and Terms of Use

The author and publisher of this book and the accompanying materials have used their best efforts in preparing this book. The author and publisher make no representation or warranties with respect to the accuracy, applicability, fitness, or completeness of the contents of this book. The information contained in this book is strictly for informational purposes. Therefore, if you wish to apply the ideas contained in this book, you are taking full responsibility for your actions.

Printed in the United States of America

TABLE OF CONTENTS

TABLE OF CONTENTS III

CHAPTER 1 1

INTRODUCTION TO SHAREPOINT 1

OVERVIEW OF SHAREPOINT 1
KEY FEATURES AND CAPABILITIES 1
DOCUMENT MANAGEMENT AND COLLABORATION 2
INTEGRATION WITH MICROSOFT 365 APPS 3
UNDERSTANDING SHAREPOINT SITES AND HIERARCHY 4
   Site Collections vs. Sites 4
   What is the difference between site collections and sites? 5
   Why create a site in SharePoint instead 5
   Why create a site collection in SharePoint instead 6
SHAREPOINT SITE TEMPLATES: TEAM SITES, COMMUNICATION SITES, AND MORE 7

CHAPTER 2 9

GETTING STARTED WITH SHAREPOINT 9

ACCESSING SHAREPOINT: WEB INTERFACE AND DESKTOP APPLICATIONS 9
   Accessing SharePoint via Web Browser 9
DISCOVER CONTENT WITH THE SHAREPOINT START PAGE 9
EXPLORING THE SHAREPOINT HOME PAGE 10
UNDERSTANDING DOCUMENT LIBRARIES, LISTS, AND SITE CONTENTS 11
UPLOADING AND MANAGING DOCUMENTS 12

CHAPTER 3 13

SHAREPOINT MOBILE ACCESS 13

ACCESSING SHAREPOINT ON MOBILE DEVICES 13
SHAREPOINT MOBILE BROWSER INTERFACE 13
LAUNCH A SHAREPOINT SITE AND EXPLORE IT 14
   Launch a Microsoft SharePoint website 14
   Browsing a SharePoint site 14
   Opening your OneDrive for Business document library 15
HOW TO SWITCH BETWEEN MOBILE AND FULL-SCREEN VIEW 15
   Toggle between the PC and mobile views. 15
   Change the view from PC to mobile 16
SHAREPOINT MOBILE APP INTERFACE 16
SHAREPOINT MOBILE APP: LOGIN SCREEN AND NEWS FEED INTERFACE 17
   The Search interface in the SharePoint App 17
   The Links Tab in the SharePoint Mobile App 18
SUPPORTING THE SHAREPOINT MOBILE APPS ONLINE AND ON-PREMISES 18

Common messages received by users 19
Is this network traffic from the SharePoint mobile app? 19

CHAPTER 4 20

COLLABORATION IN SHAREPOINT 20

DISCOVERING SHAREPOINT IN MICROSOFT TEAMS 20
Accessing SharePoint files in Teams 20
ADDING SHAREPOINT PAGES AND LISTS TO TEAMS 21
WORKING WITH SHAREPOINT TEAMS AND GROUPS 24
IN WHAT WAY DO THESE SERVICES WORK TOGETHER? 24
Groups and SharePoint 24
Teams and Groups 25
Teams and SharePoint 25
CREATING AND MANAGING SHAREPOINT TEAMS 25
Create a Microsoft Team from a SharePoint team site 25
SETTING UP DISCUSSION BOARDS FOR TEAM COMMUNICATION 27

CHAPTER 5 30

WORKING WITH LISTS AND LIBRARIES 30

UNDERSTANDING SHAREPOINT LIST 30
UNDERSTANDING SHAREPOINT LIBRARY 31
How are SharePoint Lists and Libraries Different? 31
CREATING AND CUSTOMIZING LISTS 31
Creating a List 31
CREATING A SHAREPOINT LIST FROM A TEMPLATE 32
SHAREPOINT LIST MANAGEMENT 34
Adding Columns to a List 34
Deleting Columns in a SharePoint List 35
INSERTING, EDITING, AND DELETING ITEMS IN A SHAREPOINT LIST 35
Inserting Items 35
Editing Items 36
Getting Rid of Items 36
ADDING ATTACHMENTS TO A SHAREPOINT LIST 36
Customize SharePoint List Views 37
SORTING AND FILTERING 38
GROUPING 38
Creating Custom Views 38
Conditional Formatting in List Views 39
MANAGING SHAREPOINT LIST PERMISSIONS 39
Understanding SharePoint List Permission Levels 39
GRANTING AND REVOKING SHAREPOINT LIST PERMISSIONS 40
METADATA AND CONTENT TYPES 40
Introduction to Metadata in SharePoint 40

What is managed metadata? 40
SharePoint Term Store - term set Department example 41
   Term Store - term set options for managing terms 41
   Term Store - term set management options 42
Why use metadata instead of folders 42
Why manage metadata? 43
   How to make applying metadata easier for everyone 43
Creating and Using Content Types for Document Management 45
   Purchase Order 46
   Invoice 46
   Receipt 46

CHAPTER 6 54

PERMISSIONS AND SECURITY IN SHAREPOINT 54

Managing SharePoint Online Security: A Team Effort 54
   Tenant settings 54
   Sharing settings 54
More external sharing settings 55
Site settings 55
SharePoint Groups 55
Active Directory (AD) Groups 56
Breaking permission inheritance 56
Site Sharing 56
   Sites not connected to Microsoft 365 groups 56
   Sites connected to Microsoft 365 groups 57
   Change how members can share 58
Access Requests 58
Other Security Features To Consider 59
   Multi-Factor Authentication (MFA) 59
   Security and Compliance 59
   Devices Accessing SharePoint Data 59
SharePoint Permissions 60
   SharePoint Permission Levels 60
   Copy existing Permission Level 62
   Managing Permissions in SharePoint Online 62
How Do I Manage SharePoint Online Permissions? 62
   Folder level permissions in SharePoint Online 63
   How to check user Permissions in SharePoint Online? 64
Anonymous Access in SharePoint Online 65
Best Practices for Security and Compliance 66
   Data Loss Prevention (DLP) in SharePoint 66
   Microsoft Purview Data Loss Prevention 66
   SharePoint and Data Loss Prevention 66

  SharePoint DLP Policies 66
  Sensitive Information in SharePoint 66
  Creating DLP Policies 67
 POLICY TIPS AND ALERTS 67
  Policy Tips 68

CHAPTER 7 69

CUSTOMIZING SHAREPOINT WITH APPS 69

 INTRODUCING SHAREPOINT APPS 69
  Adding Apps to Your Site 70
 REQUEST AN APP FROM THE SHAREPOINT STORE 71
 ACCESSING APP SETTINGS 72
 CONFIGURING THE GENERAL SETTINGS 74
  Changing the title, description, and navigation 74
  Versioning settings 74
 ADVANCED SETTINGS 76
 VALIDATION SETTINGS 79
  Audience targeting settings 80
  Rating settings 80
  Form settings 81

CHAPTER 8 82

UNDERSTANDING SHAREPOINT SITES 82

 ACCESSING SHAREPOINT SITES IN MICROSOFT 365 82
  Click the SharePoint site you want to open. 83
 EXPLORING THE SHAREPOINT TEAM SITE 83
 FINDING YOUR WAY AROUND 84
 UPLOADING DOCUMENTS 85
 SHARING YOUR TEAM SITE 85
  Share your site from your web browser 85
  Share your site from the SharePoint Mobile App 87
 CREATING A SHAREPOINT SITE 87
  Create a subsite from your web browser 87
  Create a site from the SharePoint Mobile App 89
 GROUPING SITES WITH HUB SITES 89

CHAPTER 9 90

BUSINESS INTELLIGENCE WITH SHAREPOINT 90

 LEARNING ABOUT THE CORE FEATURES 90
  Excel Services 90
  PerformancePoint 90
  Visio Services 91

PowerPivot *91*
Microsoft Power BI *91*
SQL SERVER REPORTING SERVICES (SSRS) 91
Business Intelligence Center *92*
THE CENTER PANEL – EXAMPLES AND LINKS TO HELPFUL INFORMATION 93
Monitor Key Performance *93*
Build and Share Reports *94*
Create Dashboards *94*
Dashboard Library *94*
Data Connections library *95*
Documents Library *95*
PERFORMANCEPOINT CONTENT LIST 95
CREATE A NEW BUSINESS INTELLIGENCE SITE 96

CHAPTER 10 97

ADVANCED DOCUMENT MANAGEMENT 97

WHAT CAN YOU DO WITH A DOCUMENT SET? 97
Enable Document Sets for a site collection *98*
Create a new Document Set content type *98*
Configure or customize a Document Set content type *99*
CONTENT ORGANIZER 100
What can the Content Organizer do? *100*
Activate the Content Organizer feature on a site *101*
Configure the Content Organizer *102*
INFORMATION RIGHTS MANAGEMENT (IRM) 103
How IRM can help protect content *103*
How IRM cannot help protect content *104*
Turn on IRM service using the SharePoint admin center *104*
IRM-enable SharePoint document libraries and lists *104*
Next steps *105*
Applying IRM to Document Libraries and Lists *105*
Administrator preparations before applying IRM *105*
Apply IRM to a list or library *106*
DOCUMENT RETENTION 107

CHAPTER 11 110

RECORDS MANAGEMENT AND ARCHIVING 110

OVERVIEW OF RECORDS MANAGEMENT PLANNING 111
Overview of SharePoint Record Centers *112*
HOW TO CONFIGURE THE RECORD CENTER ARCHIVING MECHANISM IN SHAREPOINT ONLINE? 112

CHAPTER 12 114

FINDING WHAT YOU NEED WITH SEARCH 114

- Understanding How SharePoint Search Works 114
- Searching for Content 114
  - Searching for a string using quotation marks 115
  - Wildcard searches 115
- Including and excluding terms 115
- Building compound search queries using Boolean operators 116
- Finding terms in proximity 116
- Same meaning, different terms 117
- Viewing and Refining Search Results 117
- Making Search Your Users' Best Friend 118
- Removing Content from Search Results 122

CHAPTER 13 123

SHAREPOINT FOR ENTERPRISE SOLUTIONS 123

- What not to do 123
- How you did this in the past 123
- Use a phased roll-out plan and telemetry 124
- Successful Intranet Portal with SharePoint 124
  - Why should companies adopt a SharePoint Intranet Portal? 125
- SharePoint Intranet Development 125
  - SharePoint Intranet for Enterprise Collaboration 126
- Intranet Management 126

CHAPTER 14 127

DISASTER RECOVERY AND BACKUP STRATEGIES 127

- Understanding SharePoint Backup 127
- Different Methods to Protect Your SharePoint Data 127
- Full Farm Backup 127
- Granular Backup 128
- Backup via PowerShell 128
- Third-Party Backup Solutions 129
  - Best Practices for SharePoint Backup 129
  - Determine Backup Frequency 129
  - Store Backups Securely 130
- Test Backup and Restore Processes 130
- Backup SharePoint Configuration 130
  - Restoring SharePoint from Backup 131
  - Restore from Full Farm Backup 131
  - Restore from Granular Backup 132
  - Restore via PowerShell 132
  - Restore Using Third-Party Backup Solutions 132

CHAPTER 15 134

CREATING WORKFLOWS WITH MICROSOFT POWER AUTOMATE **134**

UNDERSTANDING WORKFLOW 134
INTRODUCING MICROSOFT POWER AUTOMATE 134
   Access Microsoft Power Automate *134*
GETTING FAMILIAR WITH POWER AUTOMATE 135
BUILDING YOUR FIRST FLOW 137
USING THE TRADITIONAL SHAREPOINT-ONLY WORKFLOW 139

CHAPTER 16 .... **141**

BUILDING BUSINESS APPS WITH POWER APPS **141**

INTRODUCING POWER APPS 141
   Signing into Power Apps *141*
   Getting familiar with Power Apps *141*
BUILDING YOUR FIRST POWER APP 143
SHARING YOUR POWER APP 146
USING POWER APPS ON YOUR MOBILE DEVICE 146
EMBEDDING A POWER APP WITHIN A SHAREPOINT PAGE 146
VIEWING SHAREPOINT SITES IN A WEB BROWSER ON A MOBILE DEVICE 147
CREATING VIEWS FOR SMALL SCREENS 147
TARGETING DEVICES USING CHANNELS 148

CHAPTER 17 .... **149**

REALIZING YOU ARE A SHAREPOINT ADMINISTRATOR **149**

CHANGING YOUR SITE'S BASIC INFORMATION 149
FINDING SITE SETTINGS 149
DIGGING INTO SITE SETTINGS 150
   Look and Feel *150*
SITE ACTIONS 152
   Site Collection Administration *153*
MICROSOFT SEARCH 153
WEB DESIGNER GALLERIES 153
SITE ADMINISTRATION 155
   Search *156*
CONCLUSION 157

INDEX **158**

CHAPTER 1
INTRODUCTION TO SHAREPOINT

Overview of SharePoint

SharePoint is one of the key tools in the Microsoft 365 suite. Originally released in 2003, its primary objective was to reorganize on-premises document storage solutions for individuals and companies by transferring them to the Microsoft cloud. Any user, from any device, could **save, sort, share, and access their valuable documents and information in this way**. An Internet connection is all that is needed. Nonetheless, with continuous updates, Microsoft has improved the file storage system and expanded SharePoint's function, transforming it into a platform for managing content. Put simply, SharePoint has emerged as a top choice among current technologies for creating **private sites**. SharePoint isn't comparable to other systems like WordPress or Umbraco; the portals it enables are designed for a big audience, but one that isn't completely controllable. The objective is to provide organizations and businesses with the necessary tools to create user-friendly websites and extranets that can bring together diverse audiences in a centralized location. To sum up, SharePoint is a versatile platform that can facilitate the digitization of business operations and communication.

Key Features and Capabilities

- **Co-authoring on SharePoint Pages and News:** A new collaboration dimension will be revealed where many writers can work concurrently on a SharePoint page or news story.
- **Improvements to the Document Library Version History**: New version restrictions are being implemented to lessen the storage load imposed by versions of low-value files. Administrators will have the option to choose between an automated mode that uses age and restore likelihood to intelligently expire versions or a manual mode that allows them to define version expiry and count restrictions depending on time.
- **Microsoft Lists's Forms Experience**: A more streamlined, user-friendly design for forms that can be filled out easily on any device and shared makes data collection simpler. Once you submit your replies, they will appear on your list immediately.

- **Opening Non-Office Files in Desktop Apps via OneDrive and SharePoint:** Users will soon be able to open non-Office files in desktop apps directly from OneDrive and SharePoint web, with any changes syncing back seamlessly.
- **Centralized Branding Management:** Introducing new branding and administration features to maintain branding uniformity across numerous sites and pages: centralized branding management.
- **Resource-Specific Consent:** Introducing **new.Selected** permissions and APIs, will enable programs to be granted permissions at all levels where inheritance can be broken.
- **Application Site Creation with Reduced Permissions:** Using the new scope, **Sites.create.All,** apps will be able to build new site collections without needing access to current material. Provisioning situations with decreased tenant permissions is made easier with this functionality.

Lastly, a hopeful picture is painted by SharePoint 2024, which will deliver compelling partnerships with GitHub, integration of Copilot AI, and improved admin experiences. These upgrades highlight Microsoft's continuous dedication to improving SharePoint's features, giving it an even stronger and easier-to-use platform.

Document Management and Collaboration

Microsoft's SharePoint is a strong platform with excellent features for managing documents and collaborating with others. For several reasons, including but not limited to improved teamwork, document sharing, and version control, it has found widespread use in commercial and nonprofit organizations. **SharePoint's document management and collaboration functions are thoroughly described here:**

1. **Document Libraries:** SharePoint organizes documents into libraries, which are like folders for storing files. Each library can have its settings, permissions, and metadata.
2. **Version Control:** SharePoint automatically tracks versions of documents, allowing users to view previous versions, restore older versions, and track changes made by different users.
3. **Check-In/Check-Out:** Users can check out documents to prevent others from editing them simultaneously. This helps in avoiding conflicts and ensures that only one person can make changes at a time.
4. **Document Metadata:** SharePoint allows you to add metadata to documents, such as tags, categories, and properties, making it easier to categorize, search, and filter documents.
5. **Document Collaboration:** SharePoint supports real-time collaboration on documents. Multiple users can work on the same document simultaneously, seeing each other's changes in real-time.
6. **Co-Authoring:** SharePoint enables co-authoring, where multiple users can edit a document simultaneously without locking it for other users. This promotes collaboration and improves productivity.

7. **Integration with Microsoft Office:** SharePoint integrates seamlessly with Microsoft Office applications like Word, Excel, and PowerPoint, allowing users to open, edit, and save documents directly from these applications to SharePoint libraries.
8. **Permissions and Access Control:** SharePoint provides granular control over permissions, allowing administrators to define who can view, edit, delete, or share documents. This ensures data security and compliance with organizational policies.
9. **Document Approval Workflows:** SharePoint supports customizable approval workflows for documents. Users can submit documents for approval, and designated approvers can review, approve, or reject them, with notifications at each stage of the process.
10. **Document Search:** SharePoint's powerful search capabilities enable users to quickly find documents based on keywords, metadata, or other criteria. Advanced search features like filters, sorting, and refinement help in locating specific documents within large repositories.
11. **Mobile Accessibility:** SharePoint is accessible on mobile devices through dedicated apps, allowing users to access, view, edit, and collaborate on documents from anywhere, enhancing flexibility and productivity.
12. **Integration with External Systems:** SharePoint can be integrated with external systems and third-party applications, enabling seamless data exchange and enhancing the overall document management and collaboration experience.

All things considered, SharePoint's extensive feature set for managing documents and collaborating makes it an invaluable tool for teams and enterprises looking to increase efficiency, communication, and output.

Integration with Microsoft 365 Apps

- **Microsoft Teams:** SharePoint and Microsoft Teams work hand in hand, so users may access SharePoint files from inside Teams channels. Documents saved in SharePoint libraries can be edited in real-time by Teams users, who can then share the updated version with the rest of the team.
- **Microsoft Office Integration**: SharePoint works hand in hand with other Microsoft Office products including Word, Excel, PowerPoint, and OneNote. Documents can be opened, edited, and saved to SharePoint libraries straight from these apps. Updates made to documents are promptly reflected in SharePoint.
- **Outlook Integration**: Users can effortlessly exchange documents with colleagues by attaching SharePoint files straight to Outlook emails. The files can be accessed by recipients either by clicking on the links in the email or by going to SharePoint.
- **Microsoft Power Platform**: The Microsoft Power Platform, which includes Power Apps and Power Automate (formerly known as Microsoft Flow), is integrated with SharePoint. Incorporating SharePoint data and features into user-made applications, process automation, and business solution development is now possible thanks to this connectivity.
- **Microsoft OneDrive for Business**: SharePoint and OneDrive for Business work hand in hand to provide customers with a private cloud storage area where they can save and

share data. Facilitating frictionless communication, files saved in OneDrive can be readily shared and viewed from SharePoint.
- ❖ **Microsoft Office Online**: With SharePoint Online's connection with Microsoft Office Online, users can access and edit Word, Excel, PowerPoint, and OneNote documents without downloading or installing any desktop software. All modifications are promptly sent to SharePoint.
- ❖ **Microsoft Planner**: One of the task management tools in Microsoft 365, SharePoint interfaces with it. Users can use Planner boards to create and manage tasks associated with SharePoint documents, monitor their progress, and engage with their teammates.
- ❖ **Yammer**: This is an enterprise social networking tool developed by Microsoft and integrated with SharePoint. Yammer is a social and interactive platform where users can share SharePoint material, have ideas and discussions, and work together with coworkers.

Understanding SharePoint Sites and Hierarchy
Site Collections vs. Sites

Let's start by defining these two terms:

- ❖ **A SharePoint site**: A digital repository housing a variety of files and documents. It can include one or more pages and other web components such as a calendar, to-do list, document library, etc.
- ❖ **SharePoint site collection**: A group of SharePoint sites—the name says it all. There is one main site and many subsites that can be created below it.

The current standard for making a site (home button > create a site) really creates a collection of sites.

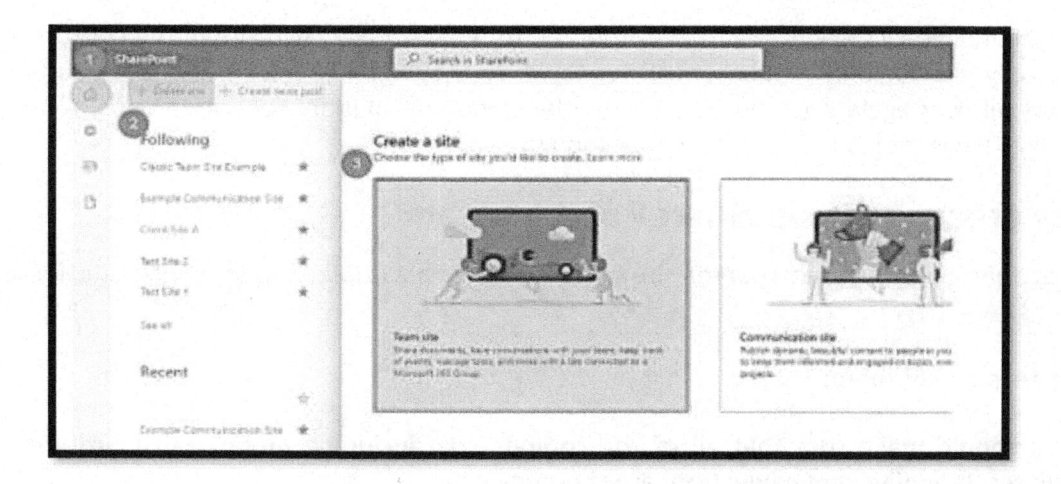

After you create a site in this manner, the first site you see is the collection's root site. You will notice an option to build subsites if you go to the "**Site contents**" page.

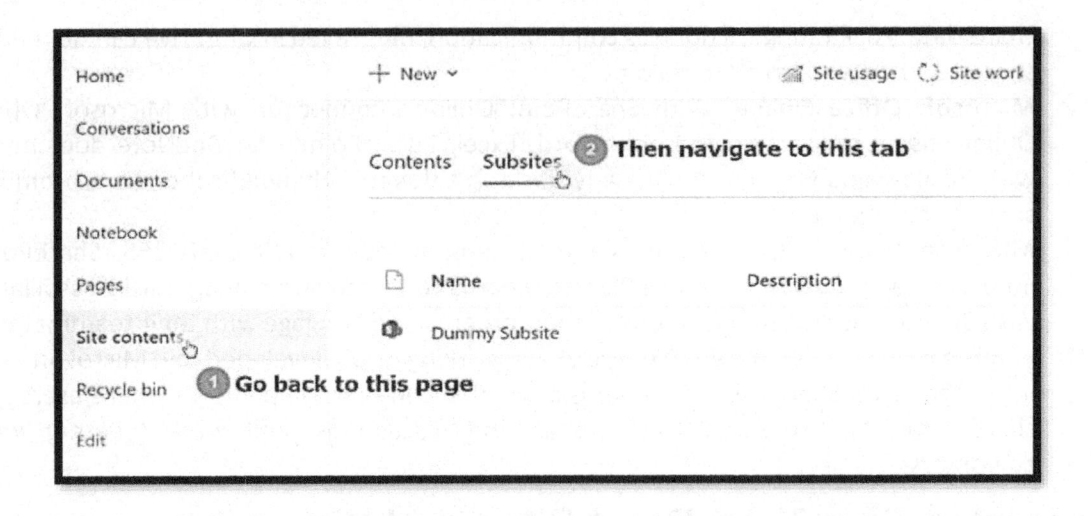

[Screenshot showing SharePoint site navigation with annotations: "① Go back to this page" pointing to Site contents in left navigation, and "② Then navigate to this tab" pointing to the Subsites tab. The screenshot displays Home, Conversations, Documents, Notebook, Pages, Site contents, Recycle bin, Edit in the left sidebar, and shows Contents/Subsites tabs with a "Dummy Subsite" listed.]

In other words, the standard method of constructing a site is more like creating a site collection, with the root site serving as its front end. The root site of a site collection and its subsites are technically sites. A subsite must be created to avoid the need for a site collection while building a site. Generally speaking, this is because the idea of sites vs. site collections is quite antiquated, dating back to before the contemporary experience was introduced in 2016.

What is the difference between site collections and sites?

Regarding the true distinctions, there aren't many since sites make up collections.

Every part of a site collection is distinct from the others, including the metadata, security groups, templates, branding, and navigation.

These characteristics are passed down from the root site to any child site in the collection. But that's only true for the specific set of sites to which they belong. This necessitates starting the process all over again if you want to apply the same information, security groups, templates, branding, navigation, etc. to another collection of sites.

Why create a site in SharePoint instead

Rather than beginning yet another site collection, it is advisable to just build a site for a few reasons.

Here are some of them:

1. You should make sure that all of the components, including metadata, security groups, templates, branding, and navigation, are the same.
- If that's the case, then establishing a subsite inside an existing site collection is the superior and more efficient option.

5

- When compared to beginning from square one, this will result in significant time savings. No items from other collections on the site may be copied and pasted.
- This is also true when you have a template site and would want all of your other sites to have the same design and layout.

2. You belong to a small organization with only a few departments and people.
- Keeping track of SharePoint site collections may be challenging. A site is preferable to hiring extra employees to oversee the whole intranet unless you need to.
- Creating an intranet without first considering all of your needs is a bad idea. The creation of those sites under a site collection will be sufficient if you simply plan to construct a few sites.

Why create a site collection in SharePoint instead

Instead of building a new site inside an existing site collection, a new site collection could be the preferable choice in certain cases. **Here are some of them:**

1. You belong to a large organization with numerous departments and multiple business units.
- It is logical to create a site collection for each of your organization's autonomous business units if they perform distinct responsibilities.
- If you anticipate that your whole firm will generate a substantial amount of information and documents, then a site collection would be the preferable option.
- Before creating any site collections, ensure that you are aware that metadata and security groups must be recreated.

2. You create documents and information that are hundreds of gigabytes in size.
- It makes sense to devote dedicated server resources and storage if your firm creates a large amount of content. This is connected to the previous point.
- There is an easy method to adjust the storage limit in the contemporary experience, even though the server resource and storage quota options are deprecated (albeit they are still on classic sites).

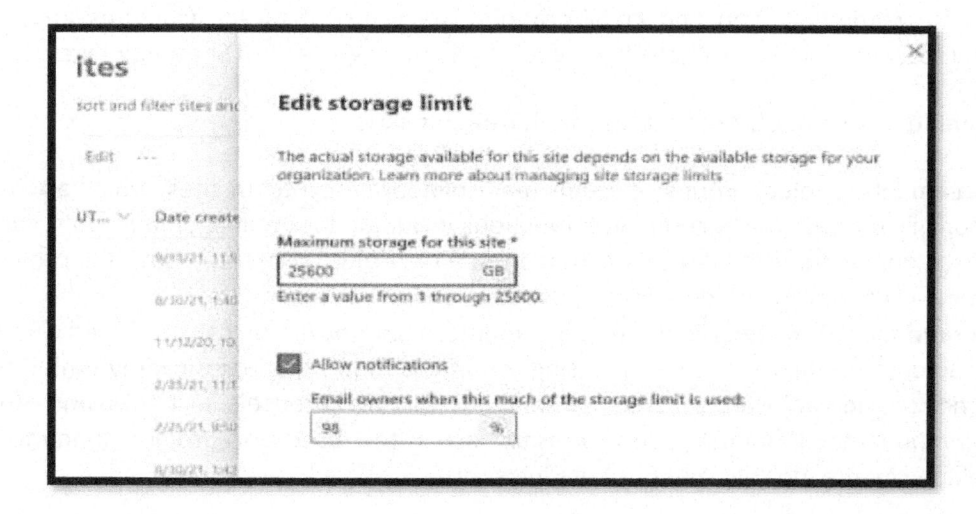

3. You must collaborate with other parties by sharing content.

- Although it may seem apparent to some, you must establish a separate collection of sites (or "site" in modern experience) for external sharing.
- Just in case you went ahead and allowed the option to let any user share outside, this is an extra safeguard.
- One beneficial aspect of the tenant is that it is possible to restrict external sharing to just certain site collections.

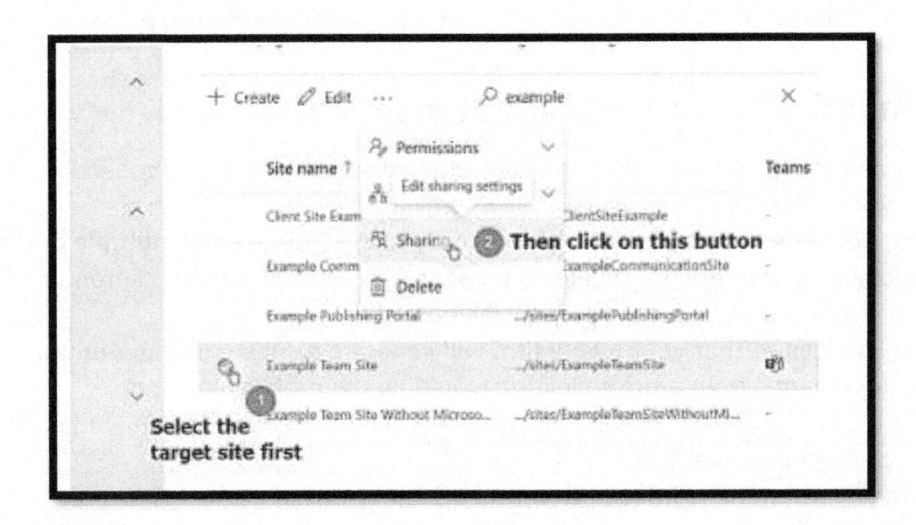

SharePoint Site Templates: Team Sites, Communication Sites, and more

A range of site templates are available in SharePoint to accommodate various organizational demands for communication and collaboration. The pre-configured structures and features offered by these templates facilitate the creation and management of SharePoint sites for users.

Let's examine a few popular templates for SharePoint sites:

- ❖ **Team Site**: Project groups or teams may collaborate on team sites, which are intended for this purpose. They come with functions including task management tools, calendars, lists, and document libraries. Within a team or project context, team sites provide real-time collaboration on documents, debates, and announcements.
- ❖ **Communication Site**: News, announcements, and information can be shared with a wider audience inside the company by using communication sites. To efficiently exhibit content, they provide adjustable layouts, news feeds, picture carousels, fast links, and other web components. Communication websites are often used for project announcements, departmental portals, and business intranets.

- ❖ **Document Center**: Managing documents, presentations, and other files is the main purpose of the Document Center template. Document processes, content kinds, metadata, and document libraries with versioning are some of its characteristics. Document centers are used for organizing and managing documents centrally.
- ❖ **Blog Site**: With SharePoint, users may establish and maintain blogs by using the Blog site template. It has attributes like categories, archives, blog entries, and comments. Users may share information, updates, and ideas with others by using blog sites, either internally or externally.
- ❖ **Project Site**: Project sites are designed specifically for task and project management. These consist of task boards, timetables, project calendars, document libraries, and lists of projects. Teams may work together on projects, monitor their progress, and exchange documents and information about the project by using project sites.
- ❖ **Community Site**: Community sites are made to encourage participation and teamwork among individuals within a community or group. They consist of social features, event calendars, user profiles, discussion boards, and forums. Community sites facilitate intra organizational networking, conversations, and knowledge exchange.
- ❖ **Enterprise Wiki**: Wiki pages with rich material, photos, links, and formatting may be created and managed by users using the Enterprise Wiki template. It may be used to build knowledge bases, repositories for documentation, and platforms for exchanging information. Wikis for businesses allow for collaborative editing and content production.
- ❖ **Blank Site**: With the help of the Blank site template, users can design bespoke SharePoint sites that meet their unique needs. It allows for flexibility in the look, content, and structure of the website, making it appropriate for a wide range of use cases.

These are some of the most popular templates for SharePoint sites that are accessible to users; each one is designed to meet certain objectives related to information management, communication, and collaboration inside businesses. Depending on their goals, the makeup of their team and the features they want, users can choose the right template.

CHAPTER 2
GETTING STARTED WITH SHAREPOINT

Accessing SharePoint: Web Interface and Desktop Applications

Accessing SharePoint via Web Browser

Accessing SharePoint using an internet browser is a practical method of getting to your sites and taking use of the many information and collaboration tools it provides. All of the main online browsers, including Internet Explorer, Google Chrome, and Mozilla Firefox, are compatible with SharePoint design. Let's look at how to use various browsers to access SharePoint:

For Internet Explorer:

1. Open Internet Explorer.
2. Enter your SharePoint site's URL in the address bar (e.g., "https://yoursharepointsite.com") and press Enter.
3. If prompted, provide your login credentials (username and password) to gain access to SharePoint.

For Google Chrome:
1. Launch Google Chrome.
2. Type the URL of your SharePoint site into the address bar and press Enter.
3. If necessary, enter your login information to log in to SharePoint.

For Mozilla Firefox:
1. Open Mozilla Firefox.
2. Enter the URL of your SharePoint site in the address bar and press Enter.
3. If authentication is required, input your username and password to sign in to SharePoint.

After successfully logging in, you'll be able to utilize all the tools and content provided on your SharePoint site, enhancing your collaborative efforts and productivity.

Discover content with the SharePoint start page

You can quickly locate and access SharePoint sites and portals inside your company by using the SharePoint start page. In addition, news from websites you follow recommended websites, and, if you use SharePoint in Microsoft 365, news from websites you often visit together with additional news suggested by the Microsoft Graph, will be available to you. See the section what you'll see on the SharePoint Microsoft 365 start page below to learn more about the frequent sites, recommended sites, news from sites, and other aspects of the SharePoint start page.

Notes:

- ❖ The SharePoint start page now has a different appearance.
- ❖ The SharePoint start page is now known as the SharePoint home page in Microsoft 365. You can create a team or communication site (video) if your administrator has granted permission to do so. Additionally from the SharePoint start page. A news post can also be made using SharePoint Online. To locate other websites, data, or individuals inside your company, use search.

To see the Microsoft 365 start page for SharePoint, go to:

- ❖ Open Microsoft 365 and log in.
- ❖ Choose the **app launcher icon** located in the upper left corner of the page, and then choose SharePoint.

Exploring the SharePoint Home Page

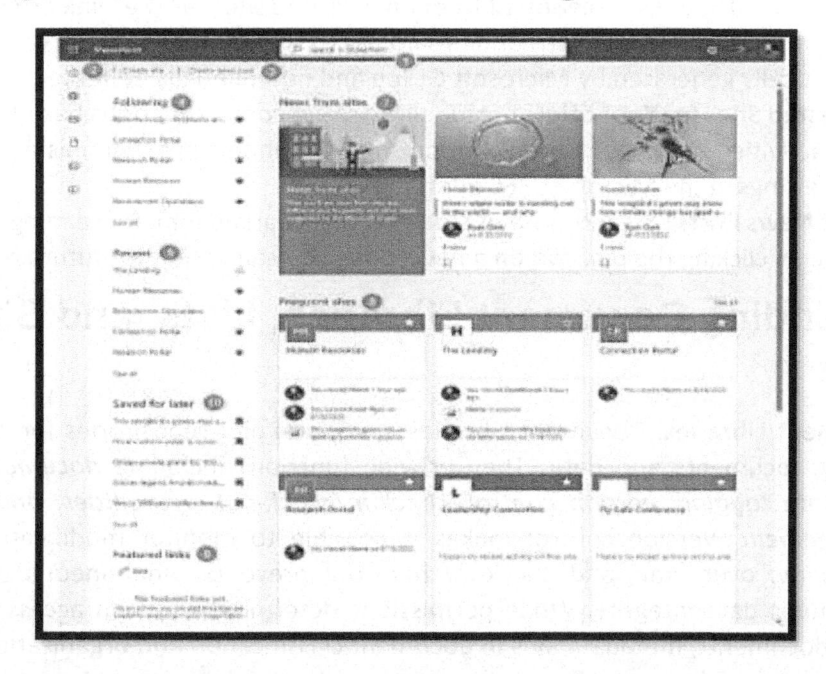

- ❖ The **search functionality** on your start page simplifies the process of locating recently accessed files and websites. It also enables you to search for other group members, as well as external websites and files. Utilizing the search tool on the start page aggregates all pertinent search results from OneDrive and other sources into a unified location.
- ❖ The **site creation feature**, contingent upon supervisor permissions, offers the ability to create a new site. This feature presents various options prompting you to choose the type of site you wish to create, such as a current conversation site or a team site.

- Adjacent to the site creation button, you'll find the **Post Creation Capability**, the option to write new news posts. A valuable resource for sharing project or team updates. As this action occurs directly from the home page, you'll need to specify the site on which you intend to post the news.
- The "**Sites You're Following**" section conveniently displays all sites you've opted to follow, ensuring easy accessibility. To follow a site, simply click the star icon on the home page.
- "**Your Recent Sites**" provides a list of recently visited sites. Selecting the "see all" link directs you to a comprehensive list of these sites.
- "**Featured Links**" highlights significant links to sites and portals curated by your organization. Microsoft 365 manager permissions allow for the personalization of these links.
- "**Latest Site News**" showcases recent updates from sites you follow or frequently visit, including selected news posts facilitated by the Office Graph. For an overview of numerous news posts, a "see all" link is available to view the most recent 100 posts.
- "**Frequently Visited Sites**" displays sites you frequent, along with recent activity reports for each site. If your list exceeds 12 frequently visited sites, a "see" link provides access to a complete list. This feature streamlines access to SharePoint sites that you regularly use, automatically generated by Microsoft Graph and not manually editable.
- "**Suggested Sites for You**" offers personalized site recommendations based on your Office Graph activities, contingent upon correct Office Graph settings. Administrators can adjust these settings in the Microsoft 365 admin center.
- "**Saved News Posts**" organizes news stories you've marked for later reading in a dedicated section. By clicking the pin icon on a news post, you can save it for future reference.

Understanding Document Libraries, Lists, and Site Contents

- **Document Libraries**: Document Libraries are SharePoint repositories for managing and storing documents and data. They provide functions including *document processes, metadata tagging, version control, check-in/check-out capabilities, and permissions management*. Version control makes it possible to monitor modifications made to documents over time, and check-in/check-out prevents simultaneous editing, which guarantees data integrity. While permissions determine who can access, change, and share documents, metadata aids in document classification and organization. Document workflows expedite procedures such as cooperation and document approval.
- **Lists**: Structured data may be managed and stored in a tabular fashion using lists in SharePoint. Users may build columns with various data kinds (text, numbers, dates, etc.) because of their customizable nature. Lists can be used for keeping track of chores, organizing contacts, maintaining inventory information, and constructing personalized forms, among other things. They include features like grouping, filtering, and sorting to effectively organize and analyze data.
- **Site Contents**: A consolidated view of all the lists, libraries, and applications housed inside a SharePoint site is offered by Site Contents in SharePoint. It functions as a dashboard

from which users can access and control any piece of material and program connected to the website. Links to subsites, lists, document libraries, and installed applications are included in the site contents. It facilitates efficient content management and navigation inside the site's hierarchy for users.

Uploading and Managing Documents

- ❖ To start, navigate to the specific SharePoint site where you intend to upload the file.
- ❖ Next, locate the **"Upload"** option, typically positioned near the top of the page.
- ❖ Click on the **"Upload"** link or button to initiate the file upload process, opening the upload box.
- ❖ In the upload box, click **"Browse"** to find and select the file on your computer that you want to share. Once chosen, click **"Open**."
- ❖ Optionally, you can add details about the file, such as a title or description, within the upload box.
- ❖ Once all necessary fields are filled, click the **"Upload"** button to start uploading the file.
- ❖ Monitor the upload progress through a progress bar, which indicates the status based on file size and internet speed.
- ❖ Upon completion, you'll receive a confirmation message or alert verifying the successful upload of the file.

CHAPTER 3
SHAREPOINT MOBILE ACCESS

Accessing SharePoint on Mobile Devices

To keep in contact with your colleagues and the office, use your mobile phone. You can download the SharePoint app for Apple iOS or Android to access your SharePoint site without using a web browser.

Utilize your tablet or mobile device to:
- ❖ **Locate SharePoint sites**. This will provide a list of websites that you have been visiting or that the administrators have informed you about using Microsoft SharePoint Online.
- ❖ **Changing site views**: You can see certain of your sites and libraries in SharePoint Online by alternating between the full-screen (also known as the PC view) and mobile views. For faster performance, it is recommended to utilize the PC View, particularly when customizing the CSS on your websites.
- ❖ **Document Management**: Check through the most recent documents that have been shared with you, such as Microsoft Word, Excel, PowerPoint, or PDF, then read and share them inside SharePoint. Additionally, you can see the documents you are viewing on Microsoft SharePoint Online.
- ❖ **Navigation**: To go between websites or from one to Microsoft OneDrive for Business, use the menus.

Let's examine the functionality of SharePoint Online on a mobile browser and a mobile application:

SharePoint Mobile Browser Interface

Launch a SharePoint site and explore it

Launch a Microsoft SharePoint website

- ❖ Open the internet browser on your phone.
- ❖ Enter the URL for SharePoint Online into the address bar. For example, if using mydock365 SharePoint as a reference, replace "mydock365" with your domain name in the URL.
- ❖ Log in using your work or school account credentials.
- ❖ If necessary, tap on the down arrow to reveal additional options, then click on "Go" located in the bottom left area of the screen.
- ❖ From the list of tiles that allow navigation, select "Sites" to access SharePoint sites and content.

A list of SharePoint sites will appear to you, divided into two groups: sites I'm monitoring and sites that have received promotion. The websites that I follow are more akin to a list of every website you visit.

Browsing a SharePoint site

- ❖ From the **Sites I'm following or Promoted sites** on the Sites page, choose the one you want to visit. Documents and lists are stored in apps, and any subsites are stored in subsites.

By glancing at the name of the view at the top of the page, you can determine which website you are now seeing.

14

- To open the OneNote notebook for a site, click on the Site Assets tile.
- To see the file on your website, choose the document library that contains it.

Opening your OneDrive for Business document library

- In the lower-left corner of the screen, touch Go and choose OneDrive if you are currently signed in to a SharePoint site on your PC. The OneDrive for Business app ought to launch.
- **Open the web browser on your application and follow these instructions if you haven't previously signed in to a SharePoint site:**
  - In the address bar, type the SharePoint Online website address (URL). Consider the following URL: **http://mydock365.sharepoint.com**. Your URL will include your domain name instead of Contoso.
  - Log in using your work or school account (joe@mydock365.onmicrosoft.com, for example).
  - Press the Play button in the lower-left corner of the screen. It's conceivable that to see the Go to button, you must press the down arrow.
  - Select OneDrive from the tile list.

How to switch between mobile and full-screen view

You can access the full-size view on your PC or phone for your SharePoint sites as well as the OneDrive for Business library.

Toggle between the PC and mobile views.

- On a site or library, choose the "More" option located in the lower right corner.
- Select "**Switch to PC view**."

15

Change the view from PC to mobile

1. Navigate to the SharePoint website and choose **Settings** from the menu in the top right corner of the page.
    ❖ You may not see the setting if you are using a full-screen view. Click the Focus on Content button located next to Edit in the upper right corner of your screen.
2. Select "**Mobile view**" from the option under **Tools**.

SharePoint Mobile App Interface

Is entering a URL every time you want to access SharePoint becoming old for you? You can access your intranet with the press of a button with the SharePoint app. Sales teams who are always on the go will find SharePoint particularly useful since it allows them to keep track of paperwork, team sites, business platforms, and other users who collaborate. On your SharePoint Team Sites, you may see and edit the documents, as well as view site activity and easily access the most current or frequently used lists. Accessing your SharePoint Online account is mandatory. Multiple accounts can be added and switched between with ease.

Important: Your business needs an active Office 365 subscription that includes SharePoint Online for this to function.

SharePoint Mobile App: Login Screen and News Feed Interface

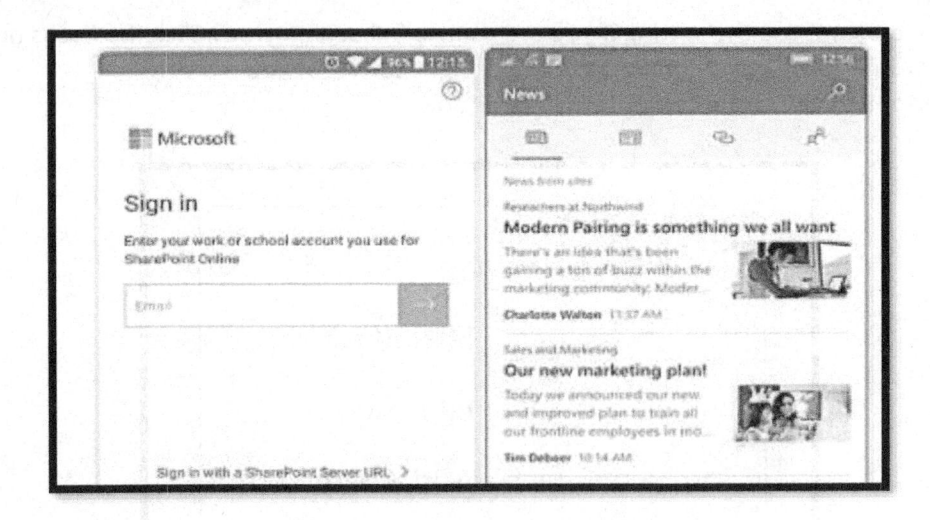

The Search interface in the SharePoint App

As shown above, the mobile app has **Enterprise Search**, which sorts the results into files, sites, and individuals.

The Links Tab in the SharePoint Mobile App

You can see the Links tab in the image. Your business advertising connections can be found here. Employees may access this via their SharePoint Administrator, and the links provided will lead you to the corporate sites and tools that interest you.

Supporting the SharePoint mobile apps online and on-premises

Your SharePoint users can access their files and data from anywhere with the SharePoint mobile app, which is compatible with iOS, Android, and Windows Mobile.

You should be familiar with these guidelines if you manage an on-premises SharePoint Server farm. With the SharePoint mobile app, you can do the following:

- ❖ Access and edit your SharePoint sites in Microsoft 365
- ❖ When connected to a corporate network, the app is most effective for users working on intranet sites. Whether you're using SharePoint on-premises or on a mobile device running iOS or Android, this remains true.

Common messages received by users

You or your users may be able to view details on the SSL/TLS certificate type and login method used while using the SharePoint mobile app. Users and supervisors are informed about permitted methods to join SharePoint with these notifications. **A few of the most common terms and their definitions are as follows:**

- ❖ **The app is incompatible with the SharePoint Server's unverified SSL certificate**. Self-signed certificates or certificates issued by an internal Certificate Authority (CA) cannot be used by the SharePoint mobile app. Your SharePoint online applications may be made safe using an SSL or TLS certificate from a public Certificate Authority.
- ❖ **This app does not yet support basic authentication, which is used by SharePoint Server**. If you prefer Forms-based authentication or NTLM security, you can utilize these with the SharePoint mobile app.

Is this network traffic from the SharePoint mobile app?

When SharePoint Server 2016 (on-premises) is connected to iOS and Android devices, administrators may see unusual data on their network monitors. Internet users may see inquiry and question-response traffic coming to and from sites such as *bl3301-g.1drv.com, bn2.vortex.data.microsoft.com.akadns.net, and even weu-breeziest-in.cloudapp.net*. The purpose of these calls is to collect data and provide tracking services. Analytics purposes make use of telemetry data to track how Microsoft 365 users interact with the service and to obtain a sense of the service's dependability. Lots of the other URLs will have Microsoft in the domain name, such *bl3301-g.1drv.com*, which is OneDrive. Any unusual data on the network should be reported to the administrators so that they can investigate. Before proceeding, ensure that you are aware that the SharePoint mobile app's data gathering and tracking services cannot be disabled. Checking the Privacy Statements can assist you in determining whether the SharePoint mobile app is suitable for your company.

CHAPTER 4
COLLABORATION IN SHAREPOINT

Discovering SharePoint in Microsoft Teams

A state-of-the-art SharePoint Team site is automatically linked with each Microsoft Teams team. The term "team" has been used quite a bit; we are aware of it. That is deliberate. For groups of individuals working together, Microsoft considers Teams as the key offering. Microsoft has gone to great lengths to include Teams in the latest Windows 11 version. You can even go so far as to claim that more individuals than ever will be using SharePoint subconsciously due to the high degree of integration between Teams and SharePoint. The SharePoint site that is created for every new team in Microsoft Teams is used for storing content. File sharing and article creation on the Teams wiki are two of the most typical uses.

Accessing SharePoint files in Teams

Various channels make up Microsoft Teams. The term "channel" simply refers to a specific chat room and serves to identify the current subject of discussion. As an example, you may create many channels for different types of discussions: General for broad themes, Carpool for specific topics like carpooling, Finance for entertaining things like that, and so on. Files are the top tab for each channel. Everyone in the channel can view the files you post by clicking the tab.

1. **Accessing Files**:
   - Upon entering a Team or creating a new one, each channel contains a "Files" tab.
   - Clicking on this tab provides access to the files stored specifically within that channel.
   - These files are stored in the associated SharePoint document library for seamless integration and organization.
2. **Uploading Files**:
   - To upload files to a Teams channel, go to the "Files" tab within the desired channel.
   - Use the "Upload" button to upload files either from your local device or directly from OneDrive for Business.
   - Alternatively, drag and drop files into the Teams channel for quick and efficient uploading.
3. **Editing Files**:
   - Edit files seamlessly within Teams using integrated Microsoft Office Online apps.
   - Simply click on a file to open it in the respective Office Online app (e.g., Word Online, Excel Online, and PowerPoint Online).
   - Any edits made to the file are automatically saved to the SharePoint document library associated with the Teams channel.
4. **Collaboration and Co-authoring**:

- Multiple team members can collaborate on files simultaneously within Teams.
- Concurrent editing allows team members to work on the same file simultaneously, with changes being synchronized and instantly visible to all collaborators.

5. **Version History and Comments**:
   - Teams integrate with SharePoint's version history and commenting features.
   - Users can view the version history of a file, revert to previous versions if needed, and add comments for feedback or discussions.
6. **Search and Navigation**:
   - Utilize the search bar within Teams to search for specific files or content within files stored in SharePoint.
   - Navigate through folders and subfolders within the SharePoint document library directly from Teams for efficient file management.
7. **Integration with OneDrive for Business**:
   - Teams seamlessly integrate with OneDrive for Business, providing direct access to files stored in your OneDrive from within Teams.
   - Share files from OneDrive and collaborate on them within Teams channels, streamlining collaboration and file management workflows.

Adding SharePoint Pages and Lists to Teams

1. Go to Microsoft Teams channel.

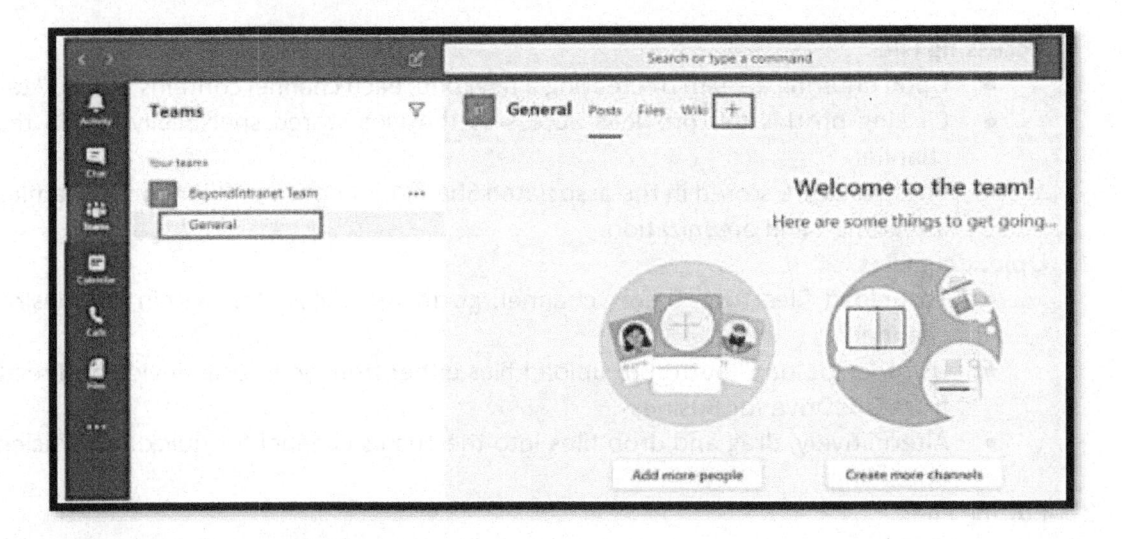

2. From the menu, choose the "+" sign.
3. It will bring up the "Add a tab" dialogue box.
4. **'Tabs for your team'** is where you'll find SharePoint. You can use the search bar on the upper right to locate SharePoint if it is not already displayed.

5. Pick out the tab's pages and list.

6. Click "**Save**" after selecting the SharePoint page you want to add to your teams. With the option to "**Post to the channel about this tab**" checked, you can also notify your team about the new tab to them.

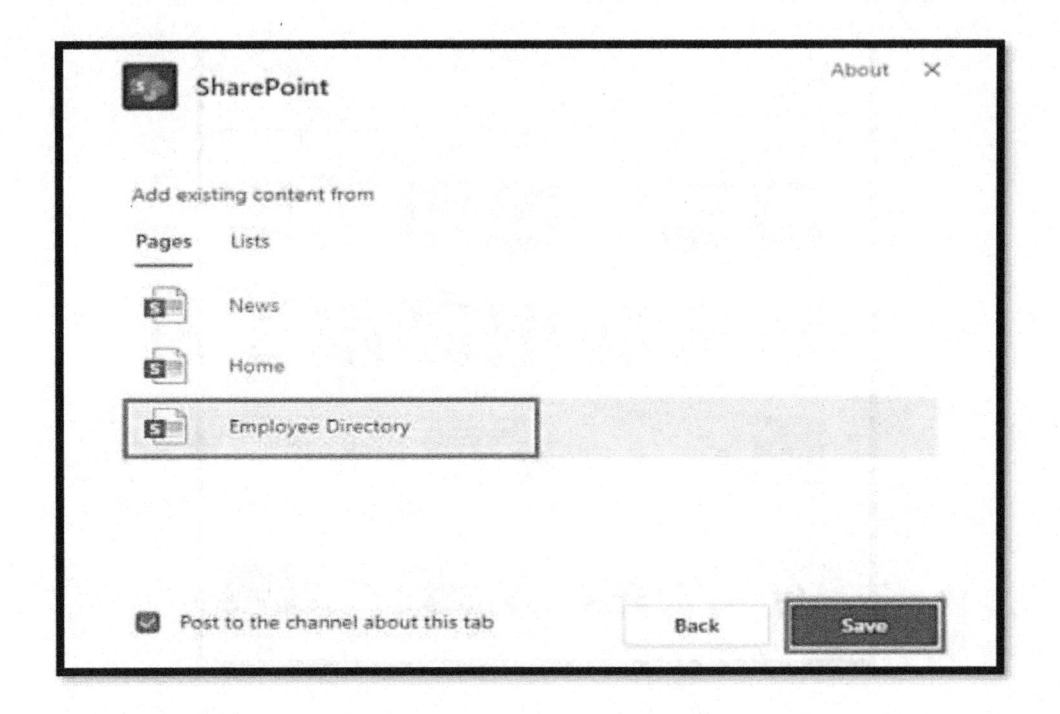

7. Teams will then display your SharePoint page as a Tab. View the picture below to see how a list will look when added as a tab.

8. By following the same steps, you can see a list in the tab. You can also click the "Open in SharePoint" button or add new entries to the list in the tab.

23

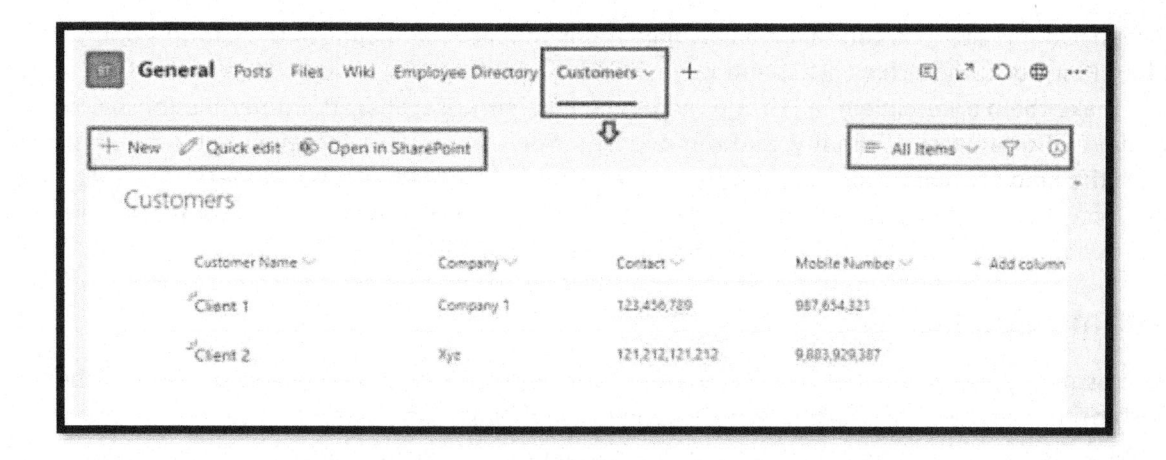

Working with SharePoint Teams and Groups

The Microsoft 365 ecosystem has three key components—Groups, SharePoint, and Teams—that can facilitate better teamwork and communication.

- ❖ **Group** allows you to consolidate individuals, discussions, and content into one location. In a communal space, you create for your team; they can work together on projects, exchange data, and hold discussions.
- ❖ Using **SharePoint**, you can save, arrange, and distribute files to your team. Collaboration and document management are made easier using this web-based service. Create web pages, documents, and lists that can be accessed from any device by everyone in your team.
- ❖ **Teams** is a chat-based collaboration solution where users can have real-time conversations, exchange information, and collaborate on projects with their teams. You can access all of your files and notes from a single location using Microsoft technologies like SharePoint and OneNote.

These three organizations provide a seamless experience for your team when it comes to cooperation. In groups, people can form teams and work together to complete projects. Things of the team's work can be stored and organized using SharePoint. You can collaborate on projects, exchange files, and have group chats all in one place with Teams.

In what way do these services work together?

Collaborative solutions like Groups, SharePoint, and Teams can greatly enhance your team's efficiency. As a whole, these services function as follows:

Groups and SharePoint

When used in tandem, Groups and SharePoint can greatly improve team collaboration. In SharePoint, a site that is relevant to the Group is automatically created whenever you create a

Group. On this site, you can save and arrange items that are significant to the Group's operations. SharePoint document files, lists, and pages can be added to the Group's SharePoint site, which will make them accessible to all Group members. Furthermore, SharePoint permissions allow you to limit who can access, modify, and remove files. You can monitor the evolution of a file's state with the help of version control. Microsoft Teams and SharePoint can be connected so that users can access their SharePoint sites directly from Teams. That is to say, you and your team members can collaborate in real-time on SharePoint files directly in Teams.

Teams and Groups

Microsoft Teams is designed to be used effectively with Groups, so you can use it to collaborate with other members of a Group. Constructing a new Team also gives you the option to form a Group. There will be real-time chatting, file sharing, and collaboration capabilities for you and your team members. Teams integrate with other Microsoft products, like OneNote and SharePoint, so you can access all of your documents and notes in a centralized location. A new folder is created on the Group's SharePoint site whenever a new Channel is created in Teams. The files and discussions associated with that Channel will be stored in that folder. With this, you can easily maintain order in your work.

Teams and SharePoint

An associated SharePoint site is automatically created whenever a new Team is created. SharePoint allows you to save and arrange team-related files, and you can then share those items directly inside Teams. Furthermore, SharePoint permissions allow you to limit who can access, modify, and remove files. You can monitor the evolution of a file's state with the help of version control. To facilitate the creation of new Channels, Teams creates a new folder on the associated SharePoint site. The files and discussions associated with that Channel will be stored in that folder. Maintaining order in your work will be a breeze with this.

Creating and Managing SharePoint Teams

One way to work with others on a project or topic is via Microsoft Teams, a messaging and collaboration app. The tool can be used to create and manage SharePoint teams. You can collaborate with other individuals using the tools that are associated with each team. The SharePoint platform is ideal for those who want to create websites, exchange content, and store information. When starting a new SharePoint site from the ground up, it is connected to the new team. A SharePoint site is associated with each team when you create a new team from an existing Microsoft 365 group. When you add Teams to an existing SharePoint site, it creates a new team and links it to the site.

Create a Microsoft Team from a SharePoint team site

- ❖ Navigate to a group-linked team site that you own.

- You can access the "Next Steps" panel, which is located in the upper right corner of your team site, or you can click on the "Add real-time chat" button in the bottom left region of your team site's main page.
- Site owners may quickly learn about the advantages of integrating Microsoft Teams into their SharePoint sites by clicking the "**Add real-time chat**" button.

- Click **Continue** to see further options for adding SharePoint files as tabs in Teams. To incorporate into Microsoft Teams, choose news articles, lists, documents, and SharePoint sites. All members of your team will be able to collaborate in one area thanks to this. No changes can be made to the default document library on the team site. You will find this library under the Files tab on the Teams channel. Although you can modify your decision, your site's homepage will also be selected for you. Select the Recommended section to see your team site's most popular tools.
- Press "**Add Teams**" to create a fresh Team channel that will include the tools you selected as tabs.

Setting Up Discussion Boards for Team Communication

Step 1: Go to the Microsoft 365 Portal.

- Navigate to the "**SharePoint**" section of your Microsoft 365 account.

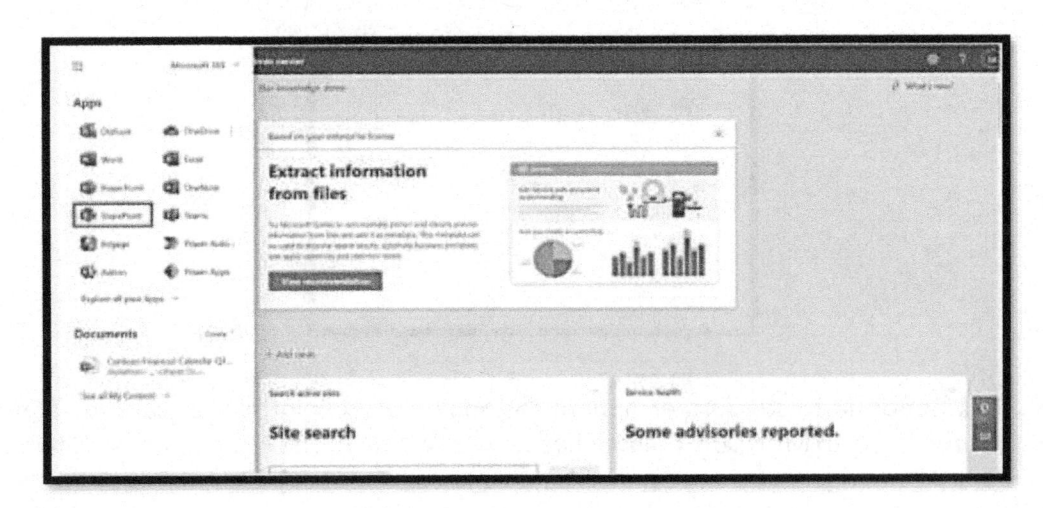

Step 2: Add an App

- Then, find the "**Add an App**" option in SharePoint's settings.

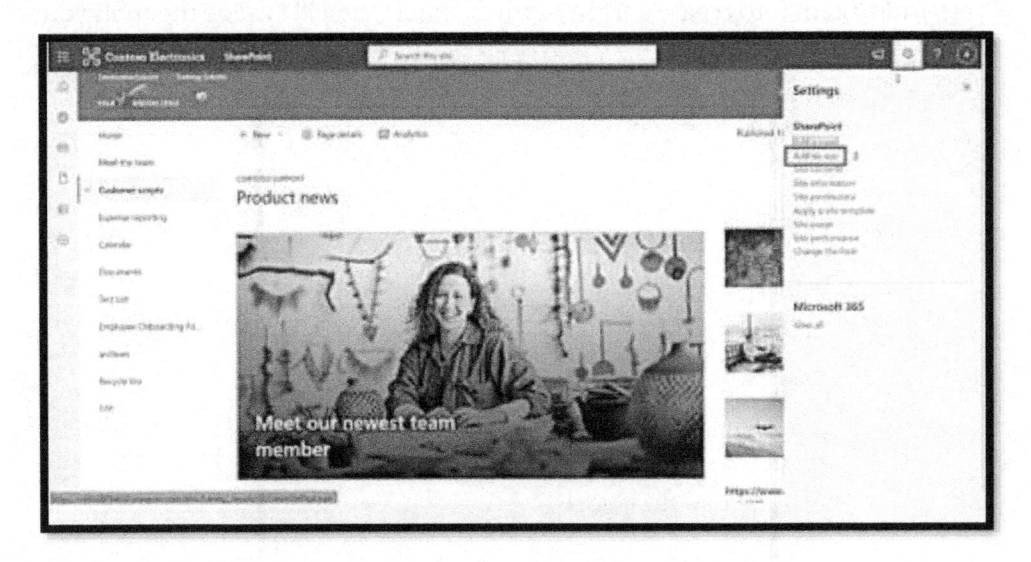

Step 3: Enable Classic Experience

- To access the app's settings, choose "**Classic Experience**."

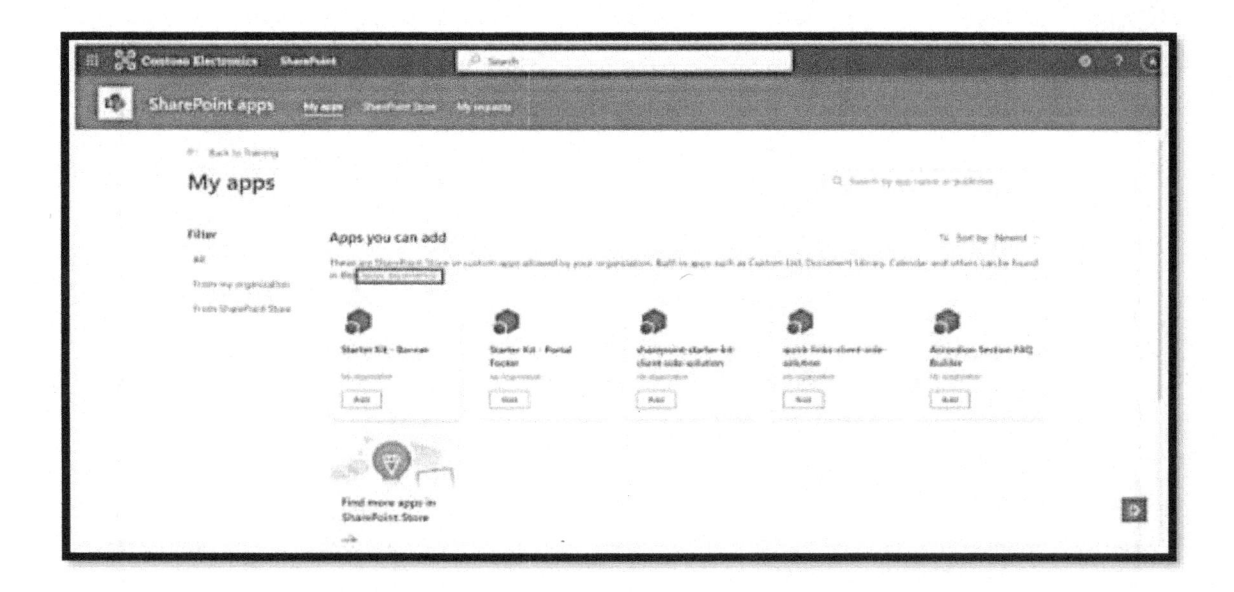

Step 4: Select "Discussion Board"
- Find "**Discussion Board**" in the Classic Experience's app list and choose it.

Step 5: Provide Board Details
- There are two options for the name of your discussion board: name it and provide a brief description of its purpose. After that, hit the "**Create**" button.

Step 6: Access Your Board
- In the list of applications, the discussion board you just created will appear. Simply click on its name to access it.

Step 7: Start a Discussion
- Click "**New**" to begin a new discussion. Then, fill in the title, type the message, and include any relevant details before saving your post.

Step 8: Engage in Discussions
- Here is the discussion board you requested. Feel free to start posting! Just by simply clicking on it, you can start a conversation with other teammates or join an existing one.

BROWSE | ITEMS | LIST

DestinationSubsite   Training Subsite   ✏ EDIT LINKS

New Project Discussion Board

Home
Meet the team
Customer scripts
   Consumer products
   Enterprise products
Expense reporting
Calendar
Documents
Recent
   New Project Discussion Board
   Wiki Library
   Wiki Page Library
   Picture Library
   Test calendar

⊕ **new discussion**

Recent   My discussions   Unanswered questions   ...

New Project Chat
Discussion about SharePoint Intranet site
By **Amit** | A few seconds ago

CHAPTER 5
WORKING WITH LISTS AND LIBRARIES

Two of SharePoint's most popular features are lists and libraries. These terms will be familiar to many SharePoint users. Is their potential and how they can expedite your work clear to you? Lists and libraries in SharePoint will be covered extensively here.

Understanding SharePoint list

A SharePoint list is a group of files that your whole organization can access and share. You can find it in other computer components as well. It has rows and sections similar to an Excel chart. Excel can provide you with the data you need for your list. There are many kinds of lists in SharePoint, including calendars, contact lists, and job lists. However, SharePoint groups can be used for a wide variety of uses. To create a data source or SharePoint list, you can begin from **square one. Alternatively, you can choose a theme from Microsoft's list:**

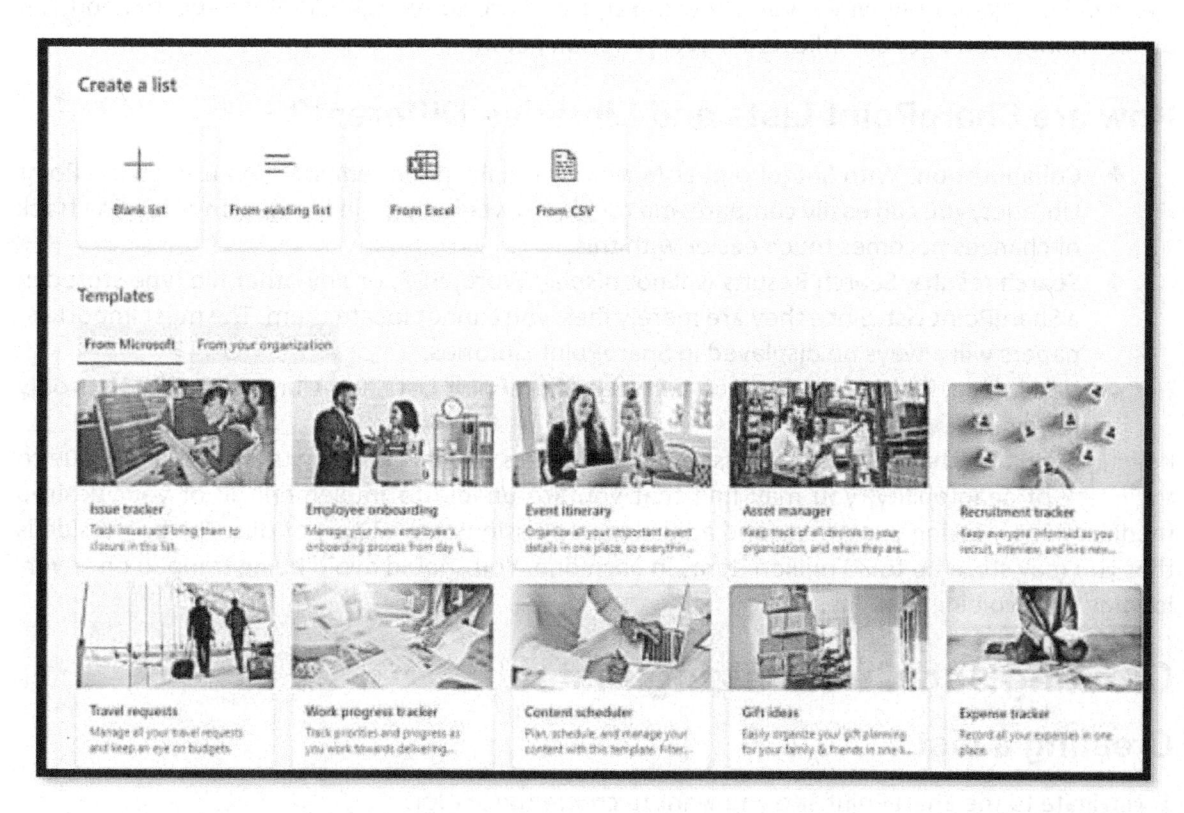

After you've customized it, you can add or delete columns and add files to a list. To have the data displayed the way you choose, you can alter the default view. It becomes much simpler to arrange the data in this way. You and your colleagues can collaborate effectively even when physically separated. On any device, you can also quickly access SharePoint groups. Their efficiency and care make the process go by quickly. Additionally, automating your work has never been easier than with the ability to create a PowerApp from a list.

Understanding SharePoint Library

One more name for SharePoint libraries is document libraries. In document libraries, people keep various papers and files. The very definition of a **"library"** is a place where you can store and arrange your information. Using versioning, you and your team can easily keep track of changes. Information contained within SharePoint folders is of utmost importance. Metadata are supplementary pieces of data that describe your files. When you add a document to a SharePoint library, all of its relevant information will be displayed. You can find out when and by whom it was posted here. Anything you think is important can be added to make this longer. It's very similar to how SharePoint lists can have fields added to them. Even while a file is open, you can edit its metadata. You can even get metadata from SharePoint lists. You can avoid repeatedly entering the same information whenever you share a new document. Information stored in SharePoint files can be organized however you choose. Yet, there are some rights that we recommend you utilize. Things won't get complicated if everyone can get in.

How are SharePoint Lists and Libraries Different?

- **Collaboration**. With SharePoint Lists, you can make direct edits. When using SharePoint Libraries, you can easily compare and toggle between multiple file versions. Keeping track of changes becomes much easier with this.
- **Search results**. Search Results will not display Word, PDF, or any other file type stored in a SharePoint List. Since they are merely files, you cannot locate them. The most important papers will always be displayed in SharePoint Libraries.
- **Versioning**. The only difference between SharePoint Lists and Libraries is that Lists only have major versions.

Keep in mind that there are limitations to the usefulness of SharePoint Lists and Libraries. Due to their lack of adaptability, you may find that you are unable to implement all of your desired modifications. Making your menu and adjusting permissions are all part of this. The bright side is that you may store up to 30 million items in each one. You should avoid being trapped on "**everloading**" by avoiding that.

Creating and Customizing Lists

Creating a List

1. Navigate to the SharePoint site you want to create the list for.
2. Select "**List**" from the list of options after clicking "**New**."

❖ Select the desired kind of list to be created.

After you've made it to the list page, you can customize it by adding columns, items, and metadata. The correct grouping and display of your data depends on your needs, so adjust your SharePoint List accordingly. There is no hard and fast rule on how you can modify the settings of your SharePoint List. At the outset, you can set up views, add or remove columns, and change the type of columns. By selecting "**New**" and then filling out the fields as needed, you can also add items to your list. Begin with a blank slate to create a SharePoint list tailored to your specific requirements; this will provide you complete control over the data structure, site contents, and style.

Creating a SharePoint List from a Template

SharePoint List templates are designed to simplify the process of creating lists by providing pre-configured sections and settings tailored for various purposes. Microsoft offers a wide range of templates to choose from, each serving specific needs.

Here are some examples:

1. **Asset Manager Template:**
    - Ideal for tracking and managing assets such as equipment, tools, or resources.
    - Includes sections for asset details, maintenance schedules, and tracking usage.
2. **Content Scheduler Template:**
    - Useful for scheduling and organizing content publishing or updating tasks.
    - Includes sections for content details, publishing dates, and responsible teams.
3. **Event Itinerary Template:**
    - Designed for planning and managing event itineraries, schedules, and related tasks.
    - Includes sections for event details, schedules, participant lists, and logistics.
4. **Issues Tracker Template:**
    - Helps in tracking and managing issues, incidents, or tickets within a project or organization.

- Includes sections for issue details, priority levels, status updates, and assigned personnel.
5. **Recruitment Tracker Template:**
   - Suitable for tracking recruitment processes, job applications, and candidate details.
   - Includes sections for job positions, applicant details, interview schedules, and hiring statuses.
6. **Work Progress Tracker Template:**
   - Designed for monitoring and tracking the progress of work tasks, projects, or assignments.
   - Includes sections for task details, timelines, progress updates, and task assignments.

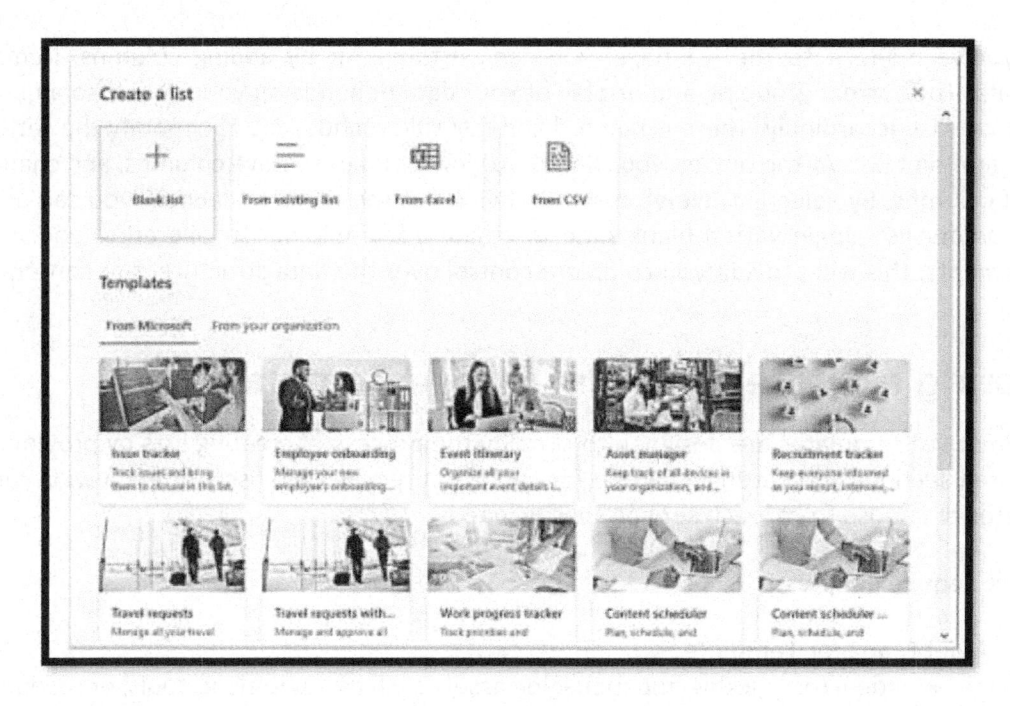

Creating a SharePoint List or an Excel table using data from an Excel file is a practical option. Good organization of the site's information page is essential for the effective maintenance of such lists. Flexibility is essential if making a personalized list template a priority. The flexibility to add or remove columns, change column types, configure views, rules, and processes, and otherwise tailor the template to individual needs is a key component of this. Not only can you save time and effort by using list templates, but you can also take use of SharePoint Lists' customization options. Instead of starting from scratch, you can quickly and easily create a SharePoint list by using pre-existing samples. A more efficient and simplified procedure of creating lists is guaranteed by this technique.

A SharePoint List can be created in this way using a template:

- ❖ Open your SharePoint site and navigate to the page that displays all the existing lists and libraries.
- ❖ Look for the "Add an App" button and click on it.
- ❖ From the list of options, select "List" to create a new list.
- ❖ Choose a template that aligns with the purpose of your list. SharePoint offers various templates such as Contacts, Tasks, Calendar, Custom List, and more.
- ❖ Once you've selected a template, you can further customize the list by adding or removing columns, adjusting settings, and configuring views to suit your specific requirements.
- ❖ After making the necessary changes, click on the "Save" button to create and save your customized list.

SharePoint List Management

Customizing SharePoint lists to meet your company's unique needs is essential for effective list management. Ensuring everything works as it should involves creating, configuring, and modifying. Setting up rights and access limits to protect data privacy and improve security measures is also an important part of list management. To work with SharePoint Lists, you can use either the simple SharePoint online interface or the more advanced SharePoint Designer. The latter offers a framework for making more intricate changes to list forms and procedures. Filtering by state or sorting by date are only two examples of how users can exercise the freedom to build their views and show data in a particular way. Thanks to SharePoint Lists' adaptability, users may make them work for their own company.

Adding Columns to a List

One of the simplest ways to alter the appearance of your SharePoint List is to add fields. Several common field kinds are available in SharePoint, including text, choice, date/time, and more, or you can create your fields. By including custom fields, you can access data tailored to your company's requirements and expedite data input.

Adding a new field to a list looks like this:

1. Go to the list where you want to add the column.
2. Click on the "Settings" button (gear icon) and choose "List settings" from the dropdown menu.
3. In the List Settings page, scroll down to the "Columns" section and click on "Add a column."
4. Choose the type of column you want to add, such as Single line of text, Number, Date and Time, Choice, etc.
5. Give the column a name that accurately describes its purpose or content.

6. Optionally, you can configure additional settings for the column, such as specifying a default value, setting column validation, adding a description, or choosing a column format.
7. Once you've configured the column settings, click on the "Save" or "OK" button to add the new column to the list.

In the list view of contemporary lists, you can include a new column by using the **"Add Column"** link.

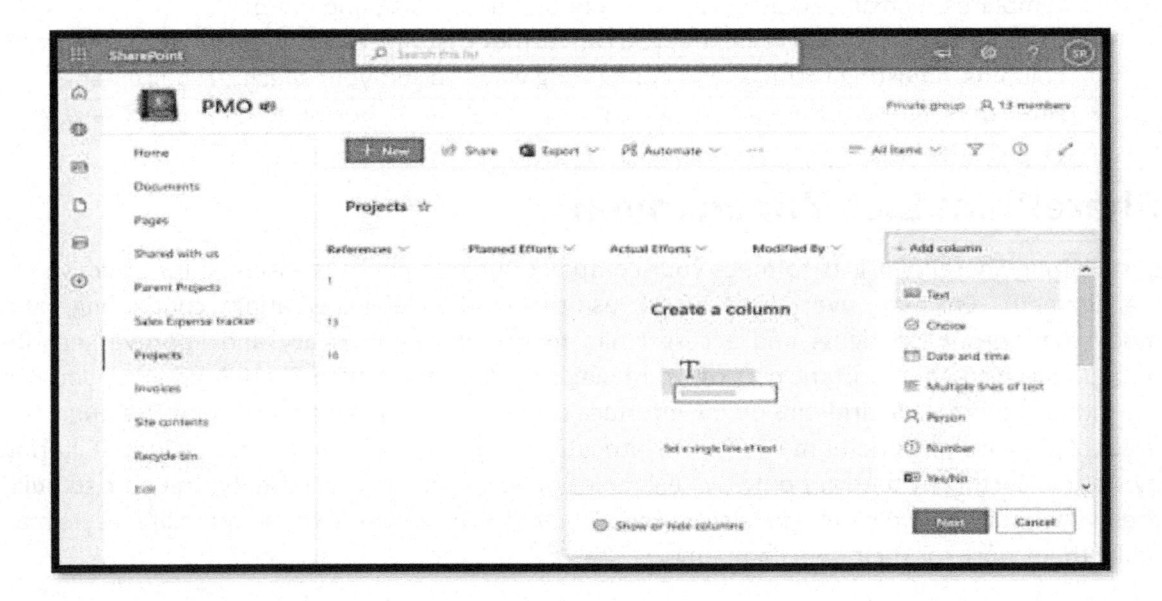

Deleting Columns in a SharePoint List

Select the unwanted column in the list's settings and then hit the **"Delete"** button. It's as simple as pie. Keep in mind that erasing a column will delete all the data contained inside it.

Inserting, editing, and deleting items in a SharePoint list

Items, which are rows of data, are what SharePoint lists employ to host data. To manage the data, users can make additions, edits, or deletions to a list. To begin managing and organizing online data in SharePoint, one of the most fundamental things to do is create a list. Anyone with any familiarity with SharePoint can pick up this technique fast because of how intuitive it is.

Step-by-step instructions for adding items to a SharePoint list are as follows:

Inserting Items

❖ Find the list you want to add the item to on your SharePoint server or SharePoint Online site. Go to the list.

- ❖ Select "**Add new item**" from the control that appears on the menu to begin adding a new item.
- ❖ A form will pop up, with fields that match the columns you set up in your list. Many other kinds of fields may be used, such as text boxes, date pickers, dropdown lists, buttons, and more.
- ❖ Fill in all the fields with the correct data. You may include the name, summary, due date, and assignee of a task in a task list, for example. Go ahead and click "**Save**" to add the item to the list. If needed, attach files.
- ❖ The **ID, Created, and Modified** columns will be filled up automatically.
- ❖ To ensure data correctness and compliance with preset criteria, validation rules can be used to prohibit submissions or demand certain forms.

Editing Items

1. Open your SharePoint site and navigate to the list containing the item you want to edit.
2. Find the item you wish to edit and click on it to open its details view.
3. In the details view, locate and click on the "**Edit Item" or "Edit**" button. This action will open the item form view with the current values preloaded.
4. You can now make changes to any text, numbers, dates, or other fields that are editable.
5. After making the desired changes, click on the "**Save**" or "**Save Changes**" button to update the item in the database.
6. SharePoint also offers versioning capabilities, allowing you to track changes and view previous versions of the item. You can access this feature to see the history of edits made to the item.
7. Alternatively, if you want to edit multiple list items simultaneously, you can switch to the Grid view. In the Grid view, you can select multiple items and apply bulk edits to update multiple items at once.

Getting Rid of Items

- ❖ Select many things at once by using the checkboxes that are adjacent to them.
- ❖ After making your selection, click "**Delete**."
- ❖ You can remove an open item using the "**Delete Item**" menu.
- ❖ Keep in mind that if anything is deleted, it cannot be recovered unless it is restored from a backup. Proceed with care to prevent the accidental deletion of data.

You can manage individual objects in SharePoint lists in the most basic way by doing these things. Acquiring the skills to add, edit, and remove data opens up several possibilities for maintaining accurate company records.

Adding Attachments to a SharePoint List

In SharePoint Lists, users can add files to a list of items, providing more information and supplementary documents.

The procedure for adding files to a SharePoint list is as follows:

1. Point your browser to the SharePoint List that you want to add files to.
2. You may connect files to specific items in the list by selecting them.
3. Open the attachments box by accessing the list item menu and clicking on the "**Attachments**" button.
4. Navigate to the file list and choose "**Attach File**."
5. Select the file on your device that you would want to attach, and then click "**OK**."
6. Just repeat steps **4 and 5** if you feel the need to add additional attachments.
7. After you've added all the files you want to attach, click "OK" to save them.

Customize SharePoint List Views

Sorting and Filtering

1. **Sorting**:
   - Sorting items through sorting allows for organizing a list based on distinct criteria like date, alphabetical order, or status.
   - To initiate sorting, select the column title representing the desired sorting criterion and click on it.
   - A single click arranges items in ascending order, while a double click arranges them in descending order.
   - Alternatively, you can click on the filter icon adjacent to the column header to sort the SharePoint List based on a particular property.
2. **Filtering**:
   - Filtering offers the capability to view items that satisfy specific conditions, such as those created within the last week or allocated to a specific individual.
   - Access filter options by clicking on the filter icon next to the column header.
   - A range of filter options is available, encompassing text filters, date filters, and number filters.
   - Leverage these filters to fine-tune the presentation of information according to your distinct criteria.

Grouping

Based on a field, such as a category or department, you can group objects in a SharePoint List. With this, you can see your data in a more structured and practical manner. Select "**Group By This Field**" from the context menu that appears when you click on the header of the column you want to group by.

Creating Custom Views

If the default views in SharePoint do not meet your needs, you can easily customize them to show just the data that is relevant to your project.

A customized view can be made in this way:

- In the list page's top right corner, you should see the gear symbol; click on it.
- To access the list's settings, choose "**List Settings**".
- Select "**Create View**" and then go with the on-screen prompts to establish your unique perspective.
- Here you can customize your view by choosing which columns to show, changing the sorting and filtering options, and giving it a name that suits your tastes.

You can customize the presentation of a list or library in SharePoint to highlight the information that is important to you. To do this, you may modify the data by adding, deleting, and rearranging columns, sorting and filtering them, and making new views according to your requirements.

Conditional Formatting in List Views

By using conditional formatting in SharePoint List views, you may highlight particular data visually under specified situations by applying alternative styles, classes, or icons to fields depending on their contents. **Custom views and conditional formatting can be implemented in the following ways:**

1. Go to the list's column settings.
2. Choose the "**Format this column**" option.
3. Navigate to the "**Format column**" menu and choose "**Conditional formatting**."
4. Get the look you want by playing around with the style settings and managing the rules.

You can make your SharePoint Lists more visually attractive and simpler to understand and analyze on a data-centric platform by adding views and conditional formatting to the data you display. This method helps make the data representation more understandable and pleasant to use.

Managing SharePoint List Permissions

Ensuring the security of your company's sensitive information and safeguarding data privacy requires effective management of SharePoint List permissions. Users and groups may be granted different degrees of access to SharePoint lists and their contents based on their permissions. Ensuring the right permissions are in place guarantees that no one other than authorized users may access, modify, or remove any material from the list. The security of your company's data and the protection of sensitive information depend on this.

Understanding SharePoint List Permission Levels

You can control who can access and interact with the list using the preset permission levels in SharePoint List. The most common permission levels are as follows:

1. **Full Control**: The ability to manage permissions, delete the list, and alter its structure and settings is granted to users with Full Control permissions.
2. **Edit**: Only users with the "**edit**" permission can make changes to the list, including adding or removing entries. They can also change the settings and layout of the list.
3. **Read**: People with Read permission can see the list, but they can't change or remove anything from it.

The default permission levels of the three groups that make up SharePoint List are:

- ❖ **Owners**: The Owners group has the ability to change the permissions of the list since they are automatically granted Full Control.
- ❖ **Members**: By default, the Members group has edit permissions, so they can update entries in the list.
- ❖ **Visitors**: By default, members of the Visitors group have read permissions, so they may see the list contents but cannot make changes.

Granting and Revoking SharePoint List Permissions

Use these procedures to set up SharePoint list permissions:

- **Go to the list settings page**: Access the desired list by visiting the SharePoint site. The gear icon "**Settings**" can be seen in the top right corner. Then, from the pop-up menu that appears, choose "**List settings**" after clicking on it.
- Click on "**Permissions for this list**": Select "**Permissions for this list**" from the list's settings page's "**Permissions and Management**" section.
- **Take care of permissions**: on the list permissions page that SharePoint will display, you can modify the permissions for individual users or groups. Various restrictions and constraints can be defined, including the amount of permission (read, contribute, or full authority) and the types of persons or groups who can get it.

Metadata and Content Types

Introduction to Metadata in SharePoint

A file can be an audio file, photo, slideshow, spreadsheet, process map, email, document, website, list item, video, or any other sort of file. Extra information about the content of a file is called metadata. Files are sorted and described using metadata, commonly referred to as "data about data" or "information about information," to make them simpler to locate and navigate inside your SharePoint sites.

There are two broad categories into which metadata can be divided:

- ❖ Administrative metadata, such as the version number, creation date, created by, and last modified date, aids in the understanding of the file by users and systems.
- ❖ Metadata such as **Location, Department, Topic, Activity, Subject, and Information Type** provide information about a file and aid in its discovery. Usually, this has to do with what your business is aware of.

You can use both to help you organize, filter, and enhance your navigation and search to discover the proper information. Metadata of many sorts can be combined and used in novel ways to improve content discovery. To put it another way, anyone can simply access or locate anything, regardless of how they search for it. Starting with where they want to live and then adding amenities like the number of rooms, bathrooms, and gardens they may like might help them narrow down their search for a rental property. Another way they may reduce their options would be to search for all apartments with gardens. If the apartment description has consistent information kept on it, this task will be simpler.

What is managed metadata?

Using metadata consistently across all of your SharePoint sites is ensured via managed metadata. You can utilize comprehensible organizational language to assist your staff in finding the correct information at the right moment. Using a common categorization, SharePoint enables you to manage this from a single location. Subsequently, the category can have more data added to it, allowing it to evolve with the company. Taxonomy is considered authoritative when it organizes data into coherent groups. With major categories and subcategories, these groups can have several levels. The information terms you've put up comprise term sets, which are created and managed using the SharePoint Term Store Management tool. This allows you to connect various categories and subcategories.

SharePoint Term Store - term set Department example

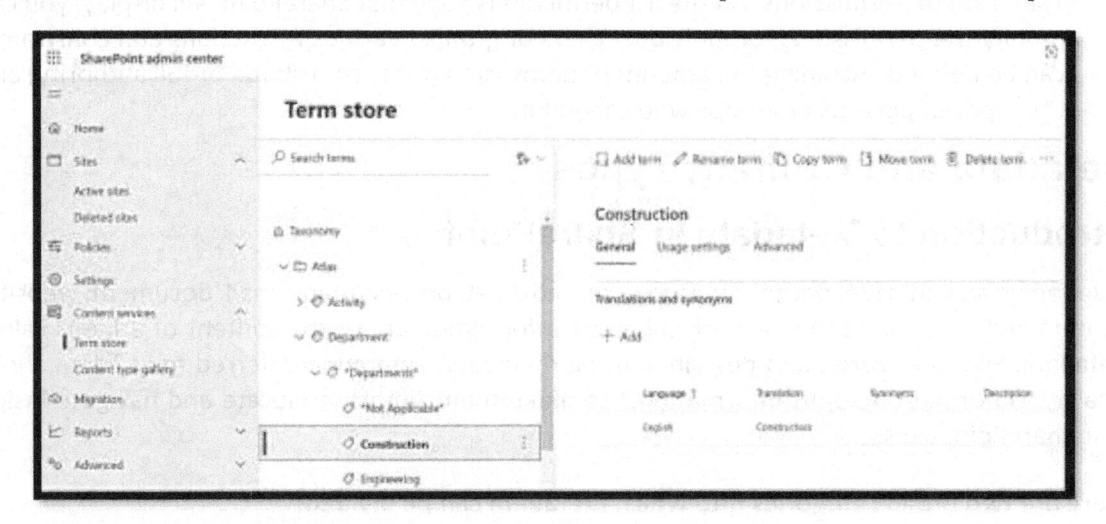

Term Store - term set options for managing terms

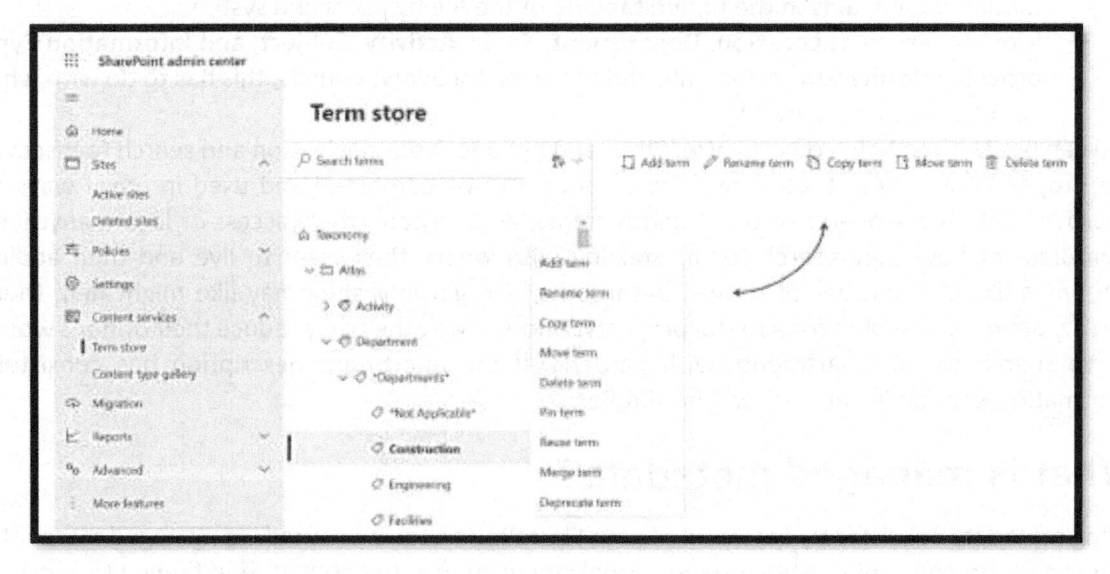

Term Store - term set management options

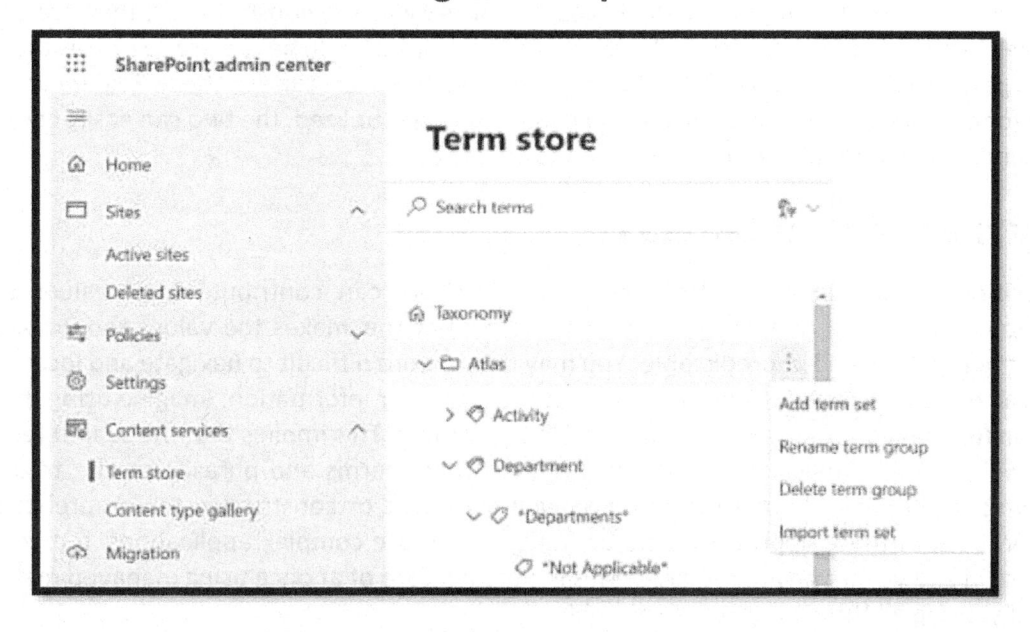

Best practice metadata management leads to:

- ❖ Users can arrange their files in more practical and aesthetically pleasing ways when metadata is managed correctly.
- ❖ Sort, filter, and group files quickly.
- ❖ Because search engines are designed to make results more relevant when they have clear information, searches are quicker.
- ❖ You can deal with files in the same manner by using file references that are consistent across your SharePoint account.

Why use metadata instead of folders

You can observe the significant difference when you compare files and information across the whole organization. Use of folders is advised. They are simple to use and obvious to anyone. With the advent of Microsoft Teams, folders are back. Now, every channel created on an MS Teams site gets its own folder under the standard SharePoint Document Library where files may be stored. **But folders do have certain restrictions:**

- ❖ To navigate across groups, you must understand their organizational structure. The majority of the time, only the creator can comprehend it.
- ❖ Not always utilized in the same manner, and when customized folder template designs are needed, they are often modified to meet specific requirements.
- ❖ Multiple files can be linked to a single file, which may cause individuals to place identical files in different directories, creating duplicate files.
- ❖ It is not simple to search, sort, or browse using folders.

When groups don't function, metadata is helpful since it addresses these issues and more. Do folders really not matter to you at all? Probably not. As was previously stated, they are used to manage channels in MS Teams sites. They can also be helpful if you have a group of files that need certain permissions to be applied so that only particular site users can see them. Folders are highly useful for organizing this kind of usage, and if information is utilized, the two can easily cooperate to maximize the benefits of both, as will be shown below.

Why manage metadata?

Information in SharePoint is often not handled. Users can contribute their values at the SharePoint site level if they are permitted to do so. But this makes the values too ambiguous, difficult to regulate, and unpredictable. You may find it more difficult to navigate and locate items across all of your SharePoint sites if you do not manage your information. Imagine using the term "**Human Resources**" in certain contexts and "**HR**" in others. This implies that the search term you enter will have an impact on the results you see. These terms and phrases can be treated as synonyms in the SharePoint Term Store as well as taught or constructed to comprehend one another. Both of these approaches can be utilized for more complex applications, but constant verification and validation are required. This is all taken care of at once using managed metadata. Naturally, using all three at once is preferable.

Inconsistent metadata and non-organizational language at a site level leads to:

- ❖ More time spent looking for anything
- ❖ More time to get new hires up to speed
- ❖ Increased probability of data silos and file duplication
- ❖ Increased probability of needing assistance from others in locating files
- ❖ A higher probability of individuals producing their collections

Through the establishment of control procedures and rules, groups can choose which values to apply. This may sometimes be the responsibility of "*metadata owners*". These are the individuals who produce, maintain, and arrange the metadata. However, everyone still has to abide by the guidelines established by the group. It can be time-consuming to coordinate and get consensus on accuracy, and implementing things site-by-site can be challenging. There are more approaches to simplify the creation and management of metadata, which will improve user experience overall for all users. Information handling has to be done better. Of course, there is. You will save time and anxiety if you let the system handle the information for you. Continue reading.

How to make applying metadata easier for everyone

The majority of the issues on the list above can be resolved with auto-tagging technologies. The user doesn't have to do anything at all since they generate information automatically. You can ensure that new material is uploaded with the correct information and that all of your SharePoint sites are consistent by utilizing these tools.

To eliminate the need for human thought while tagging files, this process is automated. At this point, the business realizes how valuable controlled metadata really is.

There are several methods that can be mixed and matched:

- ❖ Integrate your Information Architecture (managed information) into your website's design by using a solution such as ClearPeople's Atlas.
- ❖ Taxonomy ontology tools for monitoring and applying your established information architecture to each and every file.
- ❖ Artificial intelligence (AI) and machine learning tools, such as Microsoft SharePoint Syntex and Viva Topics, provide recommendations for content based on previously taught and learned patterns. You can use these tools both before and after creating a file.

The easiest approach to make metadata function in SharePoint is to include it in your site design. On top of this, you can add machine-learned and taught metadata to further enhance your controlled metadata. You can simultaneously get assistance from Syntex, Viva Topics, and Atlas. Atlas lets you apply the agreed conditions on a regular basis when constructing a site and makes necessary revisions to get you started on the road to organizationally controlled content. Viva subjects enhance this experience by proposing subjects and identifying links between content, conversations, and people's expertise. Based on previously established rule sets, Syntex can be used to enhance the quality of each file's metadata when it is created automatically during the content editing phase. Atlas dynamically adds information to files depending on where they are stored, making it quicker and simpler for users to utilize SharePoint metadata. This enables users to locate the file from any location. To accommodate changes within the organization, this information can be updated and modified centrally. To make your material simpler to locate and link with other content, Viva Topics combines fresh content with the chosen information that Atlas applies. When SharePoint Syntex enhances the quality and accuracy of information at the file level, users don't need to do additional manual tagging.

To summarize, creating, managing, and using SharePoint information doesn't have to be difficult; simply keep these pointers in mind:

- Keep things simple at first, and then as you go, make adjustments.
- Avoid inventing words only for amusement.
- Instead of requiring your staff to tag files, let them determine most of the information based on where they store the file.
- Utilize the information for your company across all of your websites in one location.
- Consider which terminology must be used interchangeably and which ones need some leeway in interpretation.
- Try to limit the number of levels in your reasonable structures (category -> subcategory) to no more than three or four.

It is important to consider what people want and how they will want to search, recognize, move, or appear. In actuality, they will combine various strategies, so whatever you decide to do has to be effective for everyone.

Creating and Using Content Types for Document Management

Step 1: Determine the types of documents you want to store in your SharePoint DMS

It is not a good idea to house all of your company's files in a single SharePoint Document Library. The primary objective of SharePoint DMS is to group documents with similar security and permissions that are relatively related. As an illustration of this kind of SharePoint DMS, consider **the following scenario You want to save various financial documents, like:**

- Invoices
- Purchase Orders
- Quotes
- Estimates
- Receipts

If you wish to store documents that belong to various sections and have distinct users, permissions, and security, then no, not in the same document library or DMS. Rather, you need to organize them into many websites or libraries.

Step 2: Categorize Documents for Your SharePoint Document Management System

Establishing discrete categories is crucial for effective organization when setting up a SharePoint Document Management System (DMS) to protect financial documents. **Let's describe the kinds of documents we want to store in this scenario:**

- ❖ **Purchase Orders**: Records pertaining to the official request for products or services, including the kind, amount, and conditions that were agreed upon.

- ❖ **Invoices**: Documents that list the costs incurred for the products or services provided, usually with itemized charges, conditions of payment, and other pertinent information.
- ❖ **Receipts**: Records attesting to the receipt of money, products, or services that are used as proof of financial transactions.

Step 3: Define metadata for each of the categories above

Each of the aforementioned groups will probably have unique information. For example, you may label every purchase order with the vendor's name, the purchase order number, and the purchase order date. The client name, the invoice number, the date of receipt, and the date of payment can all be written on bills. Lastly, labels for receipts can include the name of the supplier, the time they were provided, a description, and the name of the staff member who issued it.

In this instance, it may seem as follows:

Purchase Order

- PO #
- Vendor
- PO Date

Invoice

- Invoice #
- Client
- Date Received
- Date Paid

Receipt

- Vendor
- Receipt Date
- Description
- Employee

Step 4: For each metadata property, define the type of that property/column

Like a date, an option/drop-down menu, or a free text field. That is what we will need when we make our columns in the next step.

Step 5: Create your metadata columns

- ❖ Although you can create your column at the library level, it is usually preferable to do it at the site level. After that, libraries and other websites can utilize your content. Our plan is to construct our information sections at the site level, which will enable us to create global content kinds later.

- ❖ Click the Site Gear icon, then choose **Add Column** from the **Site Settings > Site Columns** menu (under Web Designer Galleries).
- ❖ Utilize the data obtained in Step 3 to create your notes column. As an example, I will create a seller column with a drop-down menu listing every seller's name.

- ❖ Repeat the preceding procedures for every column you discovered.

Step 6: Establish Content Types

- ❖ Go to the Site Collection's root (or the site where you made all of your site columns in Step 5).

- **Site Settings > Site Content types**.
- Press the "**Create link**" button.

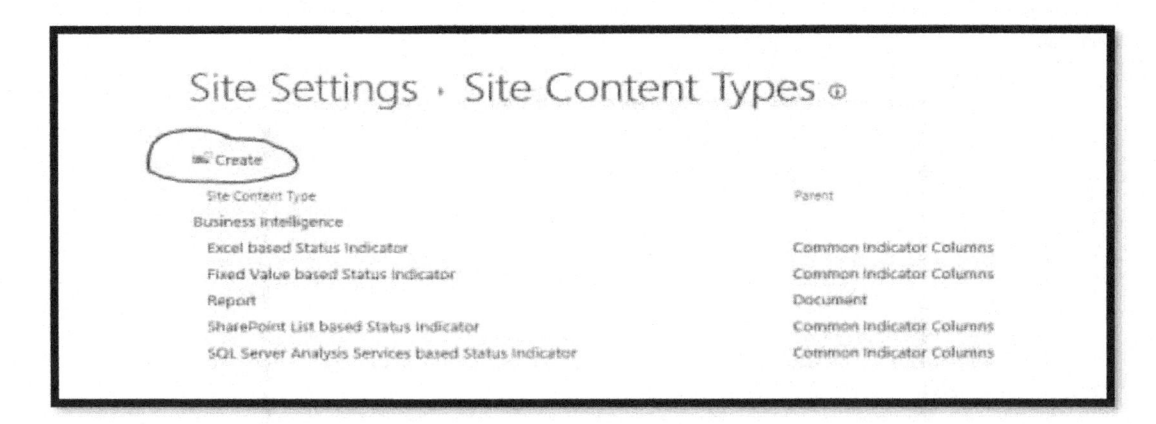

> Site Settings › Site Content Types
>
> Create
>
> | Site Content Type | Parent |
> |---|---|
> | Business Intelligence | |
> | Excel based Status Indicator | Common Indicator Columns |
> | Fixed Value based Status Indicator | Common Indicator Columns |
> | Report | Document |
> | SharePoint List based Status Indicator | Common Indicator Columns |
> | SQL Server Analysis Services based Status Indicator | Common Indicator Columns |

- Give your Content-Type a name on the next screen, such as "**Purchase Order**," and provide a short description describing its attributes and intended use. The two drop-down menus are located in the center of the page.
- Select "**Document**" from the second menu after selecting "**Document Content Types**" from the first. SharePoint is notified by this setup that the Content-Type will be in charge of handling documents inside of a Document Library.
- Choose how you want to group your Content Types in the Group area located at the bottom of the screen. Like with Site Columns, you can make your own custom group or utilize the default "**Custom group**". To save and confirm the **Purchase Order Content-Type** settings, press the **OK** button.

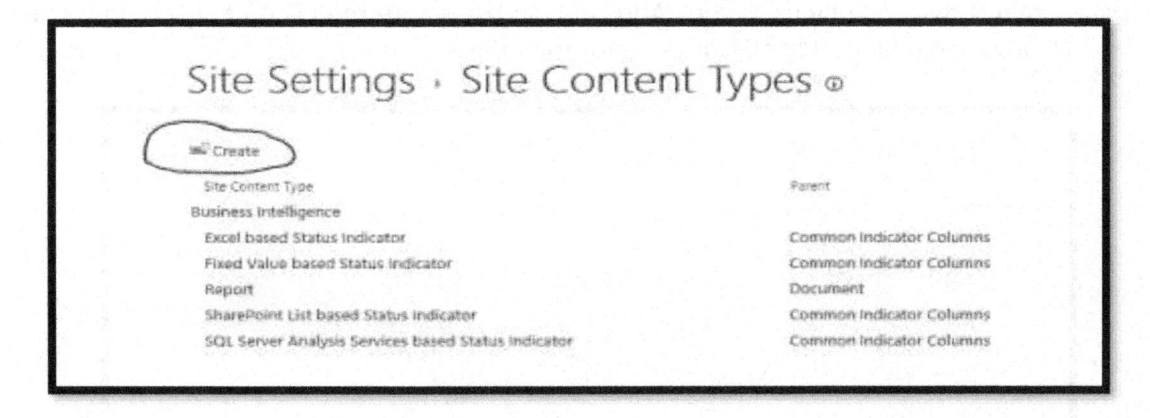

> Site Settings › Site Content Types
>
> Create
>
> | Site Content Type | Parent |
> |---|---|
> | Business Intelligence | |
> | Excel based Status Indicator | Common Indicator Columns |
> | Fixed Value based Status Indicator | Common Indicator Columns |
> | Report | Document |
> | SharePoint List based Status Indicator | Common Indicator Columns |
> | SQL Server Analysis Services based Status Indicator | Common Indicator Columns |

> The screen that follows, which looks like the one above, will show you what to do next. Right now, we want to link the newly-created Content Type—which is effectively a category—to the corresponding custom information, which is shown as columns. Although there is flexibility to change different parts of content kinds, we will be concentrating on the

interaction with site sections for the time being. For the purpose of starting this procedure, pay attention to the Title Column that is already there and choose the option "**Add from existing Site Columns**." Then, we will include the freshly created columns that we have created.

❖ The screen that appears next will be like the one below. From the drop-down option next to "Select columns from," select the group (Custom Columns) that you used to organize all of the columns on your website. By doing this, the list of site fields will be limited to those that are a part of that group. Select the site columns that correspond with the selected content type from the list of available columns. Next, add them to the selection screen's right side by using the "**Add**" button. These are the PO date, PO number, and vendor name for us. Click OK at the bottom of the screen.

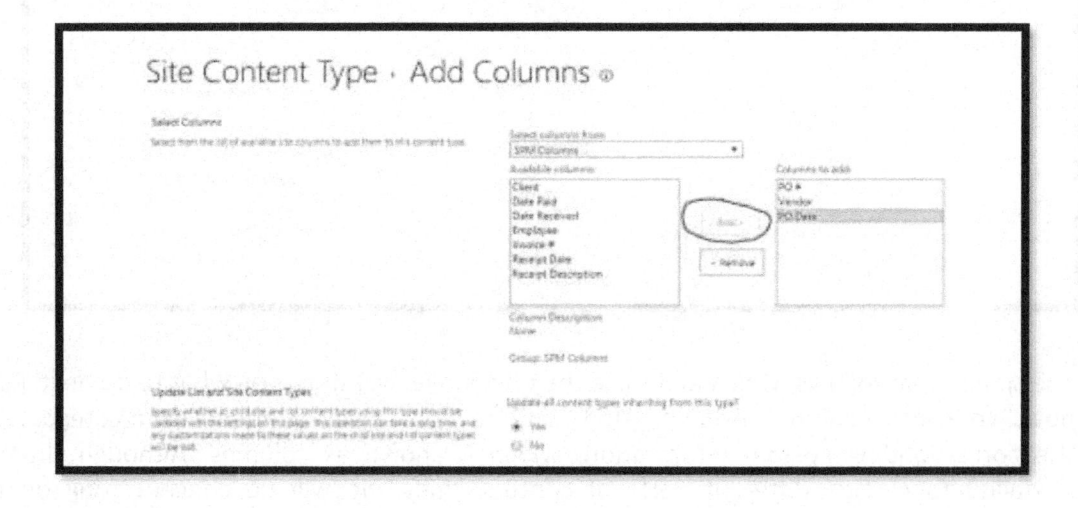

- ❖ The page below, which has the unique parts added to the Content-Type, should be the outcome.
- ❖ That concludes the first category of content. Repeat the first seven steps with every other kind of material.

Step 7: Establish a Document Library on the designated site for your SharePoint Document Management System (DMS)

Avoid using the default Document Library if you are new to building a site and adding a Document Library.

Step 8: Prepare the Document Library for Custom Content Types and Custom Metadata

A number of complex alterations are required to prepare our Document Library to include "metadata" before adding site content kinds. This is a detailed explanation:

- ❖ Go to the **Library Tab** and click on **Library Settings** to access all administrative configurations.
- ❖ Choose **Advanced Settings**.
- ❖ Set "**Allow management of content types**" to "**Yes**" to integrate designated types of site information into the document library.
- ❖ In the middle of the screen, select "**No**" next to "**Make 'New Folder'** commands available???" to prevent the creation of folders when using library information, maintaining clarity between the two entities.
- ❖ Confirm the changes by clicking the **OK** button at the bottom of the page.
- ❖ Return to the **Library Settings page** and navigate to Versioning Settings.
- ❖ Ensure that "**Create major versions**" is selected to configure versioning settings appropriately.

Step 9: Add custom content types to the document library

The exciting part is about to begin. Our document library can now have the custom content types we created in Step 6. To do this:

- ❖ To scroll down the Library Settings Page, locate its center. A section titled "Content-Type" will be placed there. After the final step of turning on content types, this section of the document library will appear. By default, the Document Content Type is the only one that is presented. Eventually, we will eliminate it. First, however, we'll list the materials we use. But let's add our material types first. Click on **Add from existing site content types**.

[Screenshot: Content Types section showing "This document library is configured to allow multiple content types. Use content types to specify the information you want to..." with Content Type "Document" checked as Visible on New Button. "Add from existing site content types" is circled. Below: "Change new button order and default content type"]

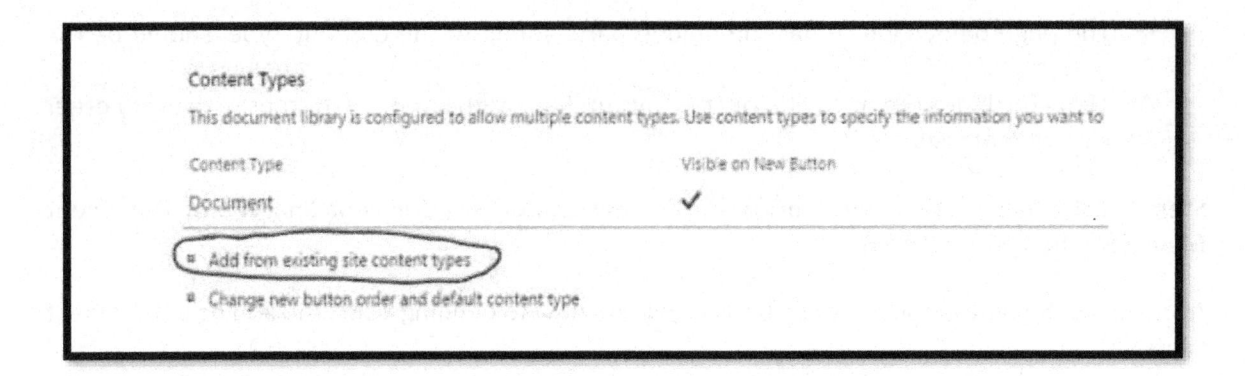

❖ Choose the different kinds of material you created on the screen that follows. Similar to how site sections are organized, you can choose the grouping used to categorize your Content Types using the drop-down option. To move the custom content types to the right side of the screen, find them and select them. Then, click the "**Add**" button. To finish, click the OK button.

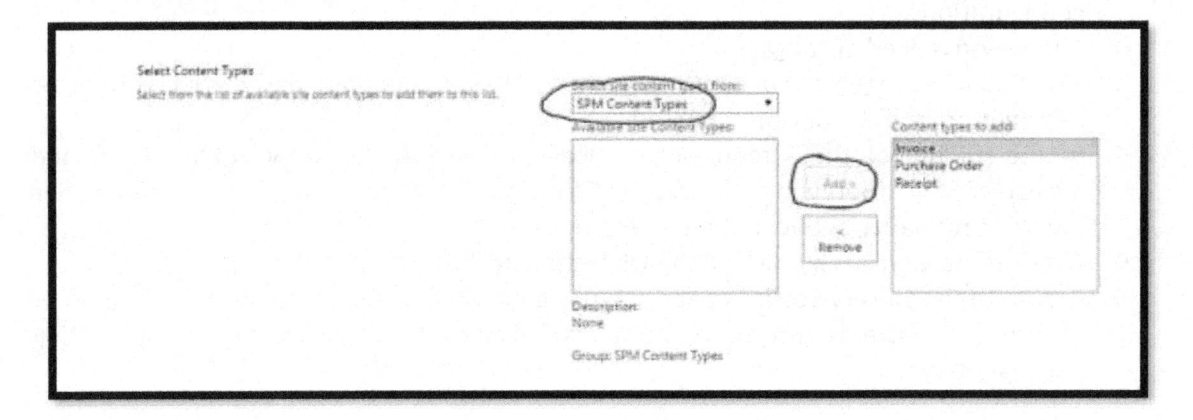

[Screenshot: Select Content Types screen with "SPM Content Types" circled in the dropdown, Available site content types list, Add/Remove buttons (Add circled), and Content types to add list showing Invoice, Purchase Order, Receipt. Description: None. Group: SPM Content Types]

❖ This is how the majority of your page will appear, with additional content kinds placed underneath the basic document type.

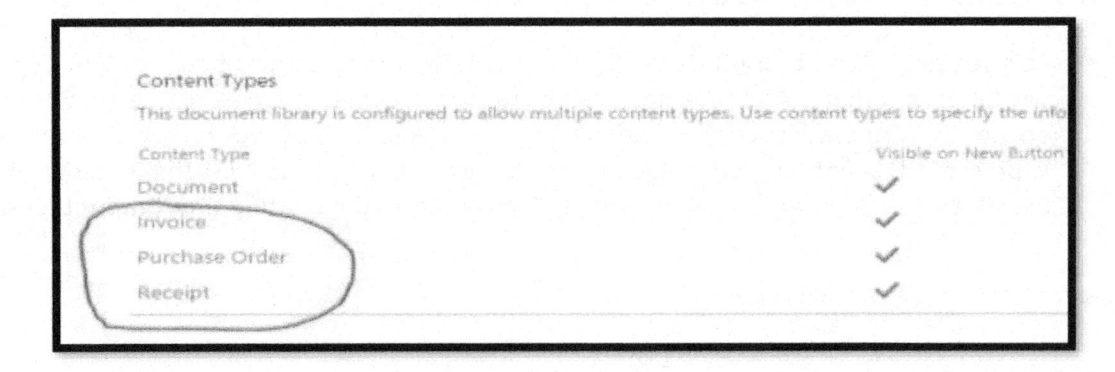

[Screenshot: Content Types section showing Document, with Invoice, Purchase Order, and Receipt circled, all checked as Visible on New Button]

❖ Not only were the document types effectively merged, but all the associated site parts were converted without a hitch, as can be seen upon closer investigation. You can easily see them in the Columns column at the bottom of the screen. This part shows the extra columns and gives some explanation of how they work; highlighting the kinds of data they hold. The seamless integration is evidence of the system's strong functioning.

❖ The basic content type may be removed from our SharePoint DMS now that it is no longer needed. To accomplish this, locate the Content Types box in the center of the screen and click on Document Content Type. Next, click on **Delete this content type**. You will be informed not to do it in a message. Please press the OK button.

❖ I like to use the extra option to hide the **title field**. A **Title Field** is pre-installed on all content types. It can sometimes include the user having to create an additional note. To me, it belongs in the dark. To make it invisible, go to the content type, find the Title Column, and then use the Hidden radio option. For all other forms of material, repeat the process.

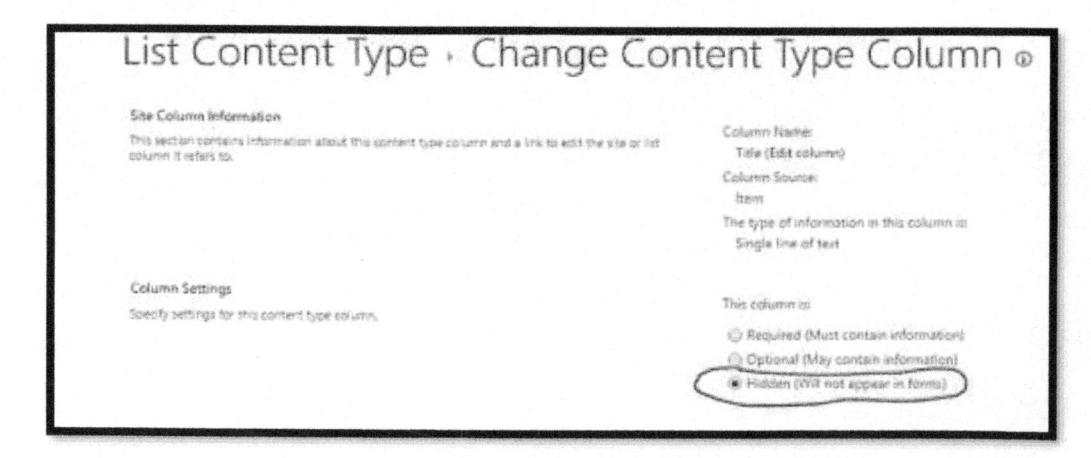

Step 10: Implement Metadata Navigation

I have a few more things to do before we finish installing our SharePoint DMS, which is our document management system. Metadata Navigation is a must-have feature for every SharePoint list or document library in my opinion. When working in settings that are heavily reliant on data, this characteristic becomes crucial. It provides aesthetically pleasing tools that users may utilize to effectively search for things, files, or documents inside the library or list. Think of it as buying on Amazon.com, where the results shown on the main page change depending on the criteria you choose on the left.

Step 11: Optimize SharePoint DMS for a 5,000 Item Limit

It is critical to optimize the document library to support a considerable volume if you want to hold a substantial number of files inside your SharePoint DMS. To do this with SharePoint, you must make sure that the document library is set up correctly, following best practices to avoid problems with the 5,000-item restriction. This preventative measure lays the groundwork for the SharePoint DMS to handle and make accessible a huge number of files with ease.

Step 12: Upload some documents

We're almost there. It is now acceptable to upload a file. A Content-Type drop-down menu and "regular" information values will be shown to you. Your information options will adapt to the position of your mouse as you hover over the drop-down menu.

Step 13: Enjoy your Document Management System in SharePoint!

And that is all! Thank goodness everything is in place now; SharePoint DMS is fantastic, and you will love using it.

CHAPTER 6

PERMISSIONS AND SECURITY IN SHAREPOINT

Managing SharePoint Online Security: A Team Effort

Tenant settings

This is the first step before granting access to SharePoint. However, it is unfortunate that the majority of users continue to use the platform with its default settings. Some rental settings, nevertheless, need your attention. Bear in mind the significance of the sharing settings. Ignoring them can lead to disastrous consequences including data breaches. To start, here is the scenario.

Sharing settings

In the **SharePoint Admin Center**, locate the **Policies section** and click on Sharing to see the sharing settings for individual tenants. The fact that SharePoint and OneDrive have a scale that is equal to "**Anyone**" should be the first thing that gets your blood pumping. You can exchange folders and files using links that don't need the other person to sign in. Isn't that crazy? **ANYONE** may be the receiver. Unless you're quite certain you want to maintain it this way, you should descend one level immediately!

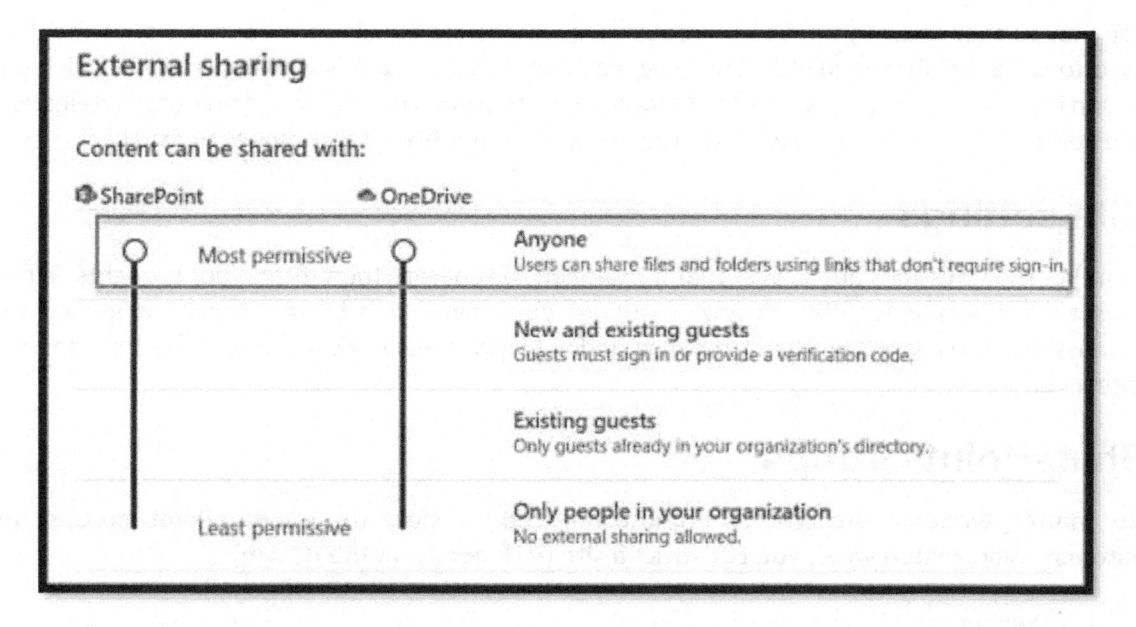

```
External sharing

Content can be shared with:

SharePoint        OneDrive

   O   Most permissive   O   Anyone
                             Users can share files and folders using links that don't require sign-in.

                             New and existing guests
                             Guests must sign in or provide a verification code.

                             Existing guests
                             Only guests already in your organization's directory.

       Least permissive      Only people in your organization
                             No external sharing allowed.
```

Take note: You are now not even required to be aware of your company's specific OneDrive for Business policies. In addition, the SharePoint option will cause the scale to descend by one level. Because OneDrive for Business can't make sharing as simple as it can on SharePoint.

Once you are aware of the company's policy, you can take these steps to choose the appropriate sharing settings:

- New and existing guests
- Existing guests
- Only people in your organization

More external sharing settings

We can obtain a bit more if we need to, and we have a few options again. If you like, you can choose all of them. The fact that you can do something doesn't imply that you should!

- **Limit external sharing by domain**. If you want to allow or block particular sites, you can do that. It is common practice to collaborate with certain clients or business associates. You can modify this option on the site level as well as the renter level.
- **Note**: Once you select "**Allow**" on one or more of the sites, the other ones will be banned immediately. You can "**Block**" certain names, but others will still be able to connect.
- Only members of certain **Security Groups** will be permitted to share with others outside of the firm.
- To access this option, make sure that the sharing settings (tenant) are set to "**New and Existing Guests**" or "**Anyone.**"

You may further secure your files by requiring guests to log in using the same account that was used to issue the sharing invites. This way, you know exactly who is viewing your files. Pick this option if you can. Guests may now log in for the duration you choose using a one-time PIN instead of a verification code; users will need to re-verify their identity after [number of days].

Site settings

SharePoint permissions are so vast that it's difficult to separate them from your thoughts. When sites are connected together in groups, things don't get much better. A peak might be the permissions. We can assign them to papers individually as we work our way down from the top (site level).

SharePoint Groups

No matter whether the site is group-connected or not, three SharePoint groups are automatically created when you construct a site (it depends on the design):

- Owners
- Members
- Visitors

Every built-in group has its own set of permissions. Prioritize using them, but if that fails, create a new SharePoint group and provide it with the appropriate amount of permission. Based on your requirements, you can choose which permission-level options to replicate and then decide which ones to employ.

Best Practice: Create your own SharePoint group and set your own permission level if necessary. The built-in groups should not be altered or removed.

Active Directory (AD) Groups

An on-premises Active Directory connected to Microsoft 365 is already in place for the majority of companies. Security groups should be introduced to SharePoint groups when permissions are granted to a SharePoint site. However, the admin area is also where you can create Microsoft 365 security groups and add them to your SharePoint site! There is a difference between Active Directory groups and SharePoint groups. Only the site where the SharePoint group was created will have access to it. The easiest way to keep things under control is to use SharePoint security groups. You may add users to sites one by one, but it will be more difficult to manage their profiles going forward.

Breaking permission inheritance

Permitting access to a certain library or document rather than the whole site may be necessary at some point. It is at this point that we can prevent the inheritance of permissions. The Site Owner, not the Site Member, is primarily responsible for this. Every person who visits your site will also have access to any libraries or documents you create or add to your lists. Do you recall the idea of the crescendo? Even if you remove the transfer of permissions from a library or list, the standard SharePoint groups—**Owners, Members, and Visitors**—will remain visible in the site permissions settings. After you've added your account (to maintain access), delete the default SharePoint groups, and provided unique permissions to this library, you may invite anybody who requires it.

Site Sharing

Without a Microsoft 365 Group connection, your site's sharing features will vary. You now have additional options when sharing and a better method to manage permissions thanks to the redesign.

Sites *not connected* to Microsoft 365 groups

For sites that aren't part of any groups, not much has changed. Despite the more modern UI, SharePoint specialists will still be able to share sites and utilize the Advanced Permissions Settings.

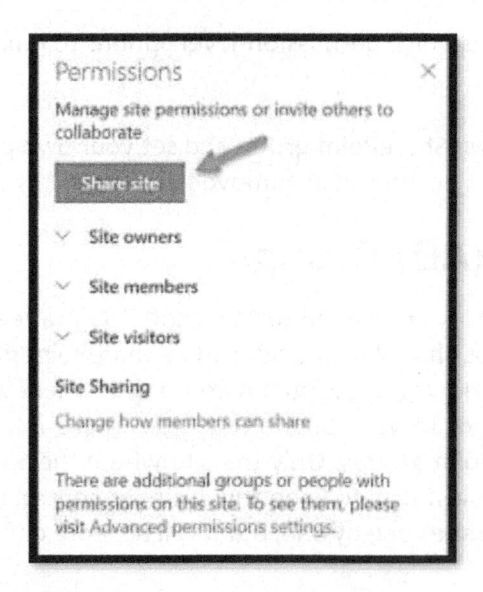

Sites *connected* to Microsoft 365 groups

After you've joined a group, you may still share the site. Put simply, you are not obligated to use any other group tools inside Microsoft 365, such as a shared inbox, Planner, etc. If you want to share the site and include the user or users in all of the Microsoft 365 group's functions, you can do so by going to the **Invite people** menu and then selecting **Add members to group**. The choice is yours!

Change how members can share

Another factor that could discourage sharing has to choose between the following three options:

- ❖ Any member-owner or owner of the site can share any folder, file, or even the site itself. Any user with Edit permissions can access shared files and folders.
- ❖ Anyone with Edit permissions, members, or the site owner can share files and folders, but only the site owner can share the site itself.
- ❖ You can't share folders, files, or the site itself unless you own it.

With option 2, the only distinction between the first two bullet points is that sharing the site will be limited to the site owner alone. No one will do it. At first, I found it difficult and had to read it many times. While the third point is easy to understand, we can see how it may hinder people's ability to accomplish their jobs. How would you go about informing a client or colleague? Additionally, this will add more work for the site owner... You can use this option if your users are new to SharePoint, if they need further training before they can confidently share, or if you choose not to let them share at all.

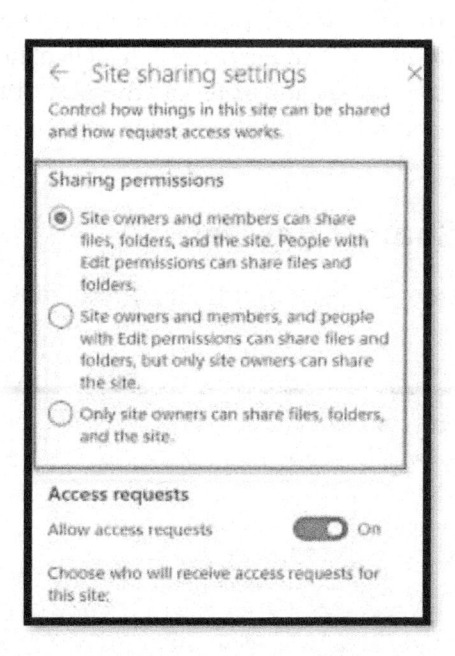

Access Requests

As you can see in the picture above, Access Requests were also turned on by default. What is it? Instead of seeing that frustrating "Access denied" warning that you can't change, you can use this long-standing functionality. SharePoint on-premises is still missing certain configuration pieces, however, SharePoint Online is completely operational! All that remains is to choose the

appropriate recipients, compose a tailored letter for the requester, and revisit the open requests.
Two options for who should receive Access Requests:
- Site Owners
- Specific email

Other Security Features To Consider

Multi-Factor Authentication (MFA)

My initial thought is multi-factor authentication (MFA) to safeguard your identities; this isn't limited to SharePoint, however. It was solely with Global Admins in mind when we first considered MFA a few years back. But the truth is that you should utilize it on every account you can.

Security and Compliance

It is only fair that we guarantee the security of SharePoint data after we have made it a secure environment to operate in. So, we'll talk about Data Loss Prevention (DLP), Sensitivity labels, categories of sensitive information, retention labels and regulations, and more. But where are they, anyway? In charge of them is the **Security and Compliance Center**. Do I need to create and manage those in my role as SharePoint Administrator? In all likelihood, no. It will need someone with permission to create labels and rules and access to the Security and Compliance center to do this. What the firm requires should ideally serve as a compass for thorough planning and execution of this.

Devices Accessing SharePoint Data

Even though they may need an Azure account, the SharePoint Online Admin Center offers additional options.

Access control
Use these settings to restrict how users are allowed to access content in SharePoint and OneDrive.

Unmanaged devices
Restrict access from devices that aren't compliant or joined to a domain.

Idle session sign-out
Automatically sign out users from inactive browser sessions.

Network location
Allow access only from specific IP addresses.

Apps that don't use modern authentication
Block access from Office 2010 and other apps that can't enforce device-based restrictions.

SharePoint Permissions

There are four main types of permissions in SharePoint Online:
1. Site Permissions:
- ❖ In SharePoint, site permissions are crucial for controlling who may see and do what on a given site. They are usually set up at the site's root level, but they can also be set up at the subsite level, which provides a more sophisticated control structure.

2. List Permissions:
- ❖ Access and modification privileges for a certain list or library on a SharePoint site are governed by list or permissions. You can customize the access control by configuring these permissions at the list or library level.

3. Folder Permissions:
- ❖ When it comes to SharePoint Online, the way folder permissions work is quite similar to how other site and document library components work. With options like Read, Contribute, and Full management, users can be granted different levels of folder access, allowing for fine-grained management.

4. Item Permissions:
- ❖ A further level of specificity is introduced by item permissions, which dictate who can see and change a particular document or item inside a library or list. You can refine access control by establishing permissions at the document or list item level, so items can have different permissions than the whole list.

Importantly, you must be the owner of the site or have the proper authorizations to establish permissions for anything. Permissions in SharePoint Online are set up at the site level, and permissions can cascade down to subsites, lists, libraries, and even individual elements within those sites. It is the responsibility of the site administrator to configure the permissions for the site. Unless specific permissions are defined for a subsite, list, library, or item, the default permissions for a site apply to all associated subsites, lists, and libraries.

SharePoint Permission Levels

What a person or group can do in SharePoint Online depends on the permission levels they have been given for a site, list, library, or item. SharePoint Online comes with some set permission levels, like Full Control, Edit, and Read. However, users can also make their own permission levels if they need to.

In SharePoint Online, the following permission levels are set by default:

- ❖ **Full Control:** If a user has Full Control permissions, they can see, add to, change, or delete any content on the site, in a list, in a library, or in an item. In addition to changing content, Full Control users can set user permissions, change item-level security settings, add or remove libraries and lists, change how the site looks, and handle site content, library, and list settings.

- **Design**: Users who have Design permissions can see and change information on the whole site, in lists, libraries, or things. They can also add to and remove categories from lists and libraries. The people who have design permission can also change the way the site looks and feels. However, they can't change the site's, lists, libraries, or things' protection settings.
- **Edit**: People who have this level of permission can see and change any data on the site, list, library, or thing. You can't change a site, list, library, or item's security settings if you have Edit permissions. Members of a SharePoint team site already have this permission.
- **Contribute**: With this level of permission, users can see and change any site material, whether it's in a list, a library, or an item. They can't add to or delete libraries or lists, though. People who only have **"Contribute"** permissions on SharePoint can't change how the site looks or how it works. They can't change the site's, a list's, a library's, or an item's security settings either.
- **Read**: This level of permission lets users see what's on the site, in the library, on the list, or in the item, but they can't change, add to, or remove anything. The safety settings for a site, list, library, or item cannot be changed by users with only Read permissions. Most of the time, given to site members.
- **View Only**: Users with this level of permission can only look at things on the site, in the library, on the list, or in an item; they can't change, remove, or add to any of the items. There are security settings for the site, a list, a library, and an item that users with "**View Only**" permissions can't change. They can look at things, set alerts, and read pages, but they can't download files to the client apps.

Here are the steps you need to take to make your own permission level in SharePoint Online:

1. Find the site where you want to set the special level of permission and go to its settings page.
2. Click on "**Settings**," then "**Site Permissions**," and finally "Advanced permissions settings."
3. Access the "**Permission levels**" link found in the menu on the Permissions page.
4. On the "**Permission Levels**" page, click "Add a Permission Level."
5. Giving the new permission level a name and a short description of what it will do is required.
6. Pick out the exact permissions you want this new level to have. You can choose from a list of set permissions, such as "**Full Control," "Edit," or "Read**." You can change these permissions to fit your needs.
7. If you want to make the new permission level official, hit the "**Create**" button.

Once you have created the unique permission level, you can give it to people or security groups as needed. This lets you change who can access and control things in SharePoint Online to fit the needs of your business.

Copy existing Permission Level

You can copy an existing permission level in SharePoint and use it to make a new one. Perform the actions mentioned in steps 1 through 3. If you click the "**Copy Permission Level**" button, you can copy any existing permission level, such as "**Contribute**." Then you can change permissions for things like "**Open items**", "**application pages**", "**Browse user information**", "**Personal web parts**", "**Client integration features**", "**Remote interfaces**" and more.

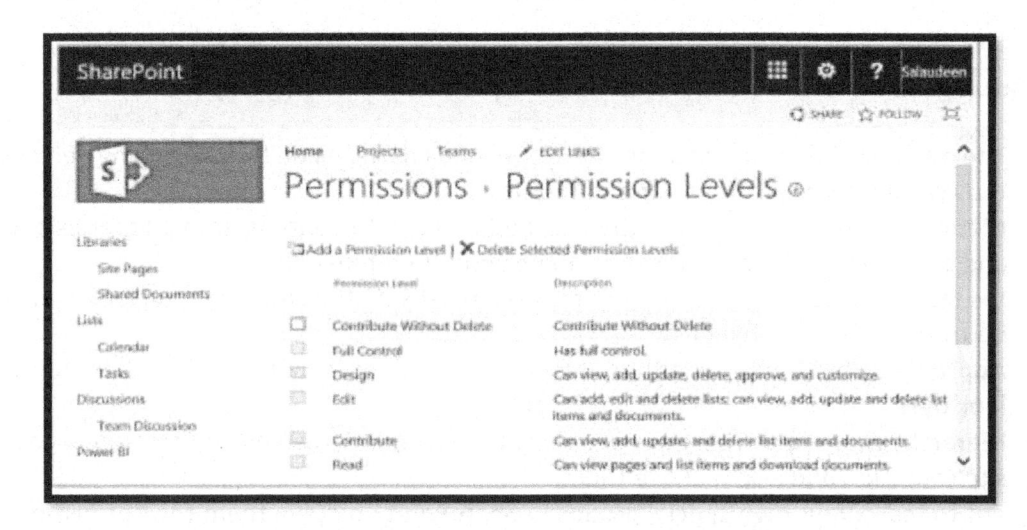

Managing Permissions in SharePoint Online

You can set and change permissions in SharePoint Online in a number of ways, including:

- ❖ **A SharePoint group** is a collection of individuals with the same permissions. You can create various groups for various purposes, such as a group for site owners and another group for project team members. You can add or remove people from groups at any time, and any changes you make to the permissions of the group will show up for everyone in it.
- ❖ **Individual Permissions**: You can also give people or groups permission to see or do things on a certain list, library, or item. When permissions are set for a person, they take precedence over permissions set for a group or level of permission.

How Do I Manage SharePoint Online Permissions?

When it comes to SharePoint Online, the User Interface (UI) is where all the permissions management happens. Through the UI, users can easily add or remove people from their site or document library, give them specific jobs and tasks, and set up groups to make managing many users at once easier. Different levels of permissions are given to users based on their job. This way, leaders have more power over the site than average users. Making Private Team Sites and Public Team Sites different gives you even more power. When managers link a Microsoft 365 group to a SharePoint site, they can choose whether the site is private or public. This choice tells SharePoint whether only certain users can access the site or whether all company users can access it by giving access to the group "Everyone except external users." In addition, when you start a new team site or discussion site in SharePoint Online, basic SharePoint groups are set up immediately. These basic groups are very important for controlling who can see the site and its material and what permissions are given to them. This organized method makes setting up SharePoint Online easier at the start and lays the groundwork for good permission management on the site.

The following is a list of the basic groups and the permissions each group has:

- **The owners**: This group runs the site and all of its parts. Aside from changing permissions, they can also change other parts of the site.
- **Members**: This group can edit the site, add and delete content, set up libraries and lists, and manage permissions for their papers and other items.
- **Visitors**: This group of people can only read what's on the site. They can look at anything on the site, but not change it.
- **Approvers**: This group can either accept or reject papers that have been sent to them to look over.
- **Hierarchy Managers**: There are people in this group who can make sites and pages in the site collection and also manage them.

If you want to make your own special groups in SharePoint and give them the permissions they need, you can set up a SharePoint group.

Folder level permissions in SharePoint Online

Indeed, you can use folder-level permissions in SharePoint Online to limit access to certain files within a list or library. **There are several ways to set permissions at the folder level. Here are some of them:**

- Go to the list or library that has the folder whose permissions you want to change.
- Pick out the folder you want from the list or library.
- On the menu, click on the "**Files**" tab. After that, press the "**Manage Access**" button.
- You can add people or SharePoint security groups and give them the right permission level in the "**Manage Access**" box. Click on the "**X**" next to someone's name to take them off the list.
- Once you've made the changes you want, click "**Save**" to apply the new permissions.

It's important to remember that in SharePoint Online, permissions at the folder level work separately from permissions at the list or library level. At the list or library level, you must set permissions for someone or a security group to be able to access all the files in a list or library.

You can add the person or group to the list of people and groups who have permissions on the "Permissions" page of the library or on the list itself. You can successfully control who can access certain files by following these steps and changing the permissions to fit your needs.

In SharePoint, how do I give someone else access to a document?

- In the list or library, find the file or folder whose permissions you want to change.
- Click on "**Share**" after picking out the file. When you do this, the "**Share with Others**" box will appear.
- Type the email address of the person or group whose permissions you want to set in the "**Invite People**" box.
- Use the drop-down menu next to "**Permission Level**" to find the right access level for your needs.
- You can add a message in the "**Add a message (optional)**" box if you want to give more information or set the scene.
- Click the "**Share**" button to send the request and set the permissions.

It's important to remember that the owner must first stop permissions from being passed down from the parent list or library to set permissions at the item level. After this is done, the manager can add people or groups to the specific thing and give them different permissions. Remember that the "**Permission Level**" dropdown may not always show the same file-level permissions based on how SharePoint is set up in your company. If the menu doesn't give you the permissions you need, you may need to ask a boss or someone else with the right access rights for more permission.

How to check user Permissions in SharePoint Online?

It is very important to check and change permissions on a SharePoint Online site on a daily basis, especially in places where people have different jobs and responsibilities. **If you want to see what permissions a site has in SharePoint Online, follow these steps:**

- You can check permissions for a SharePoint site by going to that site.
- Click on "**Settings**" in the upper right part of the page. When the choice comes up, choose "**Site settings.**"
- Find "**Users and Permissions**" on the "**Site Settings**" page and click on the "Site permissions" link.
- The "**Site permissions**" page will show a full list of all the people and security groups who have been given access to the site, along with the permission levels that have been given to them.

The same steps can be used to check the permissions on a single library or list on the site:

- Click on the name of the list or library in the library or list.

- ❖ When you do this, a box will appear that shows the exact permissions that have been given to the list or library.

Keep in mind that you need to already have the right permissions to view site, list, or library permissions. By doing these steps, you can easily check and control permissions in SharePoint Online, making sure that the right people have access based on your organization's needs.

Anonymous Access in SharePoint Online

You can make a unique link that anyone can access without a password if your external sharing settings are set to "Anyone."

Here is a step-by-step guide:

- ❖ Get the file or folder you want to share and open SharePoint Online.
- ❖ Click the "**Share**" button after right-clicking on the item.
- ❖ In the settings for the link, select "**Anyone with the link**" and enter the email names of the people you want to receive it.
- ❖ Choose the permissions you want these outside people to have from the drop-down menu, such as **Edit or View**.
- ❖ Finally, click "**Send**" to finish sharing.

This will give you a unique link that you can share with people outside of your business. This link will let them access the file or folder you specify without a password. Please keep in mind that how well these steps work will depend on how the external sharing settings for your SharePoint Online system are set up. Always make sure that the settings for sharing are in line with the security rules and guidelines of your company.

65

Best Practices for Security and Compliance

Data Loss Prevention (DLP) in SharePoint

There are rules and tools that businesses can use to keep private data from getting out to people who shouldn't have it. This is called data loss prevention. With these tools, you can keep an eye on and change data that is moving, sitting still, or being used. Strategies for stopping data loss can find people who shouldn't be viewing private data and stop them from doing so. They can also stop data from accidentally getting out. Before businesses can stop data loss, they need to know what private data they need to keep safe. This can include sensitive information about people, their finances, their ideas, and other things. Once a business knows what private data it has, it can make rules about how to keep it safe.

Microsoft Purview Data Loss Prevention

There is a cloud-based tool called Microsoft Purview that can help you keep your info safe. With Microsoft Purview, software companies can set rules for how to keep private data safe. These rules can be used to look at both live data and data that have already been saved. There are a lot of built-in rules in Microsoft Purview that can be used to protect private data in Microsoft 365 services like OneDrive, Teams, or Exchange. These rules can be changed to fit the wants of a group. Microsoft Purview has rules to keep you from losing data and tools to help you find data, organize data, and keep track of the history of data. You can find private data, keep an eye on how it is used, and make sure that laws about data security are being followed with these tools.

SharePoint and Data Loss Prevention

We understand how important it is for our business to keep our SharePoint data safe. This is why we have data loss prevention (DLP) rules in place. These rules let us find, watch, and protect private things quickly across all of our site groups.

SharePoint DLP Policies

A SharePoint DLP policy is a list of rules that are used to find and protect private data in SharePoint. PowerShell or the SharePoint admin tool can be used to make these rules and keep track of them. We need to know what the different parts of a SharePoint DLP policy are to make one that works. Some of these parts are policy rules, policy tips, acts, and circumstances. By setting these parts, we can decide how to find and keep private information safe.

Sensitive Information in SharePoint

In SharePoint, sensitive information can be anything from cash data to ***personally identifiable information (PII).*** To keep this information safe, we need to find it and use the right safety steps. One way to find secret information in SharePoint is to use DLP searches. These queries can be used to search SharePoint site groups for private data based on conditions that have already been established. Once we know it's been found, we can secure or block access to the data to keep it safe.

One more way to keep private information safe in SharePoint is to use sensitive marks. By putting sensitivity marks on SharePoint documents and other information, you can put them into groups based on how risky they are. Once this grade is given, safety measures like encryption or restricted access can be put in place.

Creating DLP Policies

To make a DLP policy in SharePoint, we need to do the following:

1. Navigate to the SharePoint center for management.
2. Select "Policies" from the left-hand menu.
3. Click on "Data loss prevention" and then choose "Create a policy."
4. Specify the types of information you want to protect and define actions for handling private information.
5. Activate policy tips and alerts to ensure compliance.
6. Save the policy rule to enforce data protection measures.

Always keep in mind that DLP rules can be tough to understand. To make sure the rule works, it's best to plan ahead and involve everyone.

Policy Tips and Alerts

The policy tips and reports that come with SharePoint's DLP rules are very important. Users are warned by policy tips when they are about to share private data, and managers are notified when private data has been shared.

To set up policy tips and alerts, we need to do the following:

- ❖ In the CMS for SharePoint, go to the "Policies" tab.
- ❖ Press "Data loss prevention" and pick the rule you need to change.
- ❖ In "Policy tip settings," we can change the message that appears when a user is about to reveal private data.
- ❖ In "Alerts," we can set up a message to appear whenever private information is shared.

You should remember that policy tips and reports can help us find possible security risks and fix them before any data is lost.

Policy Tips

Remember these policy tips when you work with DLP rules in SharePoint:

- Make sure the policy works by including people who have a stake in it in the planning process.
- Review and change the policy often to make sure it's always up-to-date.
- Show people how to find private data and how to handle it. Stress how important it is to keep data safe.
- Make sure that policy tips are written in short; easy-to-understand terms so that people know what could happen if they share private information.

By following these policy tips, we can be sure that our DLP rules will keep SharePoint data from being lost.

CHAPTER 7
CUSTOMIZING SHAREPOINT WITH APPS

Microsoft made an app for SharePoint to help people understand lists and libraries better since it can be hard to do so once you start changing them. Let's say you start with a custom list and then add fields to make it unique for each customer. What kind of list is it now? Is it still just a private list? Microsoft asked a number of focus groups this question and found that the idea of an app was clearer to them than the idea of a list or library. Because of this, now every list and library is called an app. But apps aren't just lists and libraries. Apps that do lots of cool things can be made by web writers. Anyone who knows how to code can turn any web feature into a SharePoint app because SharePoint is based on HTML standards. There is an online SharePoint App Store that you can access from inside SharePoint. This is where third parties can sell their apps.

Introducing SharePoint Apps

Apps are something you must know about if you have a smartphone. There are millions and millions of apps for every kind of smartphone. SharePoint has joined the app trend and supports the idea of an app. An App for SharePoint can be easy or hard to use. One way to make an app would be to change the Custom List app. On the other hand, you could hire a web developer to make a SharePoint app that does all of your billing. If you are using the old user interface or the new user interface changes, an app will look different in your browser. As you would expect from the standard experience, an app shows instructions on the menu that give you more setting options. These orders are local, which means that the ones that show up rely on where you are on the site. As an example, the **Document Library** app has a **Browse** tab, but it also has a **Files tab** and a **Library page**. The ribbon has been taken away from the current user interface in favor of a cleaner look at things at the top of the app. For instance, you probably add new things to a library of material all the time. You can add new documents using the first button at the top, which is called "New." Also, the **New button** is a bright color that makes it easy to find. Uploading new documents is the next button over, which you probably also use frequently.

On the page for advanced settings, you can choose whether an app gives you a new or old experience. To get to it, go to the app. From the drop-down menu next to the gear icon in the upper right corner of the page, choose List or Library settings. To get to the app's advanced settings page, go to the settings page. In the list of advanced settings, you will find a button that lets you choose between the new and old experiences. In the "**List Experience**" part, you can pick the "**New Experience**," "**Classic Experience**," or "**Default Experience**" options. It is up to the owner of the site collection to decide what the Default Experience will be. Microsoft likes to change the user experience of things quite often, which is something we talk about a lot in the book. This is shown very well by the band at the top of an app. In SharePoint, the ribbon will show up if you are using the standard view. You won't see the band if you have the most recent version. Behind the scenes, everything works the same, but the way things look and how you use them have changed. This is something that Microsoft does a lot, and it takes some time to get used to their changes. One good thing about changes is that they are generally for the better, and after the original shock goes off, we start to enjoy them.

Adding Apps to Your Site

You pick a template when you make a new SharePoint site. Your site may already have a number of apps if you choose the right template. But you can add more apps to your site. Let's say you want to add a Survey app to your site.

Now you can take these steps to add an app to your site, like the Survey app:

1. Click the **Settings button** in the upper right corner and select "**Add an App**." It shows you all the apps you can add to your site on the Your Apps page. At the top, there is an area called "**Noteworthy**" that has the most used apps.
2. Find the Survey app and click on it. The Adding Survey dialog box appears.

3. Give your Survey app a name. You can also click "**Advanced Options**" to set options that are only for that app. Right now, you can pick whether to show usernames in the poll and let users give more than one answer using the poll app.
4. Click "**Create**" to make the app and add it to your site. It shows the Site Contents page, which lists all of your site's apps. Look at your new Survey app. It has the name you gave it in Step 3.

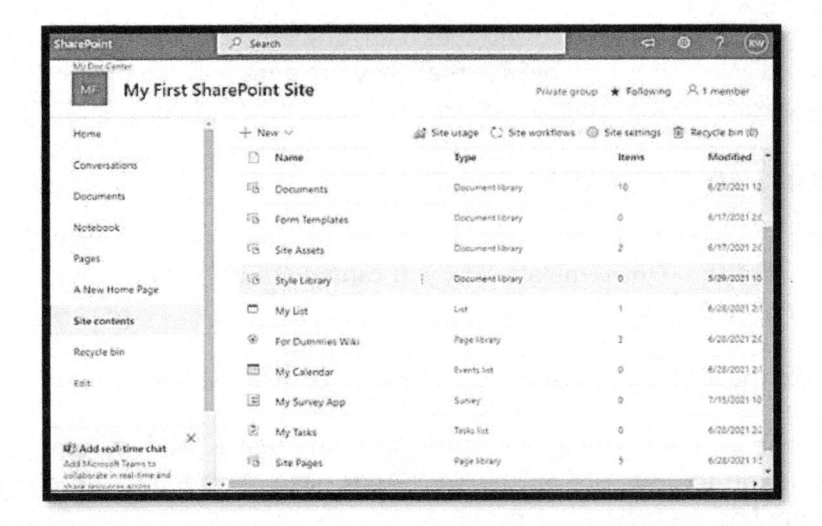

By selecting it from the Site Contents page, you can access an app. The app you just made will show up on the screen if you click on it.

Request an app from the SharePoint Store

You can ask for an app from the SharePoint Store that your company hasn't yet approved. It will let you add it to your site if it's okay.

1. Go to the site you want to add an app to and click on **Settings**. Then click on **Add an app**.
2. Click on **SharePoint Store** in the menu bar at the top of the page.
3. Use the search bar to find an app or choose a topic on the left to see a list of apps.
4. Pick out an app to add. In some cases, you may only be able to add the app through the original SharePoint Store experience. In those situations, you'll see a link that lets you go back to the classic store.
5. Click on **Request**.

6. You can add a reason for your wish if you want to. After that, click **Send request**.

7. You can add the app to your site once it's been accepted.

Accessing App Settings

A list or library is what most apps are built on. There is a settings page for each list or library where you can set up your app. Use the Library Settings page or the List Settings page to view or modify the setup settings for your Library or List apps. **This page is where you can find all the settings and customization options for your List or Library app that will work best for your business.**
1. Go to the **Site Contents** page and click on the name of your library or list to get there. The Settings gear button is where you can access the Site Contents page.
2. Click the Library or List tab on the Ribbon. The Settings area can be found on the far right.
3. Press the button that says "**Library" or "List**" Settings.

4. To change how your library is set up, click the Library Settings button. It shows the Library Settings or List Settings page.

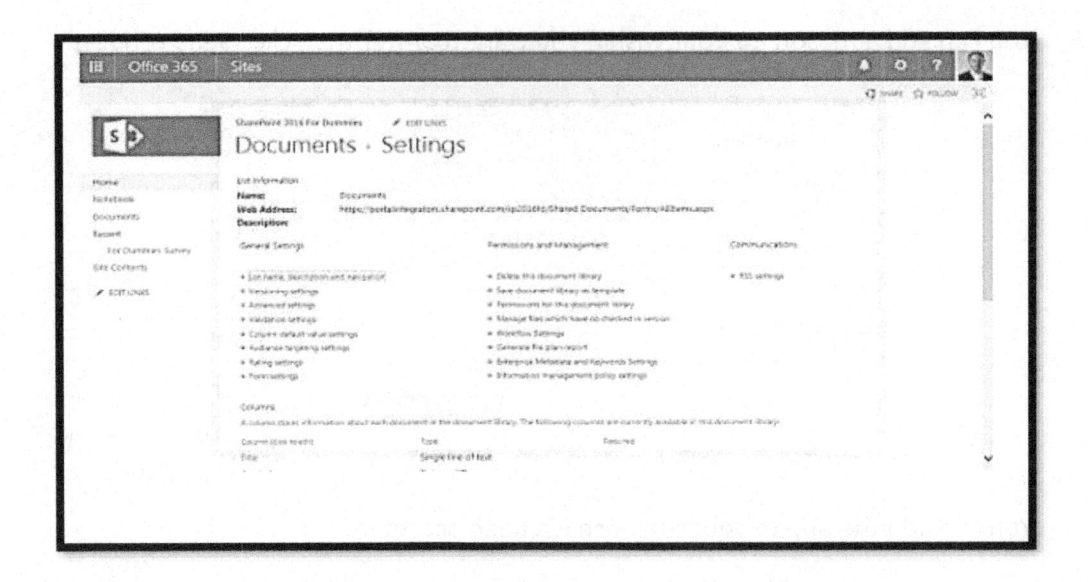

There are several parts to the Library (or List) Settings page. Each area has a lot of setting options. Look around this page for a while. Here are some of the parts you can see:

- **List Information**: Shows the name, web link, and description of the library (or list). If you click the List Name, Description, and Navigation link in the General Settings column, you can change the name and description of the list. The online address points to the list's base view. On the Library (or List) Settings page, scroll down to the Views area. This is where you can change the usual view. Use the root of the web page to link to a list or library. That way, you can always change the default view without having to change the links that point to the list.
- *General Settings:* This section has settings for Versioning, Advanced, Validation, Column Default Value, Rating, Audience Targeting, and Form. It also has the name and description of the list. For a full list of General Settings, look at Table 7-1.
- **Permissions and Management**: This section lets you save the library or list as a template and change settings for Enterprise Metadata and Keywords, Workflow, Permissions, and File Management. From this area, you can also make a file plan report.
- **Communications**: Configure RSS and incoming email settings for the library or list.
- **Content Types**: A Content Types area shows up if you have set up your library or list to accept content types. In this area, you can link different types of information to your library or list. With content types, you can use sections on different sites, in libraries, on lists, and on other sites.
- **Columns**: You can make, see, add, and change columns in the list or library. You can add a site column from the preset SharePoint site columns, make a new site column of your choice that can be added to multiple lists, or create your own column specifically for this list.
- **Views**: Show and change the list or library views. You can also get fresh views.

73

Configuring the General Settings

Recently, the Library or List app's General Settings area got a lot bigger. It now has more settings, like *Validation, Column Default Value (for libraries), Audience Targeting, Rating, and Form.*

Changing the title, description, and navigation

The General Settings page is a simple settings page that says what it does. Most of these options are set when you make the Library or List app for the first time. For example, you can choose whether the app shows up in the Quick Launch menu. The app's computer address (URL) stays the same even if the title is changed. If having the title match the URL is important or will help your team understand better, you might want to make a new app with the title you want and delete the old one. Of course, this works better at the beginning, before you share documents or make apps. You can copy documents from one Library app to another or export a List app to Excel and then put it back into a new app if you already have a lot of things in your app. But this isn't something to be taken easily. Some column setup settings, like those for a **Choice column**, need to be made over; along with the app settings we talk about here. Take some time to think about what you want to call your app before you make it if you're not sure what to call it.

Versioning settings

Some of the most-used settings in any app can be found in the Versioning Settings area. Most of the options for managing documents or information can be found in the settings for versions. The new words to remember for managing documents and material are "approve," **"version," and "check out"**. You can say it while you sleep. When you first open a Team site, the settings for *Approval, Versioning, or Check out Requirement* are not turned on. Versioning is not enabled by default because it consumes a lot of database room. The database gets bigger every time a new version is made. We do think you should turn on versioning, though, because it's important for real work. You might want to use a blogging site instead if you want these options to be available when your sites are set up. Before you choose one of these options, make sure you understand how your team does business.

You might not want or need to apply Approval settings or Check Out if documents are carefully reviewed and accepted outside of SharePoint. If your documents are pictures, you might not need to use versioning if you don't care about the versions and can go back to an older version. You might want to use more than one Document Library app and change the settings for each one as needed. Say you have 100 documents in a Library app, but you only need to version and approve 5 of them. Maybe those 5 documents can be put in a Library app with more settings. The most confusing thing about SharePoint document handling is that versions can be different from one another. Versioning is a good way to keep your work safe because you can go back to an earlier version of the file if you need to. In SharePoint, versions are copies of the same document that were made at different times while it was being edited. We recommend that you add the Versions column to your views so that people can quickly see what version of the text they are looking at.

If not, people will add the version number to the name or title of the document, like "Employee Handbook v1.0," "Employee Handbook v2.0," or my personal favorite, "Employee Handbook v3.0." The final version of the client proposal was edited by KW and reviewed by RW. It was signed off by Rosemarie on February 6, 2019, and should not be changed.

Follow these steps to apply or modify Versioning settings:

1. On the Library Settings or List Settings page, click the link that says "Versioning Settings."
- Content Approval, Document Version History, Draft Item Security, and Require Check Out are the parts of the Versioning Settings page (Library apps only).

2. Next, you need to decide if you want to require content review for things that are sent in. On the Versioning Settings page, which you can access in Step 1, you can make this choice by clicking the Yes or No radio button.
- Individuals with the Approve Items permissions can always see draft items if you choose "Yes" to the question "*Require Content Approval for Submitted Items*?"
- Users and members of the site can't see draft versions of items that haven't been accepted yet. For each draft, you can choose who can see it in the Draft Item Security area.

3. In the Document Version History area, choose a choice button to say whether to use No Versioning, Create Major Versions, Create Major and Minor (Draft) Versions, or (optionally) enter a number to say how many versions to keep.
- No Versioning is what a List or Library app is set to by default. Big Versions (1.0, 2.0, 3.0, etc.) or Big and Small Versions (1.0, 1.2, 1.3, 2.0, etc.) are what you can choose. You can set a limit for the number of versions of each type by adding a number up to 10,000 if you choose either of the last two options.

4. Select a Draft Item Security choice button in the Draft Item Security area to decide who can see drafts.
- If you don't want minor (draft) versions or need content approval for your documents or list items, this area won't work. Any User Who Can Read Items, Only Users Who Can Edit Items, or Only Users Who Can Approve (and the Author of the Item) are the three options for who can see written items.

5. Choose whether people who are changing documents should be required to check out by clicking the Yes or No radio button.
- Check out is another good safety feature that makes sure other users don't see a document in the middle of being changed or have multiple users editing at the same time (last save wins). It can be annoying, though, because people often forget that they checked out a document, sometimes months ago!
- Users can quickly see who has an item checked out by adding the Checked Out To column to your views.

6. Press "OK."
- Your Versioning settings are used after you click OK. Check them out!
- In a Library app, you can see documents by clicking the dots, which brings up a choice, as shown below. The author of a document can use this menu to check out and check in the

document, accept it, start a process, and other things. Because the menu is based on the current context, **Approve** won't show up on the menu if approval isn't set on the library or list, for example. The Discard Check Out option shows up if a paper is checked out.

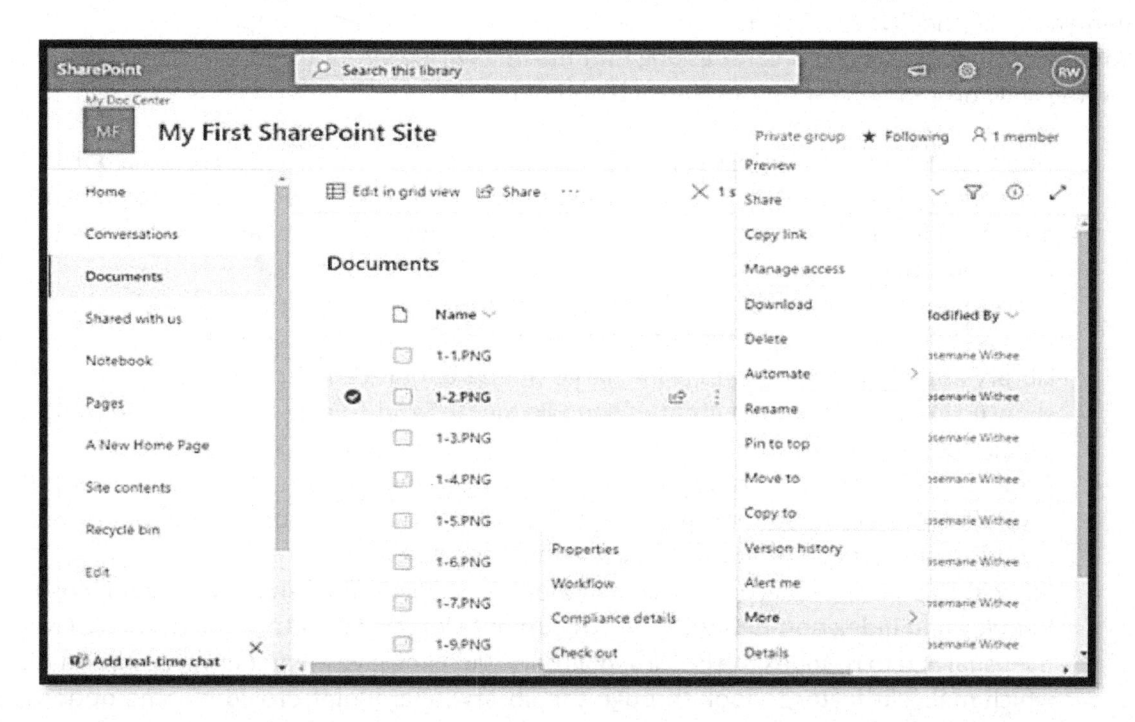

To work with list apps, most of the time, team members use browsers to get to the site. But think about how the people on your team use documents. In the browser, they might be going to an app, but they could also be linking from a bookmark or opening the file straight from an editing program like Word, Excel, or PowerPoint. Users may not know where to find the SharePoint Library app settings, even though they are supported and can be used with the latest versions of Office. It will help if you take a moment to go over the settings and options with your team. One of the best things you can do to improve SharePoint teamwork is to get training on these document management options. This is especially important for teams with a lot of members or users.

Advanced settings

Advanced settings include many powerful configuration options for Library and List apps:

- **Content Types**: This section lets you add and remove content types that are linked to an app.
- **Document Template (only in the Library app):** This lets you choose which template, like Word, Excel, or PowerPoint, is used when someone clicks the "New" button to make a new document.

It's also possible to link document templates to content types. This means that you can use a library with multiple content types to link different document templates. It might sound complicated, but in a word, having different document types and themes gives you more options when you click the "**New**" button when making documents. As an example, you could have a Word template for costs and one for asking for time off. With content types, these can both show up in the New drop-down list on the Files tab of the menu.

- **Opening Documents in the Browser (Library app only):** If someone clicks on a document to open it, you can control how the browser acts. Do not allow documents to open in the browser if you do not wish to use the Office Web apps. Users can also send straight links to the documents if they need to.
- **Custom Send to Destination (Library app only):** You can add your own web address to the Send To menu on a document's Edit menu with this great option (only available in the Library app). The person who is in charge of SharePoint can also add global names that show up in every document library's Send To menu. Send To makes a copy of your file and sends it somewhere else, like another Team site where you want to share it.
- **Folders**: This setting tells users if they can make new folders in the Library app. This option should be turned off so that people don't go folder crazy. The option can be turned on and off at any time, so you can make groups when you need to.
- **Search**: This setting lets you choose whether app things should show up in search results.
- **Reindex and index non-default views Document Library**: Ways to index views that aren't the usual and to re-index the document library. Indexing gives searches more information, which makes it faster to look through the library. SharePoint provides some options to manage the search costs, though.
- **Offline Client Availability**: This feature lets you choose if PC client software users, like those who use Outlook, can download material to view when they're not online.
- **Site Assets Library (Library app only):** This feature lets you make the Library app a Site Assets library. This makes it easy for users to find video files in the Library app.
- **Quick Property Editing**: This feature lets you choose if Quick Edit can be used on this library. With Quick Edit, users can open the view in a grid and change information right away. For comparison, this is like making changes to the metadata (information about the library documents) in real-time in an Excel-like program.
- **Dialogs:** List and library forms open in a chat box by default. You can choose this option if you want forms to open as pages instead of chat boxes in the browser window.

List app's complex settings also let you set permissions and files for each item.
To use or change, follow these steps. More advanced settings:

1. On the Library Settings or List Settings page, click the link that says "Advanced Settings." The screen for Advanced Settings shows up.

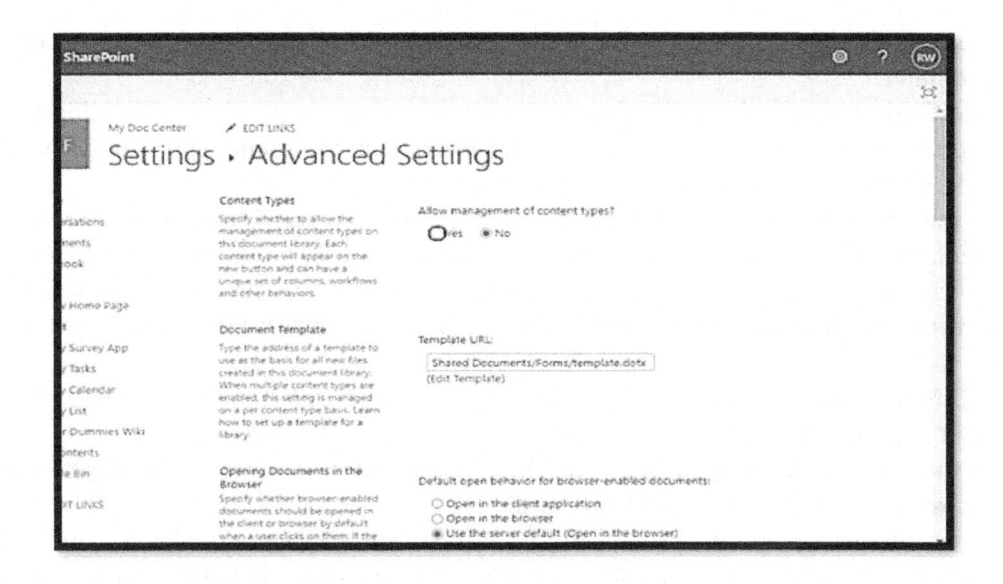

2. Click the "Yes" or "No" option button to decide if you want to allow control of material types.
You will see a new area called "**Content Types**" on your Library Settings or List App Settings page if you choose "**Yes**." No is chosen by default.

3. In the Template URL text box, type in a template URL to change the document template (only in the Library app).
Library apps come with a template that you can use to make new documents. Remember that you can make a new document in the Library app and also share documents that you have already made. In the case of a Document Library app, the usual Word template is used as the document template. This could be turned into a template for Excel or PowerPoint. You could also use a template that you made yourself in one of these programs. You can set up different templates for each type of paper when you're working with content types. In this case, your library might hold contracts and have three types of material for those contracts, each with its own template that can be found on the "New" button. You can change the Template URL in the Document Template part of the Advanced Settings page if you choose a different document template. Add the template to the Forms folder in the Document Library app.

4. Select a radio button in the Opening Documents in the Browser area to choose whether to open documents in the browser (Library app only), the client application, or as the server option.
If the client application is unavailable, the document opens in the browser.

5. Add a Custom Send to target (only in the Library app) by typing the URL target and the name that should show up on the Send To screen.
Like Windows prompts like "**Send to Desktop**," you can add an option to the Edit menu in this Library app that lets you send documents to a different SharePoint location. In the Destination Name and URL text boxes, type in a short name for the menu that shows up when you click on it and a URL for the place you want to go.

6. In the Folders area, click the Yes or No radio button to decide if this app can make folders.

Whether the New Folder action is on the New menu depends on whether you choose Yes or **No**. **Yes** is the default.

Most of the time, we turn off groups when we don't need them. We believe that folders are only useful when you need to keep a group of documents in the same app but with different permissions. People will use folders if you leave them open.

7. Choose the "Yes" or "No" radio button in the Search part to see if this app is searchable.

You can keep things in the app from showing up in search results by choosing "No" for the Search option. This is true even if the site or app is added to the Search settings. Yes is the setting.

8. Choose the Yes or No radio button in the Offline Client Availability area to make offline clients available.

With the **Offline Client Availability** option, you can choose if app items can be downloaded to offline client apps like Outlook. Yes is the default.

9. Choose the Yes or No choice button in the Site Assets Library area to add the app location to the Site Assets Library (only for the Library app).

With this new Site Assets Library option, you can choose if this Library app is used by default when you add pictures or other files to a Wiki page. This can be especially helpful for Picture Library apps or Document Library apps that have pictures in them. This prevents wiki writers from having to conduct extensive picture searches. **No** is the default.

10. Choose the Yes or No radio button in the Quick Property Editing area to see if the app can be changed with Quick Edit.

This option lets you choose if Quick Edit can be used to change a lot of data at once in this app. **Yes** is the default.

11. Choose the Yes or No option button in the Dialogs area to show whether forms should open in a modal dialog box.

We recommend that you choose the No option in this part a lot because modal window boxes get old pretty fast.

12. To apply your selections, click OK.

A Yes/No option for accepting files for a list item (the default is Yes) and item-level permissions are other advanced setup settings that can only be found in the List app and not the Library app. In a List app, all members (contributors) can read and change all things by default when it comes to item-level permissions. You can change these settings so that people can read or change only their own pieces of content.

Validation settings

Some formulas or statements need to assess TRUE before data can be saved. This is called validation. It has two kinds of validation: validation at the column level and validation at the app level. There is one main difference between column validation and app validation. Column validation only checks the data in one column against a test, like seeing if a deal is less than or equal to 50%.

= [Discount] < = .50

On the other hand, validation settings at the app level check that two or more columns are equal and must be set to TRUE before the data can be saved. You can make it so that **[Discount] < [Cost]** so that people who buy something at a price don't get something for free or get their money back.

Here's what you need to do to use validation settings:

1. Go to the Library Settings or List Settings page and click on the link that says "Validation Settings."
- There are two parts to the Validation Settings page: Formula and User Message. This is the test that your comparison of the fields must pass in order for the item to be acceptable. If the test fails, the person will see a message in the person Message area. After that, users can change the numbers until the test passes.

2. Type a formula into the Formula box to make a confirmation formula.
- In your app, the method needs to check or compare at least two fields. On the App Settings page, there is an example of correct grammar and a link to find out more.
- You can choose from a list of fields in your app to use in your code.

3. Type a message into the "User Message" box that will be shown to users who enter an incorrect item.

4. Click Save to make sure that your list is correct.

Validations don't go back in time. They only affect new and changed items in the fields that are named.

Audience targeting settings

Selecting **Enable Audience Targeting or Enable Classic Audience Targeting** for the app is an option in the **Audience Targeting** setting. For brand-new Web Parts like News, use Enable Audience Targeting. For all the Web Parts we already know and love, use Enable Classic Audience Targeting. The old books, in other words. Some Web Parts, like the Content Query Web Part, can use this field to sort list items based on whether the person is in a certain group. Targeting an audience is not the same as giving permissions. Content can still be accessed by users who aren't part of a community. Audience targeting is just a way to make sure that material is only shown to certain groups of people.

Rating settings

To allow users to review the things in the app, Rating Settings is a simple Yes/No option. A lot of people have asked for the Rating tool. A Rating box shows up in your app when it's turned on, as shown in the picture below. People can choose a star grade in the grade form. There is a "**Like**" button that you can use instead of a star number to show that you agree with something. If you know how to use social networking sites like Facebook, you already know how the "**Like**" button works. When you turn on ratings, you can change the rate from a star to a "**Like**" button on the rate Settings page.

Form settings

With the Form Settings option, you can choose to use the usual SharePoint form or use PowerApps to make your own form. If you choose the "Use a custom form created using PowerApps" radio button, you can change the form using PowerApps. A program called **InfoPath** used to let people change the way forms looked. However, Microsoft has replaced it with PowerApps, a tool that is newer and has more features. If you have an older version of SharePoint on-premises, you may still see the InfoPath option.

CHAPTER 8
UNDERSTANDING SHAREPOINT SITES

In a company, SharePoint sites are like digital meeting places where people can work together, share files, and set up information. Think about a big building with many floors. At the top is the main area, which is made up of many rooms, or sites. Each room can have smaller rooms (subsites), shelves (document libraries) to store files, lists (to-do or contact) to keep track of things, and bulletin boards (pages) to post news.

There are useful things about these sites:

- **Document Libraries**: These are like online boxes where you can store and organize your things.
- **Lists**: These are like digital to-do lists or files that you can use to keep track of things like friends, chores, and other data.
- **Pages**: These are online pages where you can post news, messages, or project information and share it with other people.
- **Web Parts**: Think of them as tools that you can change and add to pages, like movies, dates, or news feeds.

You can make these sites your own by changing the colors, adding brands, and setting things up however you like. You can control who has access to what in SharePoint sites to keep things private and safe, just like you would lock the door to your room. Because these sites work well with other Microsoft tools, it's simple to chat, share information, work together, and stay organized on different devices. It also has tools that can automatically do things like approve documents or send notes, which can help you save time and get more done. SharePoint sites help teams stay organized, share information, and work well together by being like digital workplaces.

Accessing SharePoint Sites in Microsoft 365

1. Open your web browser and navigate to www.office.com.
- Your dashboard will show up if you have already signed in. You will need to sign in here with your passwords if you haven't already.

2. In the upper left area of the screen, click the waffle sign. Then, choose SharePoint.
- The Frequent Sites page, which lists the SharePoint sites you view most often, appears.
- For quick access to the Frequent Sites page, you can also click SharePoint on the left side of the main screen. You can always use the waffle sign in the upper left area to get to SharePoint if you are in another app, like Outlook.

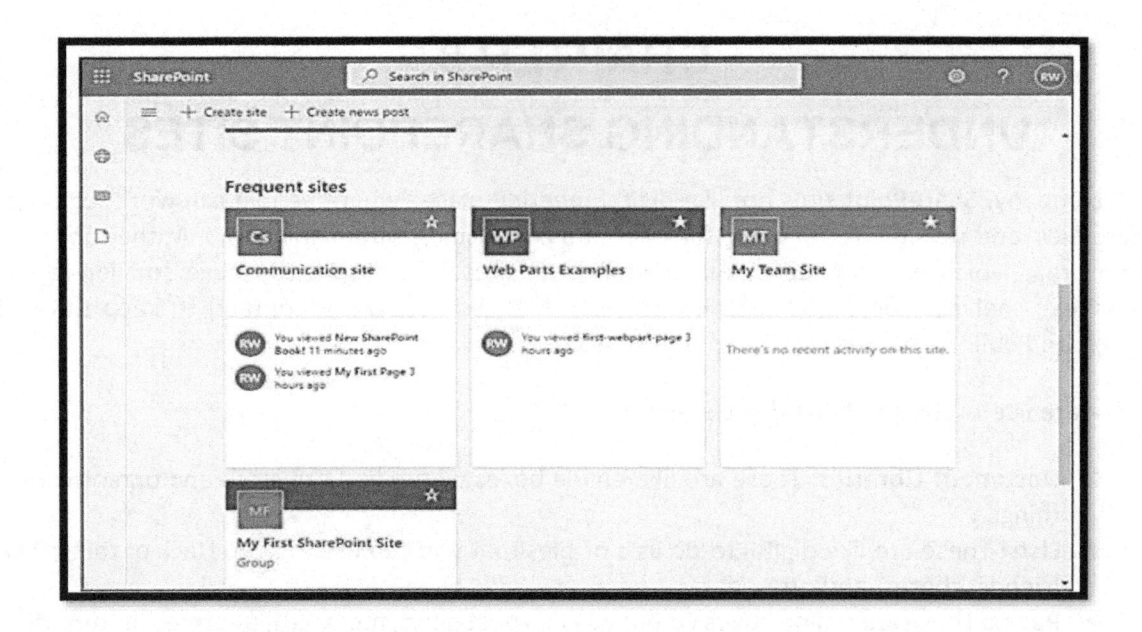

Click the SharePoint site you want to open.

- Presto! Your SharePoint site opens and you are ready to begin exploring it.

Exploring the SharePoint Team Site

When you make a SharePoint site, you can pick from a number of site designs. The most popular is the Team site template, which has a lot of features that make it easy for teams to share content and apps and work together on projects. This is what you can do when you open your brand-new Team site for the first time. You can interact with others in **Conversations** (which works with

Outlook), store your digital files in the built-in **Document Library app (Documents),** open **OneNote** to keep sharing notes (**Notebook**) and make new web pages (**Pages**) from the menu on the left. The Home page is always available by choosing Home from the navigation menu, and it is the first page that shows up when you open your Team site. The Team site's home page can do a lot of useful things. This part has sections for News, Quick Links, Activity, Documents, and Comments on the site. You can also change the parts of the Home page to suit your needs.

Finding your way around

There are the same things on all SharePoint Team sites. If you just set up a new Team site, it should look like the one in the first picture above. If you are on the usual conversation site, you will see a site that is made for conversation using that template. Your site might look a little different if it has been changed. Don't worry—everything is still the same. You might have to look around a bit to find them.

The following main parts can be found on almost all SharePoint sites:

- ❖ **Header**: The header takes up the whole top of the page. You can use the top of a SharePoint page in the same way that you use the menu in a regular Windows program, like **Microsoft Word**. Similar to how the ribbon is at the top of many Office programs, SharePoint even has the ribbon in the page header. To make it bigger, click on one of the tabs, like Files or Library. The ribbon grows in a way that looks a lot like the other Office programs when you click on a tab.
- ❖ **Left navigation pane**: The left menu pane offers quick access to the site's discussion boards, document libraries, and lists. You can even add links to things you make, like web pages and documents. You can change everything about the menu and add any links you want. You can even add links to websites that aren't in SharePoint. For example, you could add a link to the website of your partner or any other website you like.
- ❖ **Page content**: This is what shows up in the page's body. Microsoft has done a great job making the Team site's home page better. You can change the main page and add your own pages.

It's usually the case that the title and left menu pane don't change. However, the body of the page does change to show the page's content. This is a lot like how most websites work. But some sites are laid out in different ways. The Communication site, for instance, has scrolling across the top and then big tiles and parts that are meant to get information to a group. A lot of money was spent by Microsoft on user study to find the best way to arrange the pages in SharePoint. We strongly advise that you use the styles that Microsoft provides instead of making your own. More than one site has turned into a never-ending trip of changes and edits that make the site hard to use for new visitors.

Uploading documents

When you first go to a Team site, there is an area in the bottom right corner called Documents. This small part that doesn't seem important is actually an example of SharePoint at its best. On the main page, there is also a link to the Documents area. This is something that SharePoint does a lot. In SharePoint, it seems like there are an infinite number of ways to complete a single job. This can lead to some interesting conversations in the break room. Someone may be set on a certain way to use SharePoint, while someone else may be set on a different way. Both ways can be right in SharePoint! To put it simply, Documents is a place where you can store your personal files. On the inside, though, Documents is made up of pages, apps, and Web Parts. To add a new file, like a Microsoft Word file, to Documents, all you have to do is click the ellipses icon in the header of Documents and then choose New, as shown in

Sharing your Team site

Not having any people on a site isn't really useful. Your SharePoint Team site can be shared in a number of ways. Getting people to join the site is the best way to share. For those you share a site with, you will send them an email with all the information they need to access it.

Share your site from your web browser

Follow these steps to share your SharePoint site through an online browser:

1. **Open your web browser and go to the site you want to share on SharePoint Team.**
2. **Click the gear icon in the upper-right corner and select Site Permissions.**
   - The Permissions pane opens.
3. **Click the "Invite People" button and pick whether to add people to the group of people who can access the site or just share it.**
   - We will choose to share just the site in this case, which will bring up the Share Site window.

People who already have a Microsoft 365 contract will be shown on the list if you choose to add people to the group. You will only see one user if you are going along with the book (unless you have added more along the way).

4. Type in the person's email address that you want to share the site with.

To let you know that the person is not from your company, a message will show up. Remember that you shouldn't share information outside of your company if it shouldn't be shared. This warning is important. Anyone in charge of the group can stop people from sharing with anyone outside of the organization.

5. After confirming that the check box for Send Email is checked, type a message to the person with whom you are sharing the site, and then click the Add button.

The interface that you will see on your computer will be different from what we explain here if you are using the traditional SharePoint experience. In the past, for instance, a Share button would be shown at the very top of a website on the homepage. On the other hand, there are a variety of reasons why you may not be able to display this button.

There have been instances in which it does not show up in the Chrome browser but does show up in other browsers. Due to the fact that this approach is effective regardless of whether or not you see a Share button at the top of your screen, we have included an explanation of the process that is used to share a website via the Permissions window. If you do not have permission to share access to the site, the Site Permissions link will not appear when you click the gear icon because

SharePoint will delete it automatically even if you do have permission to share access. In general, if you read about anything and it does not match what you see on your site, it is typically due to one of two issues: the first problem is that the information you read about is not accurate. In the first place, it is possible that you do not possess the appropriate rights for that specific function. Secondly, it is also possible that the feature is not active or set for your website. In the event that your SharePoint instance does not have an email setup, for instance, you will not be able to see the Share button.

Share your site from the SharePoint Mobile App

The actions that you need to do to share your SharePoint site using the SharePoint Mobile App are as follows:

1. On your mobile device, either a smartphone or a tablet, launch the SharePoint Mobile App and browse the website that you want to link to.
2. In the upper-right-hand corner of the screen, tap the symbol that looks like an ellipsis.
   ❖ The site options will appear.
3. Select **Share This Site**.
From this point forward, the procedure is identical to the one you would use to share anything else from your mobile device until this point. On the iOS platform, for instance, you will find the well-known sharing mechanism shown.
4. Choose how you want to share the site.

Creating a SharePoint Site

A new SharePoint site may be created by using either your web browser or the SharePoint Mobile App on your mobile device. Before beginning the process of creating a SharePoint site, you are required to choose the site template that you want to utilize. All of the preset pieces that you need are included in each and every site design. These elements include navigation, particular functionality, and basic default pages. The Team site template continues to be the most popular site template because it has a wide variety of features that are customized for the purpose of facilitating team interaction and cooperation. However, it is essential to have a solid understanding of the different templates that are accessible to you so that you may make use of them whenever you need them.

Create a subsite from your web browser

To create a new site using your web browser, follow these steps:

1. **Open your web browser and navigate to your existing SharePoint site.**
2.   **Click the gear icon in the upper-right corner of the screen and choose Site Contents.**
   - The Contents screen for the site appears.
3. Select "**Subsite**" from the drop-down menu and click the New button.
   - There is a screen that displays the **New SharePoint Site**.

4. Create a title and description for the new website in the area labeled "**Title and Description.**"
5. In the box labeled "**Web Site Address**," add the particulars of how you would want the website to be displayed in the URL of the web browser.
6. In the area labeled "**Template Selection**," choose a site template that will be used for the website.
   - Although the default site template is the Team site template, there are a number of different site templates available for customers to choose from. To have a better understanding of how the templates function, we suggest that you make one of each and investigate it. This is essential in order for you to be able to design a website that is suitable for your specific circumstances. For the sake of this illustration, we will decide to establish a Document Center website.
7. In the section titled "**Permissions**," choose whether you want the new site to have the same rights as the parent site or if you want to generate new permissions for the new site.

8. In the area titled "**Navigator**," you will need to determine how you would want the navigation to be shown on the parent site, as well as whether or not you would like the new site to display the navigation from the parent site.
- To build the new SharePoint site, click the **Create** button.
- Following a short period of time, your brand-new website will be generated and viewed in your web browser.

Create a site from the SharePoint Mobile App

1. Launch the SharePoint Mobile App on your desktop computer, mobile device, or tablet.
2. To access the **Site Contents** menu, open the navigation window by tapping the hamburger menu located in the top-left corner of the screen.

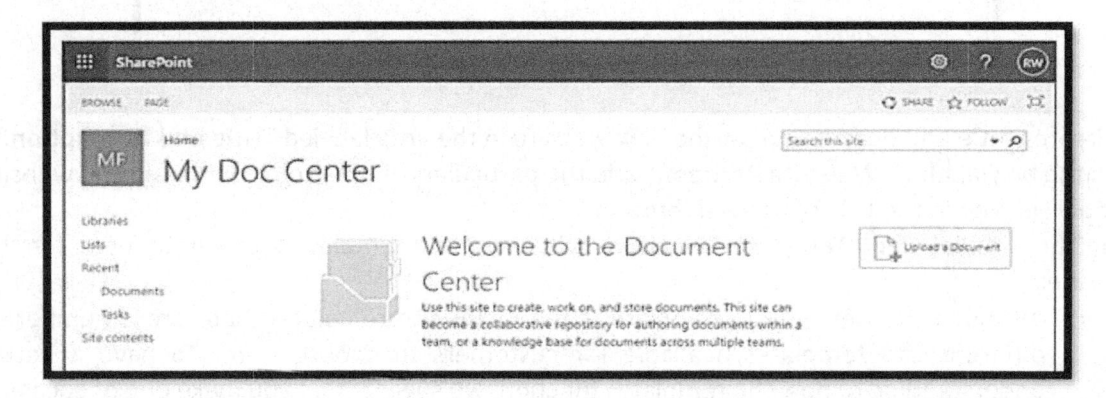

3. Select **Subsite** from the menu that appears after tapping the addition **(+)** symbol on the **Site Contents** page.
4. Click the **Create** button when you have completed the following steps: fill in the title, URL, permissions, and navigation information for your new website (as stated in the preceding section for building a website using your web browser).

Grouping Sites with Hub Sites

One of the features that are included in SharePoint is the ability to integrate many SharePoint sites into a single entity that is referred to as a hub site. With a hub site, for example, you are able to design basic content rollups and search sections, as well as combine navigation together to make it simpler to explore sites as a group. It is recommended that you use a hub site if you have a need for more than one SharePoint site, and if you want to gather all of the sites together and have a single access to all of the sites. When you are an administrator of SharePoint, you have the ability to construct hub sites by using either the new SharePoint Admin Center or PowerShell respectively. First, pick Active Sites from the Admin Center, and then choose a site to begin the process of creating a hub site. In the top menu, you will discover an item that is referred to as Hub. It is possible to register a site as a hub site or to associate a site with a hub site by using the drop-down menu located in the Hub section.

CHAPTER 9
BUSINESS INTELLIGENCE WITH SHAREPOINT

Scorecards, dashboards, and reports are the elements that come together to provide business intelligence. To make decisions and keep track of performance, several tools are used. It is possible to delegate the job of generating content that is business-savvy to a single person or to a group of people, depending on the organizational structure of your firm. Businesses really need to have a BI Center site that is comparable to SharePoint since it gives them the ability to share, consume, and manage information that is relevant to them.

Learning about the Core Features

With time, Microsoft has added the following core features:

Excel Services

If you have been employing Microsoft Excel for the purpose of organizing, displaying, and updating data, the good news is that you may easily adopt centralized business information. Centralized business intelligence is something that can be easily incorporated into your operations if you deal with relatively small volumes of data. You have the option of publishing the Excel data to a document library hosted on SharePoint, ensuring that the relevant security restrictions are in place. For those who prefer not to attach the Excel data to an email, here is an option. Employees will have an easier time seeing the data and using it in a manner that is suitable for their needs as a result of this. SharePoint is a remarkable platform because it enables Excel documents to maintain their data linkages in their original state, and it also enables the reader to observe changes as they occur inside the document in real-time. The workbooks are outfitted with data models that include information from a wide number of sources, including SQL Server, Access, and XML, amongst others. You also have the ability to customize the view of Excel to a Single PivotChart, which will make it easier for the user to look at the information that you are aiming to stress. Those who have the Office online App will be able to interact with the data from the online browser, which will help them save a large amount of time and effort. This opportunity will be available to those who have the app. Excel Services experiences just one issue, and that is the fact that it is now a component of Office Online Server rather than SharePoint services. This is the sole issue that affects Excel Services. There is no other issue with Excel Services but this one.

PerformancePoint

Thanks to PerformancePoint, which is a solution for strategic data and analysis, the Core On-Premises data may be employed and evaluated in the same manner as it is shown on the dashboards. Through the usage of PerformancePoint, it is possible to use and evaluate the data.

If one were to imply that it is the Cadillac of business intelligence at Microsoft, it would not be considered offensive. It is possible to use the core design application to send reports and data into SharePoint, which can then be used to get an in-depth study of the situation. Because of its comprehensive connection with a data warehouse, users are able to make reasonable business decisions that are tied to the organization's vision, objective, and long-term strategy. These choices may be made by users. Users are able to make these assessments because of the connection that is available to them. Additionally, the fundamental components make it easy to include web elements into SharePoint, which enables businesses to provide their services online.

Visio Services

This function, which was developed to make the viewing of data easier, was included in the revised version of SharePoint that was released in 2013. To facilitate the production of detailed diagrams and the mapping of data inside the canvas on which it is shown, it comes with a number of tools that may be used. People who do not have a local perspective of the region are nonetheless able to see and engage with the diagrams because they have a high resolution, which allows them to see and access the information. The ability to rapidly extend these diagrams, which is made possible with the support of web component connections and JavaScript, adds to an increase in the accessibility of the user experience as a whole. The inclusion of this into business intelligence was a good idea since it allows employees to produce unique ideas that are specifically customized to the company and industry in which they operate. This is a terrific notion.

PowerPivot

This component was added to SharePoint in 2013, which is an effective tool that controls the work of a large dataset. SharePoint is a platform that was named after the year it was created. Excel Data, which gives the maximum degree of control over the charts and makes it simple to pivot data with ease, is linked to it, which is the reason why this is the case. Depending on the manner in which it was developed, it might be a client-side software or an add-on feature integrated into Excel.

Microsoft Power BI

Through the use of Power BI, it is feasible to disseminate your data to all of the employees who are placed inside your organization on a range of devices. After this information has been gathered, it may be imported into Excel for further analysis. And this is the most important element. As an extra option, you have the ability to make use of a number of other visualization techniques, such as Power View, Key Performance Indicators (KPIs) in Power Pivot, and Power Map, which will make the data available to all users.

SQL Server Reporting Services (SSRS)

A number of different groups have engaged in a substantial amount of conversation on SSRS. With the support of this, both programmers and experts working in information technology have been able to develop reports that are structured. After that, these reports are published on SharePoint sites with the support of a controlled environment, which offers consumers an exceptional experience while they are using the platform.

As you are probably aware, SharePoint offers a great Business Intelligence solution; but it does not yet include some of the more advanced features that are now being provided by firms that are in direct competition with SharePoint. Even though Microsoft is making substantial investments in business intelligence, the corporation is largely focusing on cloud services, the introduction of SQL, and the acquisition of Datazen respectively.

Business Intelligence Center

There are a variety of formats in which the information that your company has is most likely kept, such as spreadsheet files, e-mail messages, and databases. For more precise information, your company is home to a substantial quantity of data. With the aid of the Business Intelligence Center website and the tools that it provides, you will be able to organize that data most beneficially and display that data as useful information. You may manage the operational parts of business intelligence (BI) reporting with the help of the Business Intelligence Center, which is a pre-built website that is also known as a site template.

This website is meant to assist you in such management. Scorecards, dashboards, data connections, status lists, status indicators, and a great deal more are some of the elements that are included in this category. You have the option of customizing a Business Intelligence Center website to your specifications, or you can start by using the capabilities that are already included in the platform. The Business Intelligence Center is a wonderful place to go if you are looking to get started. An Excel Services worksheet for analysis, charts, and various types of dashboards are some examples of important business intelligence pieces that can be seen here. Other examples include dashboards.

Furthermore, to get extra information in any case, you may learn more about it by clicking on links that are conveniently located and connecting to publications that provide additional information. The construction of data connections, the administration of information for PerformancePoint Services or SharePoint BI, and the storage of final dashboards are all things that may be accomplished with the assistance of special-purpose libraries that are already prepared for access.

On the homepage of Business Intelligence, there are two basic panels: the **Center panel** is where information resources are available, and the **Quick Launch panel**, which is situated on the left side of the screen, is where links to pre-built libraries are located.

The center panel – examples and links to helpful information

If you look at the panel that is located in the center of the home page, you will be able to get a concise summary of the distinctive characteristics of the Business Intelligence middle. The information panels provide a few instances of business intelligence (BI) tools that may be used. Dashboards, other types of analytical tools, and spreadsheets are some examples of these. In addition to this, status indicators are given. Individuals who own an Enterprise license for SharePoint can get knowledge on the straightforward but powerful capabilities that are included in each installation of the platform. In addition, these information panels provide access to more information on PerformancePoint Services. These services offer instruments for performance monitoring and analysis that are outstanding in terms of their power and level of complexity.

Monitor Key Performance

- ❖ Within the Monitor Key Performance panel of PerformancePoint Services, you will discover links that provide information on different techniques of monitoring performance, as well as scorecards and SharePoint Status Lists. The panel contains these links for your convenience.
- ❖ When it comes to the construction of SharePoint Status Lists, the procedure is both straightforward and fast.
- ❖ Additional elements that are provided by PerformancePoint scorecards include a complete hierarchical structure as well as a connection to specialist analytical reports.

Build and Share Reports

- ❖ The Build and Share Reports panel has links to information about Excel Services and the interactive visualization tools that are included in PerformancePoint Services. These connections can be accessed under the Build and Share Reports panel.
- ❖ Excel Services provides you with the opportunity to design your problem solution in Excel, which is the business intelligence tool that is used the most in the world. Excel is the most extensively used application. Spreadsheets, PivotTables, and charts may be built in Excel, and the reports that you make can be published to SharePoint once they have been prepared.
- ❖ There is a broad range of data visualization tools that are accessible in PerformancePoint Services. These tools include charts and graphs that are related to establish Key Performance Indicators, Strategy Maps linked to geographic maps, and a comprehensive assortment of other possibilities.

Create Dashboards

- ❖ You can find specific links that provide information on how to construct dashboards. These links may be found by using the tools that are available in SharePoint or by utilizing the tools that are available in PerformancePoint Services. You will be able to get the information that you need by clicking on these links.
- ❖ One of the buttons on this panel is labeled "**Start using PerformancePoint Services**," and it is designed to take the user to the homepage of the website that is dedicated to PerformancePoint Services.
- ❖ Either click the **Run button** on Dashboard Designer or follow the links to the **Getting Started articles** if you want to get started right away. Both of these options are available via Dashboard Designer. Scorecards, decomposition trees, dashboards, and analytical charts and grids are all examples of the types of tools that may be created with the help of these articles.

Dashboard Library

When it comes to SharePoint, a dashboard is just a plain Web Part page that is meant to display a collection of indications, data, or graphic components. A dashboard is comprised of these core components, which make up its fundamental structure. SharePoint contains a library called Dashboards, which is specially built to store and produce Web Part pages that are devoted to dashboard material. This library was created to make the process of creating and managing dashboards easier. Dashboards that were developed using PerformancePoint and Web Part pages that had Status Lists for SharePoint status indicators are both examples of what might fall under this category. PerformancePoint Services dashboards are automatically stored in the Dashboards collection anytime they are produced using Dashboard Designer. This happens regardless of whether or not the dashboards were built using Dashboard Designer. Importing dashboards that you have already created is something that PerformancePoint Services makes possible for you to do. There is also the possibility of constructing a new dashboard from a Web Part page by using the Ribbon commands that are accessible on the Dashboard list page. Additionally, the Ribbon commands that are located on the Dashboard list page may be used to generate a Web Part page that incorporates a Status List to show SharePoint status indications. Following the completion of this development, you will have the ability to improve the dashboard by including other components such as charts, filters, and other content web elements that are tailored to your particular needs. Using this adaptable method, users can personalize dashboards to meet their requirements, including a wide variety of components to effectively communicate information and insights.

Data Connections library

With the assistance of the Data Connection library, you can declare connections to data sources just once, and then you can reuse those connections in every Web Part that you create on the website. Files that are associated with the **Universal Data Connection (UDC),** files that are associated with the **Office Data Connection (.odc)** format, and PerformancePoint Data Sources are all supported by the Data Connection library.

Documents Library

It is possible to locate a wide variety of documents, including spreadsheets, SharePoint lists, text documents, and other sorts of documents, inside the Documents library, which functions as a central library. It will be much easier for you to find the information you want if you create folders inside this library. To give you an example, you could want to create a folder that is titled "**Excel Reports - financial**" or "**Status Lists for tracking**," depending on your preferences.

PerformancePoint Content list

An analyst can design a scorecard and report items for PerformancePoint Services with the assistance of Dashboard Designer. These things may then be saved in the PerformancePoint Content list. As an instance, this specific image displays a PerformancePoint Content library that comprises a scorecard, a report, and **Key Performance Indicators (KPIs).**

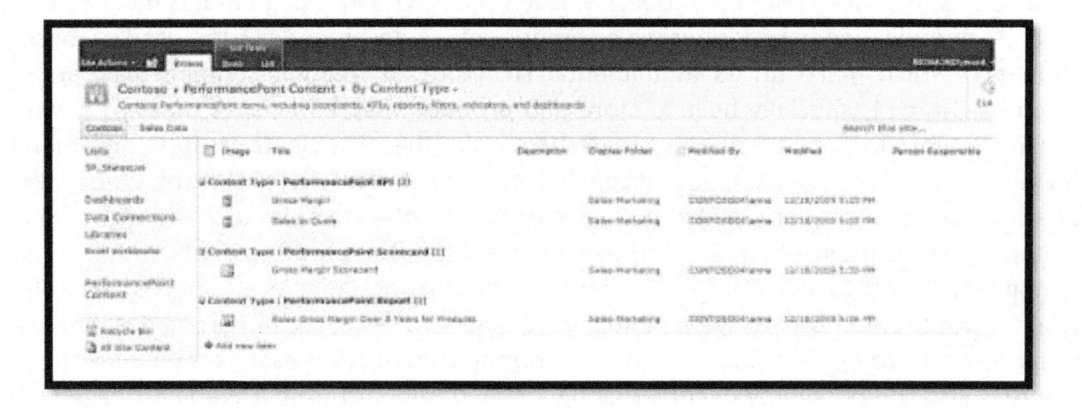

Create a new Business Intelligence Site

The Business Intelligence Center site template in SharePoint offers a specialized and well-organized platform for the development and administration of business intelligence solutions. By using the New Site dialog box, SharePoint Site Owners can get access to this template, which enables them to simply establish a Business Intelligence Center that is suited to the requirements of their firm.

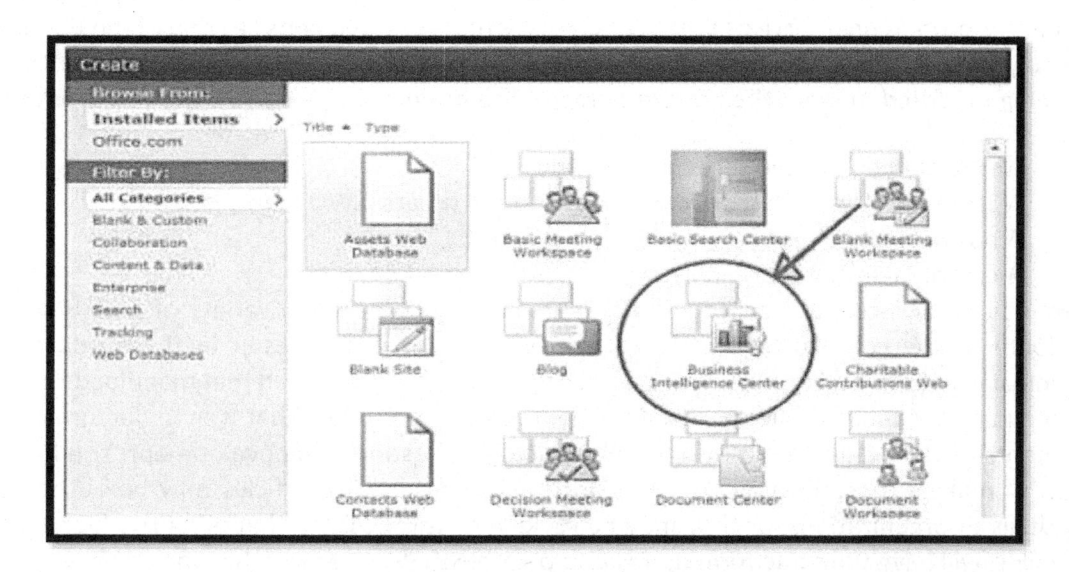

The capability of the Business Intelligence Center to provide users with the opportunity to personalize data displays is a valuable feature. On a dashboard page, this is accomplished by linking some different Filter Web Parts to Web Parts that are already there. Doing so enables users to tailor the data that is shown, making it more relevant to certain people or groups and making it more accessible to them. Consider, for instance, a situation in which several different sales managers are responsible for overseeing separate territories. Each sales manager can get a tailored view of sales data that are particular to their area if they link Filter Web Parts to relevant Web Parts on the dashboard. The degree of customization that is available here improves the usability of the Business Intelligence Center, which in turn enables stakeholders to concentrate on the data that is most interesting to them.

CHAPTER 10
ADVANCED DOCUMENT MANAGEMENT

People create a collection of documents that are linked together for a variety of different kinds of undertakings. Certain projects come to a close with this collection of documents, which is also referred to as the "deliverable." When responding to a request for a proposal from a potential customer, a professional services organization may create a "pitch book" as one of the things that they may create. **The following sections may always be included in the pitch book, with each one being modified to meet the requirements of the project that is currently being worked on:**

- An introduction to the services company
- A Strengths, Weaknesses, Opportunities, and Threats (SWOT) analysis
- A business plan
- A comparable company analysis

In other circumstances, this collection of papers could just include a variety of data types that contribute to the completion of a larger project and ultimately result in the production or dissemination of something else. To provide one example, a corporation that manufactures items would create a standard collection of documents for each product that it manufactures. These documents would include topics such as manufacturing, testing, and development. You have the option of making these documents all at once or in phases. The articles may be authored by individuals or organizations, or they may be reviewers. It is possible that all of the files, such as Word files, will have the same format. It is also possible that there are other sorts of files, such as Word documents, OneNote notes, PowerPoint presentations, Visio models, Excel spreadsheets, and so on. Document Sets have the potential to simplify how corporations deal with situations like this. Using the Document Set, many documents that are linked together are compiled into a single view. This allows the documents to be worked on and managed as a single unit throughout the process. In the process of creating a new Document Set, you will create a new content type using this method. When this occurs, the content type is accessible over the whole of the site collection. You can create a new content type for the Document Set format for each multi-document work product. After adding a Document Set content type to a library, users can create new instances of the Document Set in the same manner that they create new instances of a single document.

What can you do with a Document Set?

Work products including numerous documents are simpler to create and manage due to certain features of the Document Set content type. **When you configure a Document Set content type, you may conduct any of the following actions:**

- **Customize a Welcome Page**: Make sure the Welcome Page for the Document collection has all the information a person might need about the collection. A Web Part Page called the Welcome Page may be configured to provide information about the project or links

to useful resources for team members working on a document collection. It could display the project timetable or resource links, for instance. A list of the recently added files to the collection is also shown.
- **Specify default content**: Every time a new copy of the Document Set is created, you may decide what basic material should be created and added. You can control which designs are used and make certain sheets appear instantaneously. You can be certain that the fundamental papers' content types are correct. As an example, you may exchange distinct files that your business utilizes for certain kinds of communication when you build up a Document build content type.
- **Specify allowed content types**: Select the content kinds (text, images, sounds, and videos) that may be included in the document collection.
- **Specify shared metadata**: Select the fields of data and shared metadata you want to have for every document in a collection. The metadata is instantly added to the default documents upon creation of the Document Set. The Welcome page displays the shared information as well.
- **Specify shared metadata**: Configure the procedures you want to apply to the Document Set. You may utilize the usual Review or Approval procedures with Document Sets. The workflow will process the whole Document Set as if it were a single file. Furthermore, your business may design its own Document Set procedures.

Send Document Sets to the Content Organizer so that they can be sent to a specific library, site, or area.

Enable Document Sets for a site collection

Make sure that the Document Sets functionality is enabled for your site collection before creating or configuring new Document Set content types. **You must be a Site Collection Administrator to utilize the Document Sets tool.**

- Within the collection of sites, identify the primary site you want to utilize Document Sets for.
- Choose **Site Settings** from the site's action menu.
- Click on Site Group Features after selecting Site Collection Administration.
- Find Document Sets in the list, select it, and click Activate.

Create a new Document Set content type

For any work product you want to manage, you must first create and configure a Document Set content type before allowing site users to utilize Document Sets to create new multi-document work products. Next, the document library containing the Document Set content type has to be added. Once you've created and configured it, you must add the Document Set content type to the library so that users may create their own Document Sets.

You must be a Site Owner or a Site Collection Administrator to create or modify Document Set content types.

- Select **Site Settings** from the **Site Actions** menu.
- Select **Site content types** from the list of galleries.
- Go to the page with the Site Content Types and press the Create button.
- In the "Name" box under "**Name and Description**," enter the name you choose to give your new Document Set. When someone creates a new Document Set, they will see these names.
- Type a brief description of the Document Set in the "**Description**" box.
- Select the parent content type by clicking Document Set Content Types. If **Document Set Content Types** is not selected, **Document Sets** may not be enabled for this site group.
- Select whether to add your new Document Set content type to an existing group or a new one in the Group section.
- Press the **OK** button.

You may make further changes to the Site Content Type information page for a newly created Document Set content type after being redirected to it.

Configure or customize a Document Set content type

- Select **Site Settings** from the **Site Actions** menu.
- Select **Site content types** from the galleries section.
- On the **Site Content Types** page, click the name of the **Document Set content** type that you want to modify.
- Select **Document Set settings** by going to Settings.
- From the list of Available Site Content Types in the Allowed Content Types section, choose the content type you want to allow into this Document Set. Next, click the "**Add**" button to include it in the Document Set box's permitted Content Types list. Repeat this process for each kind of data that you want to include in the Document Set.

It should be noted that only documents added to the document set using the "New" button are eligible for the **Allowed Content Types** option.

- Select the kind of material you want to add default content for in the Default material section. Next, choose **Browse** to locate the file you want to include. Immediately upon creating a new copy of a Document Set, authors are assigned default content.

Assume for the moment that you are creating a Document Set to record the steps involved in product design. This document set could include a Microsoft Word file for the Product Design Document, a Microsoft Visio file for the Design Drawing, and a Microsoft Excel worksheet for Performance Specs. Some of the common information that authors need to fill in may already be included in a standard Microsoft Word example of a product design document that exists in your organization. This design may be made the default text. When authors update the product design Document Set, they get a copy of the Product Design Document. It may be altered to provide extra details. When writers create a new instance of a Document Set, they won't be able to automatically generate files if you don't provide default content for the content types in the Document Set. **Rather, writers will need to create them from the beginning within the Document Set or add papers to it.**

- Click "**Add new default content**," select the kind of material you want to add default content for, and then click "**Browse**" to locate the file you want to share if this Document Set has several content types and you want to add default content for each one. Do this step again and again until you've set all of the default content you want for each type of content in this Document Set.
- Tick the box next to **Add the name of the Document Set** to **each file name** if you want the name of the Document Set to appear in the names of the files that are part of a Document Set. When adding this information, users may find it easier to locate files in certain library views, particularly if the library contains many Document Set types.
- Select the columns that you wish to be shared by all content categories in the Document Set under "Shared Columns."

Only the Document Set itself can modify shared fields; the documents inside it can only read them. Changes made to the values of the shared columns for the Document Set will also affect the values of the shared columns for the individual documents that make up the set.

- In the **Welcome Page Columns** section, choose the columns you want to display on the **Document Set's Welcome Page**.
- To alter the Welcome Page's appearance for every edition of the Document Set, choose Customize the Welcome Page in the Welcome Page section elsewhere in the Document Set.
- Select the checkbox next to **Update the Welcome Page of Document Sets inheriting from this content type** if you want these modifications to be applied to all Document Sets that derive from this Document Set.
- Select the content categories from this Document Set you wish to have the modifications you made applied to in the **Update List and Site Content** categories section.
- Click "**OK**."

Once you've created and configured it, you must add the Document Set content type to the library so that users may create their own Document Sets.

Content Organizer

One feature of SharePoint that may take care of some significant library tasks quickly is the Content Organizer. In addition to saving time, this may guarantee that a document library is maintained regularly.

What can the Content Organizer do?

SharePoint's Content Organizer functions as an automated system that can handle several jobs on its own, improving document organization and administration.

The following are the main features of the Content Organizer:

1. Route Documents to Different Libraries or Folders

- The Content Organizer, which serves as a document guardian, uses preset criteria to decide automatically where a new document should go.
- Documents can be directed based on metadata and other predefined criteria to various libraries or folders, even across site collections.

2. **Upload Documents to a Drop-Off Library:**
    - All incoming documents can be directed by the Content Organizer to a specific Drop-Off Library.
    - This Drop-Off Library acts as a central location where documents can be completed for submission before being further distributed.

3. **Manage Folder Size**:
    - Content Organizer can keep an eye on folder capacity and stop them from going above a certain limit, which is often set to 2500 items by default.
    - To preserve an orderly structure, the Content Organizer automatically generates a new folder and transfers the document when a folder exceeds its limit.
    - The system can be configured by administrators to limit the number of objects that can fit in a single folder.

4. **Handle Duplicate Submissions:**
    - The Content Organizer offers duplicate submission management tools to address scenarios in which a user uploads a document that is already in the library.
    - To ensure that the original and the copy are safely stored, administrators may direct the system to utilize a different version of the file or add special characters to the file name.

5. **Keep Up Audit Records:**
    - For every document it processes, Content Organizer can create and preserve audit logs. These logs include details about the document's route and provide an audit trail that may be useful for tracking and compliance needs.

Activate the Content Organizer feature on a site

Use these procedures to activate and set up the Content Organizer tool on a SharePoint site:

- **Ensure Prerequisites**: Verify that you have at least Site Owner capabilities to change settings and that the posting tools are on.
- **Go to Site Settings**: Open the website for which you want to make changes.
- To see the site settings, click "**Settings**." Then, choose "**Site settings**" from the drop-down menu. As an alternative, choose "**Site contents,**" then "**Settings**," and finally "**Site settings**."
- **Go to Manage Site Features**: Find the "**Site Actions**" group on the Site Settings page. In this category, choose "**Manage site features**".
- **Turn on Content Organizer**: Search the features list for the Content Organizer option. Select the Content Organizer function by clicking the "Activate" button next to its name.
- **Confirm Activation**: The Content Organizer function is now enabled for the website when the term "**Active**" appears in the Status section after it has been activated.

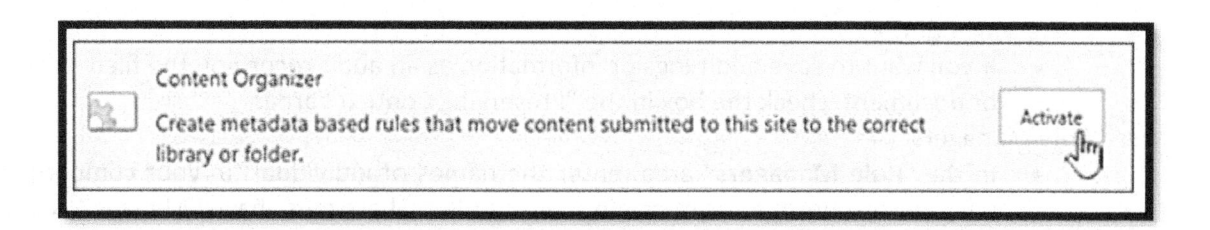

> **Content Organizer**
> Create metadata based rules that move content submitted to this site to the correct library or folder.   **Activate**

Configure the Content Organizer

To set up the Content Organizer in SharePoint, follow these steps:

1. **Ensure Permissions:**
   - Make sure you have at least Site Owner permissions to set up the Content Organizer.
2. **Navigate to Site Settings:**
   - Go to the site where you want to configure the Content Organizer.
3. **Access Site Settings:**
   - Click on "Settings" (gear icon), and from the drop-down menu, select "Site settings."
   - Alternatively, go to "**Settings**," click on "**Site contents**," and then click on "Site settings."
4. **Access Content Organizer Settings:**
   - Click on "**Content Organizer Settings**" in the Site Administration group.
   - Note: The Content Organizer settings link will only be visible if the tool is turned on for the site.
5. **Configure Content Organizer Settings:**
   - Check the box to make the Content Organizer mandatory in the "**Redirect Users to the Drop Off Library**" section. This ensures that when users attempt to share a file, they are directed immediately to the Drop-Off Library.
   - Check the "**Allow Rules to Send Documents to a Different Site**" box in the "**Sending to Another Site**" section.
   - In the "**Folder Partitioning**" section:
     - Check the box next to "Create subfolders after a target location has too many items." This creates subfolders when a location surpasses a specified item limit.
     - Specify the number of items in a single folder before a new one is created in the "Number of things in a single folder" box.
     - Choose the desired format for the new folder names in the "Format of folder name" box.

6. **Manage Duplicate Submissions:**
   - Under "**Duplicate Submissions**," choose whether duplicates should use versioning or have file names that always start with a different set of characters.

7. **Preserving Context:**
   - If you want to save audit logs or information as an audit record on the filed item or document, check the box in the "Preserving Context" area.
8. **Rule Managers:**
   - In the "**Rule Managers**" area, enter the names of individuals in your company who are responsible for managing rules. Rule makers must have "Manage Web Site" permissions to access the Content Organizer rules setting page.
   - If configured correctly, emails can be sent immediately to rule makers when content is sent to the Content Organizer or when content doesn't meet a rule. Note: Email options require proper setup by your SharePoint or network administrator.
9. **Submission Points:**
   - Fill out the "**Submission Points**" area with information about other websites or email clients that can send content to this one.

Information Rights Management (IRM)

When you use information rights management (IRM), people who take files from lists or libraries can't do certain things with them. Through IRM, some people and apps are not able to decrypt files that have been saved. While IRM can limit who can read files, it can also limit who can write to them. They can't copy the files or take text from them, for example. IRM can be used on lists or libraries to keep secret data from too many people. One example is IRM can be used to stop marketing reps from sharing information about new products with other employees of the business. This could happen if you're making a document library to share information about new products with certain reps. IRM can be used on a site's list or library as a whole, not just on single files. You can now be surer that all of your files and papers are always safe at the same level. Because of this, IRM can help your business follow the rules that say how to share and use private or secret info. In SharePoint Online, files are protected with IRM at both the list and library levels. Before your business can use IRM safety, you need to set up Rights Management. IRM uses Azure Information Protection's Azure Rights Management tool to keep data safe and tell people how they can use it. Azure Rights Management isn't included in all Microsoft 365 plans. You can try Microsoft Purview products for free for 90 days if you don't already use E5. This way, you can see how other Purview tools can help your business with data security and compliance.

How IRM can help protect content

In the following ways, IRM helps protect material that isn't open to everyone:
- Helps keep people who are allowed to see the information from copying, changing, printing, faxing, or copying and pasting it for illegal purposes.
- Use of the Print Screen tool in Microsoft Windows is limited to protect information from being copied by approved users.
- Helps keep material from being seen by people who aren't supposed to if it is sent by email after being downloaded from the computer.

- Users must log out after having access to material for a set time.
- Helps your company follow the rules for how the staff can use and share information

How IRM cannot help protect content

IRM cannot protect restricted content from the following:

- Threats like Trojan horses, keystroke hackers, and some types of software can send, remove, record, or steal data.
- A computer bug can also erase or damage data.
- Writing down or copying things that are on a screen;
- Taking pictures of what's on a screen, either on film or digitally;
- Making copies with screen-capture programs from outside sources;
- Copying content information (column values) by hand or with third-party screen grab software.

Turn on IRM service using the SharePoint admin center

Before you can IRM-protect SharePoint libraries and lists, you need to make sure that your company's Rights Management service is up and running. You need a work or school account with world control rights to use the Rights control service. Not doing this will stop you from using IRM tools with SharePoint Online.

To turn on IRM, go to the SharePoint admin center and log in after the Rights Management service is up and running.

- Log in as a SharePoint manager or a global admin.
- The app launcher button is in the upper left area. Click it and choose **Admin** to open the Microsoft 365 admin center. If the **Admin tile** isn't there, it means that your work or school account doesn't have the right permissions to run your business.
- Find the SharePoint admin area on the left side of the screen and click on it.
- Pick out the old settings page from the menu on the left side of the screen.
- There is a section called "**Use the IRM service that was set up in your setup.**" Click on that. After that, click on **Refresh IRM Settings**. Folks in your business can use IRM in their SharePoint lists and files after you change the settings. It could take up to an hour for the options to show up in **Library Settings** and List Settings before you can do that.

IRM-enable SharePoint document libraries and lists

After making changes to their IRM settings, site owners can protect their SharePoint lists and files with IRM. Any file type that is allowed by that list or library can be protected if the site owner turns on IRM for that list or library. When IRM is turned on for a library, all of its files are subject to rights management. IRM only takes care of the files that are linked to list items when you turn it on for a list. It doesn't keep track of the list of things. Users who are allowed to see the files are the only ones who can open them when they download them from an IRM-enabled list or library.

Every file that is managed by rights also has a license that says who can/can't see it. Making a file read-only, stopping people from copying text, stopping them from saving a local copy, and stopping them from printing the file are all usual limits. These limits are put in place by client programs that can read IRM-supported file types and the license that was given in the rights-managed file. This keeps a rights-managed file safe even after you download it. You can't make or change documents in a library that has IRM if you use Office in a browser. One person at a time can only download and change IRM-encrypted files. Co-authoring, or when more than one person writes the same thing, is handled by check-in and check-out. When you use Microsoft 365 to download a PDF file from an IRM-protected library, it turns it into a protected PDF file. The file is safe and won't change its name. To see this file, you'll need the Azure Information Protection browser, the full Azure Information Protection client, or another tool that can open protected PDF files.

The following file types can be encrypted in SharePoint Online:

- PDF
- The Microsoft Office 97–2003 file types for the following programs: There's PowerPoint, Word, and Excel.
- The Office Open XML file types for these Microsoft Office programs: There's PowerPoint, Word, and Excel.
- The XML Paper Specification (XPS) format

Keep in mind that IRM protection can't be used on protected files like digitally signed PDFs because SharePoint needs to open the file when it is uploaded.

Next steps

Once IRM is turned on for SharePoint Online, you can start controlling who has access to lists and libraries. The new OneDrive sync app for Windows can now sync IRM-protected SharePoint document libraries with OneDrive folders, as long as the IRM setting for the library doesn't end document access rights.

Applying IRM to Document Libraries and Lists

You can use Information Rights Management (IRM) to protect the files you download from lists or libraries. This tool only works in the Microsoft global cloud. In national cloud apps, IRM doesn't work with libraries and lists in SharePoint.

Administrator preparations before applying IRM

- The Azure Rights Management service (Azure RMS) from Azure Information Protection and the on-premises version, Active Directory Rights Management Services (AD RMS), can both be used to manage information rights for sites. There's no need for any other or different installations.

- Your site needs to be set up with IRM before it can be used on a list or library. You need management permissions to enable IRM.
- You must have management permissions for a library or list to add IRM to it.
- Your users may run into timeouts when they try to download larger IRM-protected files in SharePoint Online. Protect larger files in Office with IRM and store them in a SharePoint library that doesn't use IRM to get around timeouts.

Apply IRM to a list or library

- ❖ You need to find the list or library that you want to add IRM to.
- ❖ Then, go to the menu and click on the Library tab. Finally, click on Library Settings. Go to the List tab and select List Settings to modify the settings for a specific list.

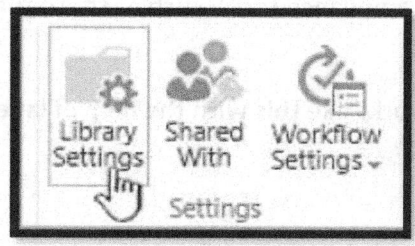

- ❖ Scroll down and select **Information Rights Management** from the list of **Management and Permissions**. If the Information Rights Management link doesn't show up, it's possible that IRM isn't turned on for your site. Find out if you can turn on IRM for your site from the person who runs the server. The Information Rights Management link doesn't show up for photo galleries.
- ❖ Check the box next to **Restrict permission to documents in this library on download** on the page for Information Rights Management Settings. Users' access to the documents they download from this list or library will be restricted as a result.
- ❖ In the box that says "**Create a permission policy title**," name the policy something that makes sense. Use a name that stands out from other strategies to help people understand it. You could use business Confidential to give a list or library of private business files with restricted permissions.
- ❖ In the "**Add a permission policy description**" box, type a description of how users of this list or library should handle the documents in it. These words will be shown to people who use the list or library. For example, if you only want workers within your company to see the information in these documents, you can type **Discuss the contents of this document only with other employees**.
- ❖ Follow the on-screen steps to add more limits to the files in this list or library after you click "**Show Options**."
- ❖ Click **OK** when you're done picking all the options you want.

Document Retention

You can keep all the files saved in SharePoint sites if you use a retention plan or retention label. You can use both live and stored sites.

You can get rid of the following files:

- When you have a system for keeping records: all the files in document libraries, even those that are created automatically in SharePoint, like Site Assets document libraries.
- Every file in every document library and every file at the top level that isn't in a folder is when you need to use preservation marks.

SharePoint will add a Preservation Hold library to the site if it doesn't already have one. This way, important information can be kept safe. The Preservation Hold library is a hidden part of the system that shouldn't be used directly. Instead, it saves files automatically when that's what the rules say it needs to do. If you keep these files, you can't change them, delete them, or move them. Instead, you should use compliance tools, such as those that work with eDiscovery, to get to these files.

The Preservation Hold library works like this with the help of labels and rules for keeping things safe:

People can add to or take away from things that need to be saved because of a policy or a sign that says they are records. The first copy of the material is sent to the Preservation Hold library when they do either of those things. With this behavior, users can add or remove data from their app, but legally they need to keep a copy of the original. The **Preservation Hold library** has a job that runs at set times. This job checks the item against all the questions that were used by the items retention settings if it has been in the Preservation Hold library for more than 30 days. When their time is up, items that aren't waiting for a disposition review are taken out of both the Preservation Hold library and the original location, if they are still there. The items will not be taken out of the Preservation Hold library for at least 30 days if this job is done every week. It might take up to 37 days altogether. This is how it works for files that were already in the Preservation Hold library when the settings were made for preservation. It is important to remember that any new material made or added to the site after the policy went into effect will also be kept in the Preservation Hold library. When new information is changed for the first time, it is not added to the Preservation Hold library. New information is only copied when it is lost. For the parent site to keep all copies of a file, versioning must be turned on. When a user tries to delete a site, library, list, or folder that can be kept, they are told. The person can get rid of a folder that doesn't have a name as long as they move or delete any important files that are in it. Plus, users will get a message if they try to delete a named item in any of the following scenarios. The item doesn't get copied to the Preservation Hold library; it stays where it was found.

- ❖ The change that lets users get rid of named things in records has been turned off.

If you want to change this setting in Microsoft Purview Compliance, go to the Records Administration option and do so. Then, go to ***Records management > Records management settings > Retention labels > Deletion of items***. SharePoint and OneDrive each have their own settings. Let's say you don't have access to the Records control system. You can still use ***AllowFilesWithKeepLabelToBeD.***You can use Get-PnPTenant and Set-PnPTenant to select SPO and A***lowFilesWithKeepLabelToBeDeletedOD***B.

- The hold sticker locks the thing and says that it is a record.

The most current version is kept in the Preservation Hold library until the record is opened.

- ❖ The mark on the item's keeping means it's a legal record and can't be changed or taken away.

It depends on whether the settings for a OneDrive account or SharePoint site are to keep and delete, keep only, or delete only that information. After that, the information can go in three different paths. We will see that material that has been changed is sent to the Preservation Hold library so that records can be kept per the rules. With retention marks, things are marked as records and the information inside is made public. The Preservation Hold library makes copies of things that are taken away, but not of things that are changed with retention labels that don't mark them as records.

When the settings for keeping are to keep and delete:

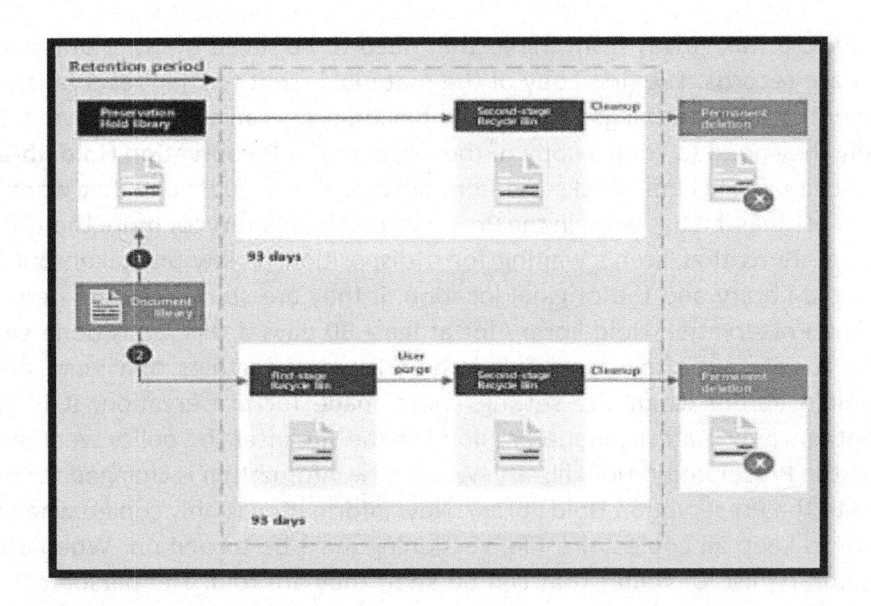

- The Preservation Hold library makes a copy of the original content. This copy is the same as it was when the retention settings were made, in case the content is changed or removed during the retention time. That's where the timer job looks for things whose hold time has passed. These kinds of things are sent to the second-stage Recycle Bin. After 93 days, they are taken away for good. End users can only see the first-stage Recycle Bin. The second-stage Recycle Bin is hidden from them. But site collection administrators can look through that bin and get things back.

Note: We no longer delete items from the Preservation Hold library for good, so information doesn't get lost. The only thing we do is delete items from the recycle bin for good. All the files in the Preservation Hold library will now go through the second-stage Recycle Bin.

- The timer job sends the content to the first-stage trash bin at the end of the waiting period if it wasn't changed or deleted. People who empty this Recycle Bin (also known as "purging") or remove the items in it move the document to the next round of Recycle Bins. The trash stays in the first- and second-stage recycle bins for 93 days each. After 93 days, the file is permanently erased from either the first-stage or second-stage recycle bin. You can't look in the Recycle Bin because it's not on the list. This means that an eDiscovery search can't find anything in the Recycle Bin that should be kept.

Note: The first principle of retention says that the final deletion of an item must always be put on hold if it needs to be kept because of another retention policy or label, or if it needs to be kept for law or research reasons in eDiscovery.

CHAPTER 11
RECORDS MANAGEMENT AND ARCHIVING

In a business, a record is something that needs to be kept for a certain amount of time. It could be a paper copy or a computer file that shows what the business did or bought. It is up to the company to decide what kinds of records to keep as it grows. **Management of records is the word for this.**

- Figures out what kinds of data fit in the "records" group.
- Figures out how to handle and collect current documents that will be labeled records, as well as how to treat them while they are being used.
- Finds the right way and length of time to keep each type of record to meet legal, business, or government requirements.
- Looks into and uses business practices and technology solutions to help the company meet its records management needs affordably and straightforwardly.
- Completes duties related to records, such as locating and keeping records of documents related to outside events like lawsuits or getting rid of old records.

There are corporate compliance officers, records managers, and lawyers whose job it is to figure out what papers and other things in your company, whether they are digital or physical, are records. You can trust these people to help you keep papers for the right amount of time by organizing all of your business's items with care. A well-designed records management system can help with legal defense, following the rules, and speeding up the work of the company. This is because it makes people more likely to get rid of old things that aren't records in the right way.

A records management system includes the following elements:

- **A content analysis** that sorts and lists the business's content that can be turned into records. It also shows where the content came from and how it will get to the records management app.
- A **file plan** should be in place that lists where each kind of business record should be kept, the rules that apply, how long it should be kept, how it should be thrown away, and who is responsible for handling it.
- **A document that lays out compliance standards** and the rules that the company's IT systems must follow to make sure they are compliant. It also explains how to get business team members involved.
- **One way to get old files and records from all record sources**, like email systems, collaboration servers, and file servers.
- Another way to check records while they are still being used.
- A way to keep track of records' metadata and check logs.
- A way to keep records (not delete them) until certain events happen, like lawsuits.

❖ Finally, a way to keep an eye on and report on how records are being handled is to make sure that workers are following the rules.

Some parts of SharePoint can help businesses set up ways to manage records that work with each other.

Overview of records management planning

When planning, what steps should you take to be sure that the SharePoint-based records management system you set up will help your company reach its records management goals? **This article talks about them. Here's a quick look at how the planning process for managing records works:**

1. **Identify records management roles**: There needs to be a person in charge of organizing the organization's data and running the records management process for it to work well. Examples of these people are compliance officers and records managers.
   ❖ For good record-keeping, IT staff set up the right tools. Content managers need to know where the company's records are saved and make sure their teams follow the rules for handling records.

2. **Analyze organizational content**: The content manager and the records manager look at how the company uses paper to see which ones can be turned into records before they make a file plan.

3. **Make a file plan**. After you've looked at what's in your group and decided how long to keep things, fill in the rest of the file plan. Each business has its file plan, but in general, it lists the kinds of things that the company keeps as records, where they are kept, how long they are kept, and other information like who is in charge of them and what bigger group of records they are a part of.

4. **Develop retention schedules**. Figure out when each type of record is no longer important, how long it should be kept, and how it should be thrown away at the end.

5. **Evaluate and improve document management practices**. Keep an eye out for places where documents are kept that don't follow the rules. For example, make sure that the right reports are kept with the records and that the right information is being looked over.

6. **Design the records management solution**. Pick whether to back up the records, deal with them the way they are now, or do a mix of the two. Plan the record collection around your file plan, or figure out how to store records on sites you already have. You can set up rules, content types, libraries, and, if needed, information that tells the system where to send a file.

7. **Plan how content turns into records**: As long as you use SharePoint for both managing live documents and managing records, you can set up steps to move documents to a library for records. You can plan and build links that move content from other systems to the records folder or that mark a document as a record but don't move it. This works whether you use SharePoint or a different system. You also plan how people will learn how to use records and make records.

8. **Plan email integration**. Select whether SharePoint or the email tool itself will be used to manage your email records.

9. Plan compliance for social content. Figure out how the material from blogs, wikis, or other social media sites used by your business will be saved as records.

10. Plan compliance reporting and documentation. By writing down your plans and procedures for managing records, you can make sure that your company is following the rules for managing records and let other people know about these rules. For example, if your company is sued over records, you might need to show these rules, goals, and data on how well they worked.

Overview of SharePoint Record Centers

We can say that the record center site gathering handles the process of automatically saving old documents in one place, which is known as record preservation. Many things can be done with it. The first method is to use it as a central location to store documents. Let's say you have a lot of documents in the current document library. After a few days, it might become too full, which could lead to the well-known SharePoint list view barrier error. To stop this from happening, the old documents must be moved to a new site, which is merely a document center.

As long as certain conditions in the content type IRM policy are met, the document will be sent to the record center site. This is something I will talk about more in the next part. If you want to keep track of all your documents in one place, you could also use it. You could, for instance, send all of your law documents, sales order documents, buy order documents, finance documents, sales documents, and so on to one place and have them sent immediately to the right sites. You can set up content manager rules in the record center site to do this.

Note:

- ❖ You can't delete a document that is already in the record library. The record center does this for us.
- ❖ We can even turn a paper on the team site into a record, but we have to set up a process or use Power Automate to do it.
- ❖ The last stage in a document's lifecycle is the record stage, so it is locked.

We know what a SharePoint Online record center is and why we need one now. Now we will talk about how to set up the system for storing.

How to configure the record center archiving mechanism in SharePoint Online?

There are three steps to setting up the record center in SharePoint Online:

- ❖ Gather records from the record center site
- ❖ For Microsoft 365 Record Center, set up the link to the record center.
- ❖ For the record center site collection, make and set up the content manager rule.

As part of the test, I made the sites below for the record center.

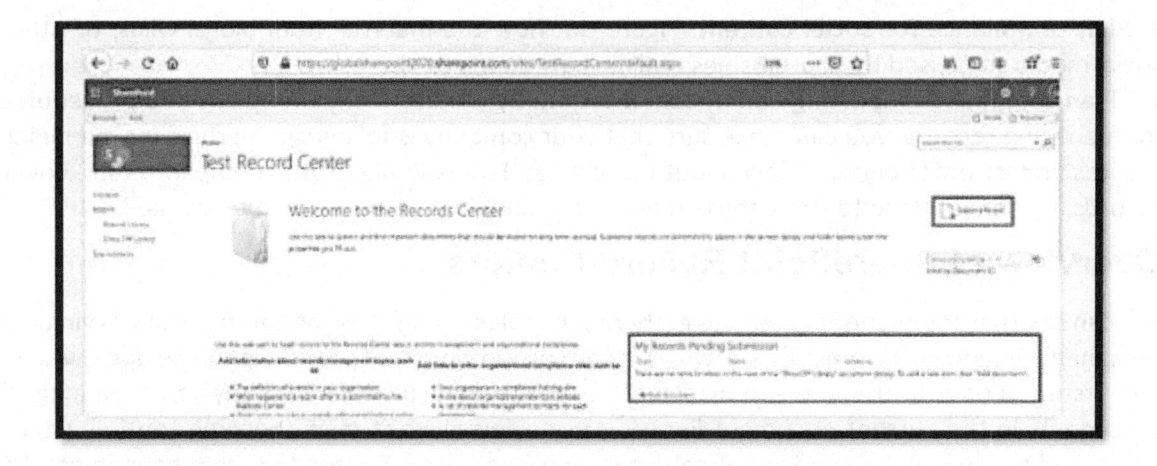

- ❖ Visit the **site's settings** page.
- ❖ Click on "**Content organizer settings**" in the "Site Administration" area.
- ❖ Following that, we will reach the page where we can change the settings for the Content manager.
- ❖ We can see the URL for the web service that was sent at the very bottom of this page.

Note down the web service URL:
- *https://globalsharepoint2020.sharepoint.com/sites/TestRecordCenter/_vti_bin/OfficialFile.asmx*

This web service URL is what we will need to connect to the record center in the Microsoft 365 admin center. Please remember this.

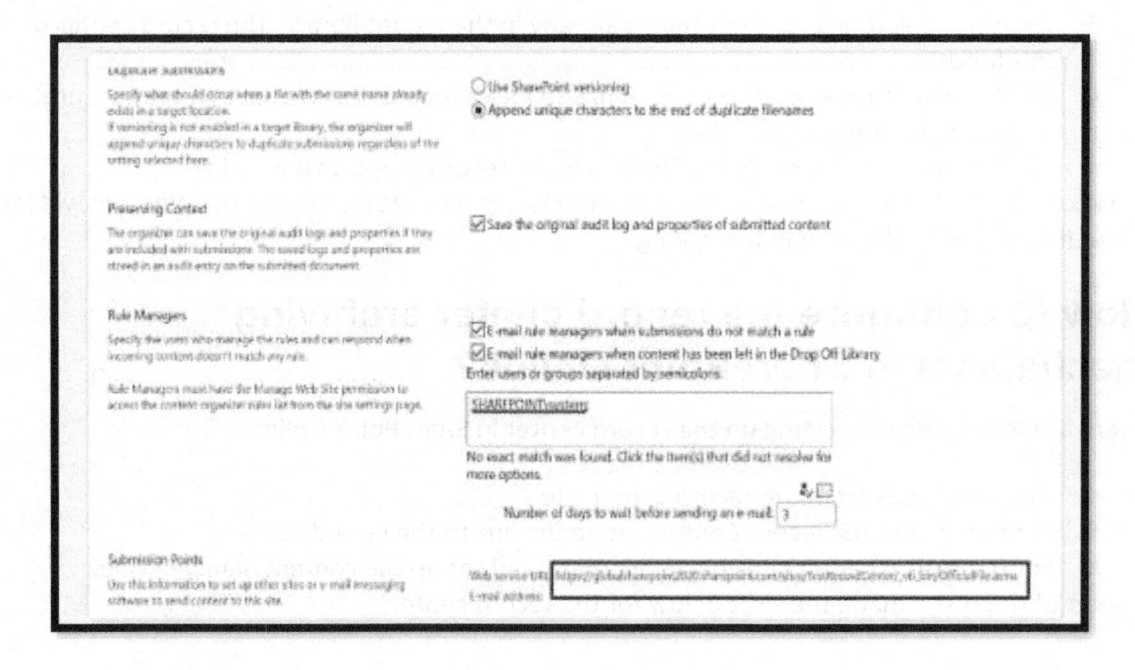

CHAPTER 12
FINDING WHAT YOU NEED WITH SEARCH

The SharePoint search tool is both powerful and easy to use to find information. SharePoint lets users search for information and narrow down the results right away. You can set up and tweak SharePoint search to make it work best for your business. You can think of search this way: as a platform instead of a tool that you can turn on or off.

Understanding How SharePoint Search Works

A lot of people don't understand how search works in SharePoint. A lot of people think that search is either on or off. Search can be set up and works very well. For instance, query rules can be used to change the results of a SharePoint search so that users get the best results possible. The Marketing app, which has the company's entire official marketing documents, may be what users are looking for when they search for marketing. Query rules can be used to put the Marketing app at the top of the search records. The addition of **FAST** search is one of the best changes to search in SharePoint. Microsoft bought the company FAST, which was based in Oslo, Norway. FAST search was a different tool in earlier versions of SharePoint. The **FAST** technology is built right into modern SharePoint. So even if you don't know it, **FAST** technology is being used when you search in SharePoint. Behind the scenes, SharePoint search is handled by a service called Search. The Search service reads all the material and builds an index. After a search question, the index is used to give results. When a person writes a word into the Search box and hits Enter, the Search service looks it up in the index and sends back a web page with the results. If you add a new file or item and then can't find it in a search result, it means that the Search service hasn't crawled and indexed it yet. If your company uses SharePoint On-Premises, your owner can decide when it will happen. If your company has a Microsoft 365 contract and uses SharePoint Online, Microsoft will take care of the Search service for you. We've found that new things usually show up in the search results about an hour after we add them.

Searching for Content

With SharePoint, it's easy to look for information. There is a Search box at the top of every website. Type your search word into the text box and click the magnifying glass to the right of the Search text box to conduct a content search. The SharePoint search engine uses your words to search and shows you the results. You will also notice that the search engine gives you suggestions as you type. You can tell the search engine to do different things when it runs the question in different ways, not just by typing in search words. Because of this, you can use special characters and narrow the search results in SharePoint based on features.

Searching for a string using quotation marks

When you type more than one word into the Search box, the SharePoint search engine looks through the material and shows you any examples that have those words in them. That's what you do when you want a string of two or more words: you put quote marks around the string. For instance, the following search phrase finds any material that has either "Annual" or "Report" in it.

- *Annual Report*

If you're looking for content where the words are found together, then you would type the search string in quotation marks.

- *"Annual Report"*

The search engine takes anything within the quotation marks and looks for that entire string in the content.

Wildcard searches

In a search, the star (*) can be used to stand for a blank space. For instance, you might need to find a file that starts with "Quarter," but you can't remember if it's "Quarters" or "Quarterly." To **search for anything that starts with the word Quarter, you could use the "*" symbol as shown below:**
- *Quarter **

This search would show everything that starts with "Quarter," such as Quarterly and Quarters. In the same way, you might know that the first word is Quarterly but not whether the second word is Reports or Results. Following the question mark and the wildcard character, you would tell the search engine that you want all content that has the word "Quarterly" followed by any word that starts with the letter "R." This would be the question:
- *"Quarterly R*"*

You can get a lot of search results with random characters when you don't know the exact word.

Including and excluding terms

By using the plus sign (+), you can tell the search engine to only show results that have a certain word in them. One way to write your search would be:
- *Annual Reports +Marketing*

If you click on the plus sign, it means that the information you get back must include the word marketing along with either Annual or Reports. A drawback of search is that you frequently receive far more results than you can handle. You can also cut down your search results by leaving out certain words. For instance, you might be looking for content about product marketing but don't want to find any that has the word "**internal**" in it. This is how you could write your search: "**Product Marketing**" –internal. The search engine then shows all the results that have either "Product" or "Marketing" in them and gets rid of any results that also have "internal."

Building compound search queries using Boolean operators

Multiple search phrases are needed to make compound search questions. With the Boolean operators, you can put together phrases to make full queries.

The following are the Boolean operators:

- **AND**: It only gives you content if both claims are true.
- **NOT**: Only gives back data when the statement is false. As we saw in the last part, this is the same thing as using the minus sign.
- **OR**: A value is returned when at least one of the statements is true.

Putting two words into the Search text box is the same as putting in one word, then OR, and then the second word. When used with braces, Boolean operators are very useful. There are times when you use brackets and Boolean operators together to tell the search engine how to group the query lines, which we'll talk about next.

Finding terms in proximity

There are times when you need to find text where you know two words are close to each other but not exactly next to each other.

As an example, look at this sentence:

The sales figures for China are excellent. The words **"sales"** and **"China"** are very close to each other in this line. Yes, you would get this content if you just typed "sales China" into the Search box. But you might also get a lot of other content that isn't related. This is how you could use the NEAR function to find the answer you want:

- *"sales" NEAR(5) "China"*

NEAR will only turn up findings where the words are within five words of each other. The number in the braces tells it this. But you don't have to give the number. It would be just as easy to write the question:

- *"sales" NEAR "China"*

If you don't tell the search engine how many words to use, it will use eight by default. In other words, the words are close if they are within eight words of each other. In some cases, it might not be enough for two terms to be close to each other; they also need to be in a certain order. You might want to only get results where the word "sales" comes after the word "China" within a certain number of words. ORDER BY is the Boolean function that lets you do this. The ONEAR operator does the same thing as the NEAR operator, but it takes an order. The search engine is told to only show results where the word "sales" is followed by "China" in a span of five words.

- *"sales" ONEAR(5) "China"*

Same meaning, different terms

You could have said **"television"** or **"television."** Where did you go to the theater? It wouldn't matter if you watched or went; it would still mean the same thing. It is easy for people to understand homonyms. It's so simple that we don't give many of the clear ones much thought. There are times when people answer the question by saying they watch TV but don't answer the question. Computers should be able to think that well. You tell the search engine that two words mean the same thing with the WORDS function. For instance, if you want to find all material that talk about California, you could write the question like this:

- ***WORDS(CA, California)***

Because of this, the search engine knows that CA and California mean the same thing and shows the right results. Why not just put the two words into the Search box? The answer is in how the scores are ranked. The search engine will show the same results if it knows that these words mean the same thing. It might return content that has both California and CA at the top of the list if it doesn't know this. However, content that only has the word CA further down the list might be more useful. When you type these words into the search engine, it knows that they all mean the same thing and will give you the best answers.

Viewing and Refining Search Results

After a query is run, you are presented with the results page, as shown in the image below;

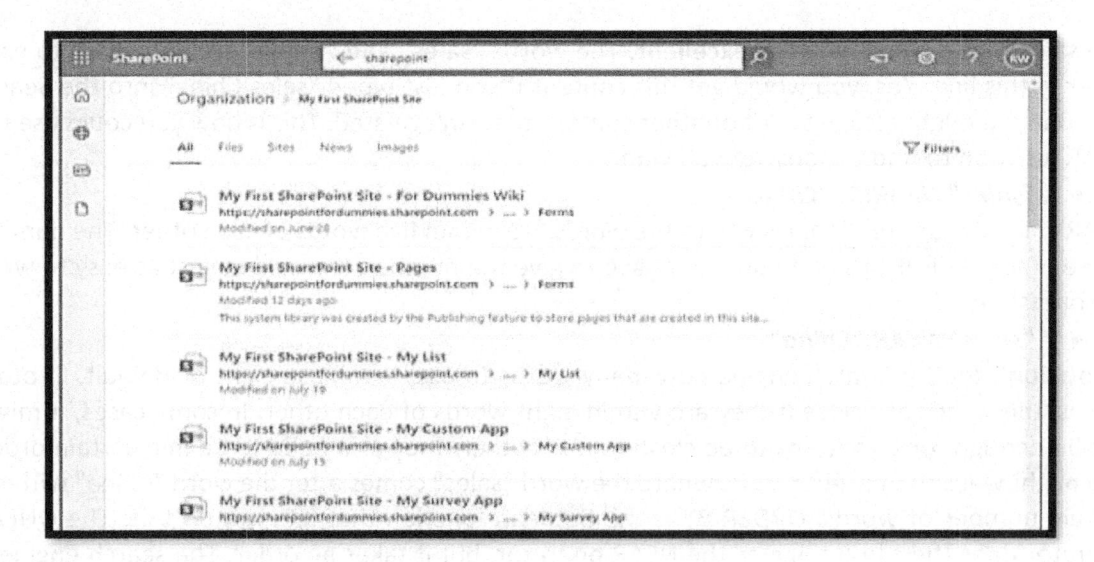

The results page has a lot going on, but it's mostly easy to understand. You will see a thumbnail peek to the right of the search result if the result is an Office document (like Word or Excel) or another type of document that has a preview option. In the first picture, you can see a SharePoint site. In the second picture, the first thing that comes up is an Office Word document, with a sample of the file's contents to the right of the result.

You can narrow down the results by clicking on the buttons at the top of the page that look like filters. You can click on a certain type of content or use the date the content was last changed to narrow down the results. It's very helpful to be able to narrow down content based on when it was last changed since old content can be a real problem in search results.

Making Search Your Users' Best Friend

It can be very frustrating to try to find the right material. Internet tracking and search engine access are what companies like Google were built on. You could find different kinds of material on the Internet before Google, but only on services like AOL. When Google first came out, all you had to do was go to www.google.com and put your search query into the Search box. The result would usually be right there in the first few pages of the results. How did Google do that? To list all the material on the Internet, it used special algorithms. If you are in charge of a site, you can change the search results in SharePoint to fit your business. Let's say you have a website for people who work in call centers to use. When people search for product documentation, you don't want the official sites for that documentation to get lost among other material that talk about products. You can set up SharePoint search so that approved pages show up higher than other pages. You can even make searches that are similar to the ones people are already looking for. These will appear right next to the search results. Query rules allow all of this to happen. A query rule is a set of rules that SharePoint search uses to answer a search question. This means that as a site owner, you can use a query rule to tell the search engine how to handle certain questions.

The search question function gives the same result as the Best Bets function did in older versions of SharePoint. New features have been added to Best Bets, such as linked search blocks and result ranking. All of these features can now be used in search results. To help you learn how a query rule works, try this out. There are two parts to this case. The first is that you want an app called Employee Onboarding to come up whenever someone looks for "new employee" or "onboarding." In this case, the Onboarding app is a list that has all the steps that new employees need to take to get started at the company. You want to add a result block to the search results whenever someone types in "onboarding" or "new employee." Is that all? If you choose, a results block is just a secondary question that will show up in the search results.

Follow these steps to get people to the Onboarding app whenever they search for "onboarding" or "new employee":

1. Click the Settings gear icon in the upper right corner of the screen and select Site Contents to go to the Site Settings page. Then click the Site Settings button.
- It shows the Site Settings page.

2. Select "Search" and click on the "Query Rules" link.
- It shows the Manage Query Rules page.
- In the Site Settings page, if you are in charge of a site collection, you can also find the Search Query Rules link under "Site Collection Administration." These two Query Rules settings are different because one only affects the site and the other affects all sites in the same group. Click the Query Rules link in the Search area of the Site Settings page. In this case, you only want to build the query for your site.

3. Select Local SharePoint Results (System) from the Result Source drop-down list.
- You can see that the Query Rules load for the Local SharePoint Results source.

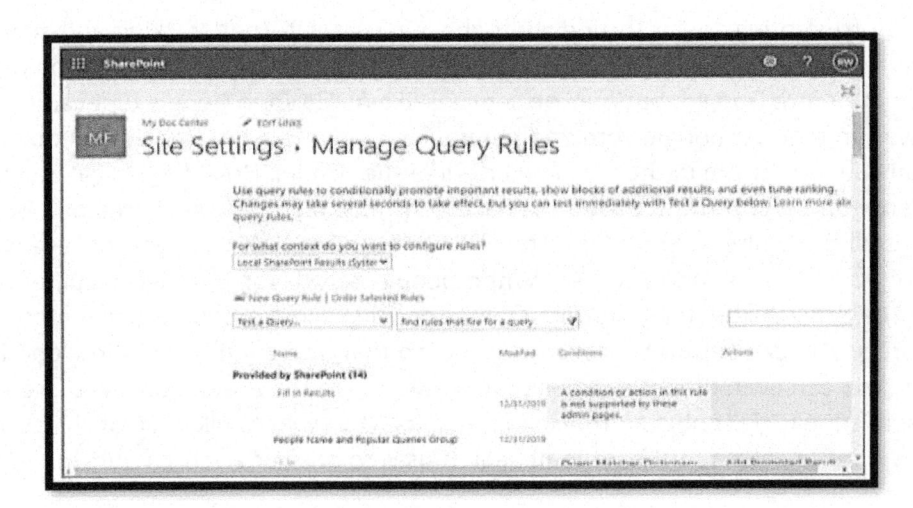

119

- You can choose the context of the query rule you're making from the Result Source drop-down list. Take note of how many answer source options there are. These let you make very specific question rules. One example of a rule you could make is for people search or discussions. You pick Local SharePoint Results (System) because you only want results for the local SharePoint site in this case.

4. Click the New Query Rule button.
- The Add Query Rule page is displayed.

5. In the Rule Name text box, give the rule a name. In the Search Term text box, separate the search words "new employee" and "onboarding" with a break.
- The exact text you should type is new employee; onboarding

6. Click the Add Promoted Result link.
- The **Add Promoted Result** dialog box is displayed.
- There is no difference between a recommended result and a Best Bet in older versions of SharePoint. The featured result is at the top of the search results page when someone types in the exact words "**new employee" or "onboarding**."

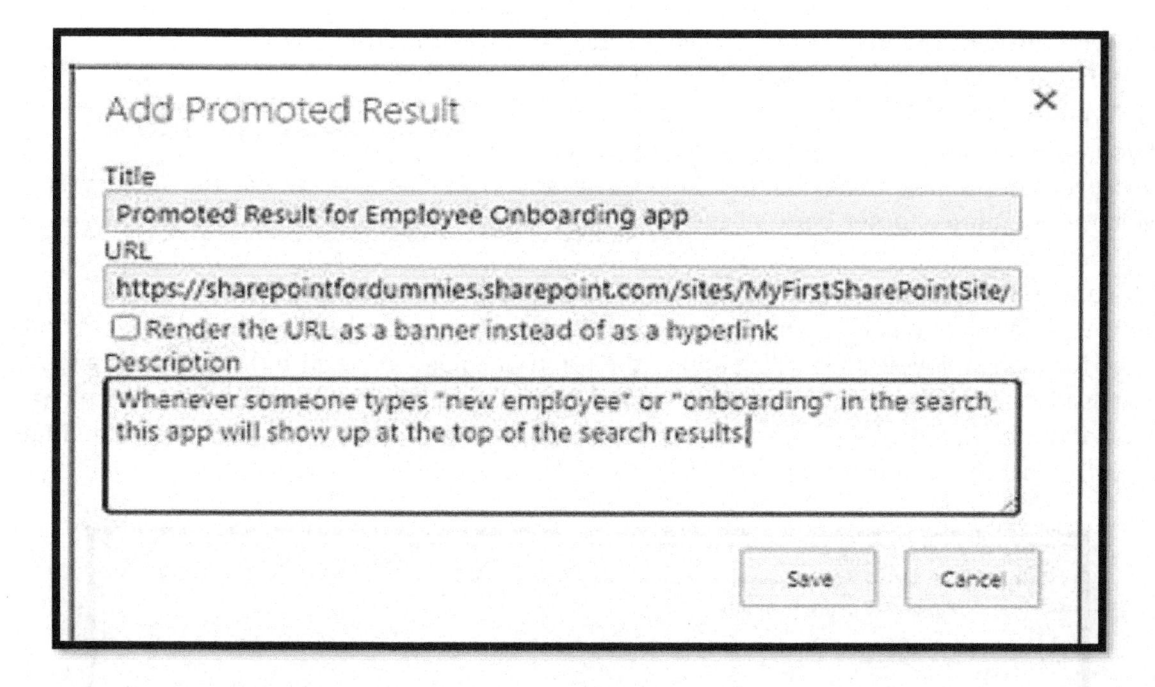

```
Add Promoted Result                                    ×

Title
[ Promoted Result for Employee Onboarding app        ]
URL
[ https://sharepointfordummies.sharepoint.com/sites/MyFirstSharePointSite/ ]
☐ Render the URL as a banner instead of as a hyperlink
Description
[ Whenever someone types "new employee" or "onboarding" in the search,
  this app will show up at the top of the search results ]

                                         [ Save ]  [ Cancel ]
```

7. In the Title text box, give your promoted result a title. In the URL text box, type the URL to the content you want to show. In the Description text box, write a description of the promoted result.
8. Click "**Save**" to add the advanced result to the query rule.
9. Click the link that says "**Add Result Block**" to add a linked search to the search results that have the words "**new employee" or "onboarding**" in them.

10. Type the description of the result block into the description text box.
By default, it shows the search words that were used for the report.
11. Type the search terms you want to use in the result block into the "Configure Query" box.
If you are searching the SharePoint site and want to add this second search to a search for new employees or training, think about these terms that way. In this case, we use the subject terms, which is the norm, to get back all the material that has the exact string "new employee" or "onboarding."
12. To save the query rule, click Save after clicking OK to save the result block.
Now, when someone puts **"new employee" or "onboarding"** into the site's Search box, they see an ad for the Employee Onboarding app at the top of the page along with the results of a search that used the same words. The outcome is shown in the picture below. Since our site doesn't have a lot of material, we only get one result. But as your content grows, you can understand how powerful this behavior can become.

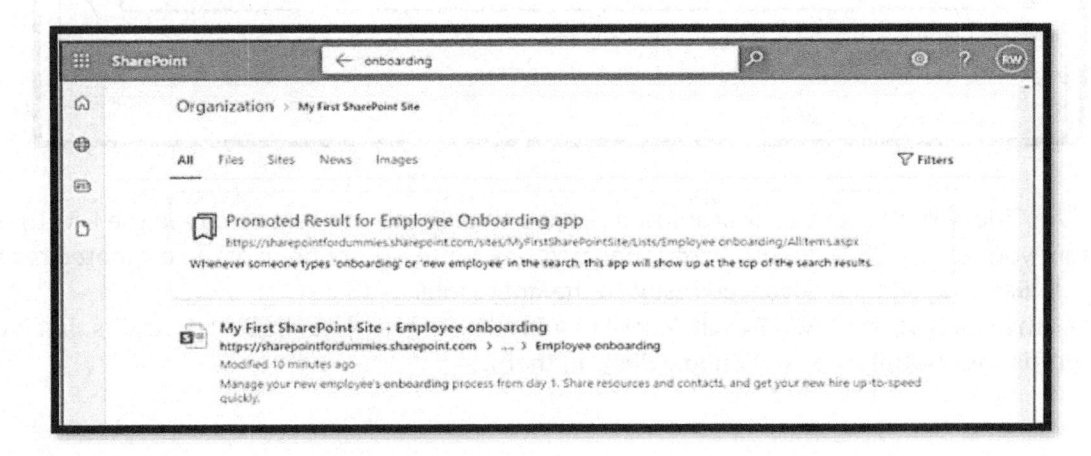

121

Removing Content from Search Results

When you search, things and documents in apps will show up by default. These things might not be what you want to show up in search results.

Follow these steps to keep things and documents in apps out of search results:

1. Click the gear button in the upper right corner of the screen and select Site Contents. This will take you to the app that you want to remove from search. There is a list of all the apps.
2. Click the app to open it and then open the app settings page by clicking the gear icon again and clicking **List Settings** or **Library Settings**. The App Settings page appears.
3. Go to the **General Settings** part and click on the link that says "Advanced Settings." The screen for Advanced Settings shows up.
4. In the Search box, click the "**No**" radio button.
5. To save the settings, click "**OK**." This app's information will not be searched by the search engine the next time it does so.

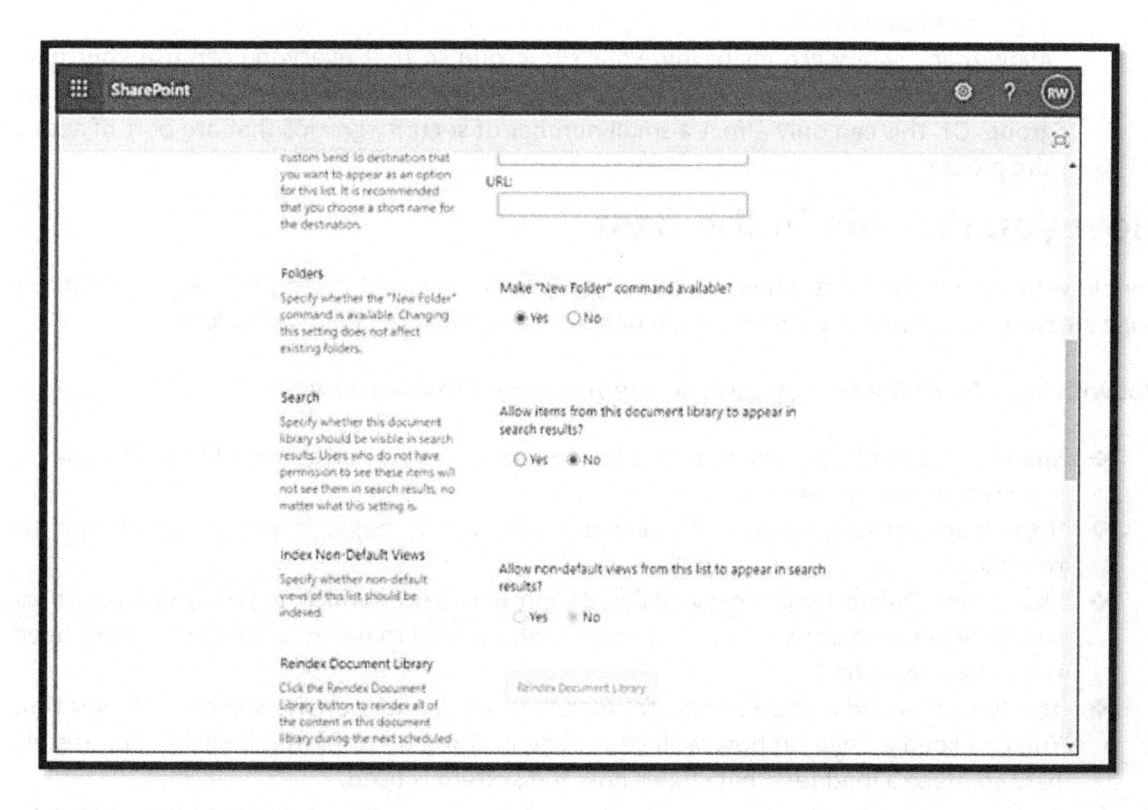

122

CHAPTER 13
SHAREPOINT FOR ENTERPRISE SOLUTIONS

After all the work you put into it, you want that new SharePoint site to be up and running as soon as possible. But how should that be done in the best way? These tips are mostly for SharePoint Online, but most of them also work for websites that are stored in an on-premises SharePoint system.

What not to do

Here is a list of the most important things you should not do when setting up your platform.

Don't:

- Test your gateway under a lot of stress with a SharePoint Online user.
- Have a "big bang release," which means that all of your customers should see your new page at the same time.
- Allow many safety groups to join your site group so that everyone can use your page. That's a lot of security groups (30–40,000), but each one can only be a part of one site group. Or, this can only affect a small number of security groups that are part of a lot of site groups.

How you did this in the past

People who used SharePoint when it was still on-premises would often put their sites through huge stress tests to see if the system could handle it and still let pages load quickly.

But with SharePoint Online, you can't do a normal stress test because:

- ❖ SharePoint Online sees the load test as a denial-of-service attack and blocks the user or, even worse, the whole tenant;
- ❖ If the load test isn't blocked, it's slowed down, which makes it hard to understand the results;
- ❖ SharePoint Online dynamically scales its infrastructure, which is great, but not if you suddenly put a lot of work into it. The back-end model that can handle more work needs time to get used to it.
- ❖ This type of speed test only looks for mistakes once, but your site will change over time. You can keep an eye on how well your page is doing by using the built-in data. It's also hard to make a load test that shows how the system is used.

The best way to get your new portal up and running is to use a staged roll-out plan and built-in portal data to keep track of progress as more users are added. The next part talks about this method in more depth.

Use a phased roll-out plan and telemetry

You should use a planned method if you want to add new features. This involves steps like these:

- ❖ **A pilot wave**: A small group of important people can now access the site for the first time. Get a group of reps, or important, key users, who can give you feedback right away.
- ❖ **One or more end-user waves**: If you're following a plan, the number of waves you have will depend on how many people are there. The roll-out steps for some businesses are based on how their business is set up, while the steps for others are based on the country or area. Finally, the most important thing is that new people are slowly joining the site.

The picture below shows a plan for a slow roll-out. Remember that this is why end-user waves generally have fewer busy users than invited-user waves.

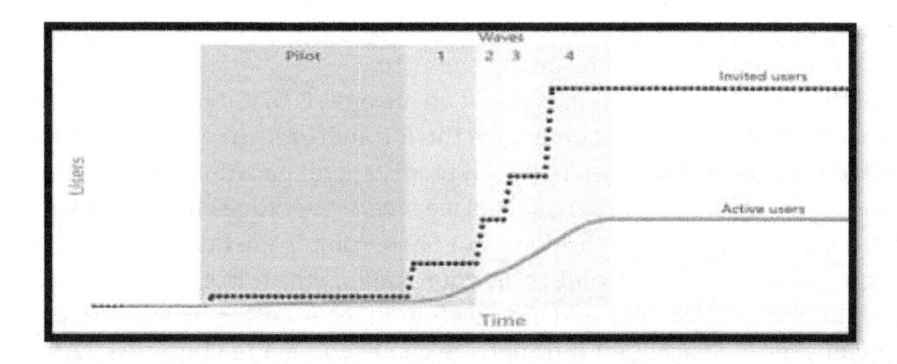

Before you make any changes to your site, this step-by-step process gives you time to think about the feedback you're getting. But how do you keep track of and measure success with this phased roll-out? The best way to do this is to add site info to your app. If you keep track of how the site is doing, you can see if the speed changes as the number of users grows. The next time you change the site, this can also help.

Successful Intranet Portal with SharePoint

When it comes to business communication, intranet sites top the list. The intranet is being used by more and more businesses to help people work together. The market is also going up. Statista says the market for teamwork software will keep growing and bring in around $13.58 billion US in 2023. These numbers show how much money businesses spend on different tools for working together. Because it is used by more employees of all ages, the intranet site will probably be the most expensive thing on this list. The list of the best websites available includes Microsoft SharePoint at the top. In 2001, Microsoft launched SharePoint for the first time. Since then, it's had a lot of changes and updates that have made it the best choice for businesses that want to work together. SharePoint has been the most famous tool for working together for almost 20 years. Why is SharePoint so great? The first thing is how simple it is to use. The flexibility of SharePoint means that it can perfectly meet the needs of any business. It is also very easy to set up and use. SharePoint is also great because it's easy to set up and businesses can rely on the service quality.

Why should companies adopt a SharePoint Intranet Portal?

Businesses can buy a lot of tools for teamwork these days to help their workers work together. But why would they pick an intranet? An intranet site is unique because it can hold all the tools for working together in one place. By putting it all together, businesses can make sure that information is uniform, knowledge is shared centrally, and they can support a language-free workplace. They can also benefit because it is easy for them to find and use the information with the united information store. The internet portal cuts down on the number of clicks a person needs to make to find something. **A site for a community can also do the following.**

- ❖ On many levels, an intranet can talk to each other. There will be many departments in a business, and it should be simple for folks from different departments to talk to each other. This is made possible by an intranet site.
- ❖ One of the most important things about an intranet is that it lets you control the content. You can store and access documents in the intranet, which will be the main location.
- ❖ It's easy to manage teamwork between teams and departments with an intranet.
- ❖ Intranets are the best way to make a place where everyone can work together.

There are many intranet connection options, but SharePoint is the best. Let's find out why that is happening. You can change SharePoint to fit your wants, which is its best feature. It has many web parts built in, and you can also add your own to make it better. These groups can use these to build their websites. A SharePoint intranet site can become a full business system that can do many things because it can change or adapt. What you might find here ranges from an HR management system to a simple paper management system.

SharePoint Intranet Development

SharePoint has been the best program on the market for 20 years. Also, it's changed a great deal since then. Also, Microsoft adds to SharePoint every day to make it a better tool for intranets. **Based on the versions that Microsoft makes public, the SharePoint intranet can be built in four different ways.**

1. SharePoint Intranet On-Premises Solution
2. SharePoint Online (Stand-alone)
3. SharePoint Online (part of O365)
4. SharePoint Online (Part of M365)

You should know what you want from building a SharePoint group. The intranet needs to be able to meet these work needs. In on-premise versions, this can be done through **"My Site,"** which is an employee's area with information about their work and the projects they are working on. Their work should be in it. In some versions of Office 365, you can look at an employee's profile in Delve to see what they are working on, who they are talking to, and other things. Now you can do this with Microsoft Delve. There should also be a way for teams to work together on the website. The **"Team Sites"** part of SharePoint lets you do this. Teams can store and look at papers here, as well as share ideas and discuss what's happening. Setting up and making changes to team sites is very easy. Simple changes can be made to the site by anyone, even if they don't know much about SharePoint. The web parts that come with SharePoint can also be used to change these pages. The people who run the site can easily decide who can read these pages and make changes to the information on them. You can improve the appearance of teams' websites with "Communication Sites." One cool thing about it is the Hero Web part, which is a content slider where you can put videos and pictures. You can change communication sites in any way you want, just like you can change Teams. Something else great about SharePoint Online right now is that it has something called "Hub Sites." **Links to other sites**, like Team sites and Communication sites, are used to make these sites. It's like the hub of your neighborhood. SharePoint has many different types of sites that can help teams work together better. These include a business wiki, blogs, community sites, community platforms, and project sites. You need to use these tools to make a collaboration site that works for your teams, meets user needs, and helps workers do their jobs better. You can get more done as a team by making it easier for people to work together. If you want to work together better, you can always have SharePoint experts make and build your team sites.

SharePoint Intranet for Enterprise Collaboration

Enterprise collaboration's only goal is to make getting information simple and quick for everyone. With SharePoint Intranet, you can show company-wide data on your site with personalized web parts. You should give it a lot of thought because it will be the home page for the company's community. The group's news, important links, and ways to get to important papers and other material should all be on the first page. A company can use the useful parts of the SharePoint site. Among these is *HR management, project management solutions, contract management, document management, asset management, project management solutions*, and many more.

Intranet Management

The right way to use an intranet is important once your business has picked one. The information should be kept up to date and made more interesting so that people will use the answer. To get more people to use your website, show them how to use it, add new features, and ask for feedback on a regular basis. People don't use the intranet even though companies spend a lot of time and money making it better. This makes no one use the intranet, and the business loses a lot of money. Keep an eye on the solution and make sure it's well taken care of. Last but not least, you should always keep the answer up to date with any new features or bug fixes. There's no need for these changes to be big. When you're in charge of the website, you need to keep it safe and up to date. SharePoint Intranets are the source of all of these perks. Give them some thought before you decide.

CHAPTER 14
DISASTER RECOVERY AND BACKUP STRATEGIES

Understanding SharePoint Backup

Every business needs to back up SharePoint. How to keep your info safe and get it back if something goes wrong. To back up, you can use SharePoint's tool, a third-party tool, or do it by hand. Before the process can begin, the SharePoint farm, all of its files and settings must be fully backed up. A good backup plan keeps your business going and makes sure you don't lose any data. You should think about how often, what kind of backup (full or partial), where, and how long to keep the data when you make a plan. Make sure your copies are always right. To make sure you backup all the important parts, you can talk to a professional if you need to. Forbes said that 60% of small businesses that lose their records close down within six months. Plan and carry out the backup plan for SharePoint to keep the business running smoothly. Don't worry about losing your SharePoint data; just make sure you back it up.

Different Methods to Protect Your SharePoint Data

The information in SharePoint will be safe as long as you back it up. These tips have been shown to work in the past to keep your SharePoint setting safe.

- ❖ **Full Backup**: When you choose this option, the site's content, settings, and permissions are all saved to a backup file.
- ❖ **Differential Backup**: When you use differential backup, it keeps track of all the changes that have been made since the last full backup.
- ❖ **Incremental Backup**: What changes have been made to site collections since the last full or partial backup? This type of backup keeps track of those changes.
- ❖ **Granular Backup**: As the name suggests, this type of backup only keeps certain SharePoint sites, lists, or document stores safe.

Some third-party tools, such as CloudAlly, Veeam, and AvePoint, can back up your SharePoint data. You can also use the tools that come with SharePoint. Performing regular backups and recoveries is important to ensure that the saved files can be viewed and used in case of a disaster.

Full Farm Backup

SharePoint is great for working together as a team and managing info. Make sure you backup your SharePoint data often to keep it safe. **The "Full Farm Backup" option is one you can select.**

- ❖ Visit the Central Administration website. Select "**Backup and Restore.**"
- ❖ Choose "**Farm Backup**" and then click "**Start Backup.**"

- ❖ Choose where to save the copy.
- ❖ Check the settings. Press "**Back Up Now**."

Wait, because it takes time to do a Full Farm Backup. After these steps, the backup is done. Set up backups for times when not much is going on, like when you're not working. Store the second copy somewhere else to be safe. People use SharePoint Health Analyzer to check for issues or warnings. Things you store in SharePoint will be safe if you do this. It takes a long time to do granular backup, but it's worth it in the end.

Granular Backup

Granular backup is needed for SharePoint to work. It saves time and room and keeps files safe. This can be done with PowerShell or Central Admin, which are both part of SharePoint. Backing up can also be done with third-party tools that are easier for most people to use. With detailed backup, you can back up specific books, sites, lists, and even papers. With your own rules and goals, it can run itself. There's less chance that info will be lost. More than that, cloud-based services like Microsoft 365 let you back up a lot of information.

Pro Tip: Make sure you test your backups often. It will ensure that things will be fixed in a situation.

Backup via PowerShell

Would you like to make a copy of your SharePoint data? We need Microsoft PowerShell to fix this! You can do quick jobs with the command line, and this tool is strong and adjustable.

Here are the steps you need to take to make a good backup with PowerShell.

- o To log in to SharePoint, run "**Add-PSSnapin Microsoft.SharePoint.Powershell**" in Windows PowerShell.
- o Pick the page or site group that you want to save. "**New-Item E:\Backup -type directory**" will create a new backup folder.
- o To make a new backup object, use cmdlets such as **Export-SPWeb, Backup-SPFarm, or Backup-SPConfigurationDatabase.**
- o Decide whether you want a full or split copy.
- o Type "**Backup-SPFarm -Directory E:\Backup -BackupMethod Full**" to start the backup.

If you want to back up more than one subsite or group of sites, you have to do steps 2, 3, 4, and 5 again. PowerShell makes it simple to keep an eye on backups of SharePoint data. The backups are small, so they are easy to get and store. If something goes wrong, these steps will help you feel safe and save time. Backup SharePoint today with PowerShell so bad things don't happen to Simple Things Publishing!

Third-Party Backup Solutions

There may be features in third-party backup options that aren't in the backup tools that come with SharePoint. With these options, you can back up and restore everything, as well as back up only certain files or parts of files. There are also options for scheduling and reporting to be done automatically, as well as more detailed information on the status and health of files. It is important to think about how easy, scalable, and well-integrated a third-party backup option is when choosing one. **Commvault Complete Backup & Recovery for SharePoint, Veeam Backup & Replication for Microsoft SharePoint, and Druva inSync** for SharePoint are the ones you can pick from. These advanced features keep your SharePoint data safe so that you don't lose it or delete it by accident. Remember to back up your SharePoint. It's like saving your ex's number in case you need it.

Best Practices for SharePoint Backup

The business needs to keep files of SharePoint information. For backup and emergency recovery plans, we need Best Practices for SharePoint Backup. What we think about SharePoint Backup is this:

- If you want regular backups, make sure you have a plan in place.
- If you want to save time and space on backups, use incremental backups instead of full backups. Check the backup data by running a restore job.
- Keep multiple copies of backups in different places to lower the risk of losing data.
- Set up security rules to keep people out without permission and encrypt backups for privacy.

How to deal with lost data and removed sites is one of the many twists and turns of SharePoint Backup. If you want to make SharePoint Backup rules that work well and are useful, you should fully understand these changes.

Determine Backup Frequency

You should back up your SharePoint data in case something bad happens, the system crashes, or you delete something by accident. **Figure out how often you need to back up your data by looking at how much it's worth and how often it changes.**

- **Daily Back-Ups**—If you make changes every day, it's best to back up every day.
- **Backups Every Week**: Backing up every week is enough for data that doesn't change very often.
- **Backing up every month**: Backing up data can save time and space for files that don't change often.
- **Backups every three months, six months, or a year:** Every three, six, or twelve months, you can back up data that you don't use very often for legal reasons or to store it.

Back up your data more than once so that you have extra copies in case of fires, storms, or other natural disasters. Make sure that the service that backs up SharePoint can bring back all of its information, not just a few files.

Store Backups Securely

It is important to keep backups in a safe place so that your SharePoint system stays safe and works well. To do this, you should secure your files and put them somewhere safe. To make things safer, role-based access control can be used to make sure that only the right people can get in. To guard against data loss from technological malfunctions or natural disasters, it is recommended that you have multiple copies saved in different safe sites. You can also be sure that the backup method will work when you need it by using it often. When you store your SharePoint backups in this way, you can be sure that no one else can access your data without your permission and that it is safe in case something bad happens. Like relationships, things that backup and recovery: you won't know if they work until it's too late.

Test Backup and Restore Processes

For data access and dependability, you must test your backup and recovery methods. Use this as a guide:

- Make a copy of the real setting and put it in the test case.
- To test, make fake data.
- Make a full copy of the test site.
- Get rid of at least one fake set.
- Get the stuff you lost back from the full copy.
- Check that the info that was sent back works by doing what it does.

Just because you backed up something doesn't mean it worked. Add and test your escape plans for emergencies. Don't plan your training, but do them anyway as tests. You never know when bad things will happen, so be ready for them. This business was shocked when its server crashed. Some of the saved files they tried to recover were broken or lost, so they failed. They fixed old files for hours instead of doing important work. This might not have happened if tests were done more often. Keeping SharePoint settings safe is like putting on a helmet while riding a bike: it's annoying, but you have to do it to stay safe.

Backup SharePoint Configuration

Backing up your SharePoint config files is a must for smooth operation. Here's how to do it!

- Go to the **Start menu** and click on **Administrative Tools**. Then, click on SharePoint Central Administration.
- Go to the left menu and pick "**Backup and Restore**." After that, click "**Back up now**."

- On the "**Backup Options**" page, choose "**Farm Backup**." Pick out all the parts in Farm Selection. Pick "**Full**" as the Type and make a backup plan.

Making sure backups are up to date is very important if you don't want to lose info.

One pro tip: Give each backup a name so you don't delete the wrong one.

Restoring SharePoint from Backup

Every business needs to back up its data these days because we count on it so much. It comes with SharePoint, a famous tool for managing documents and working together. It's very important to be able to quickly get back backed-up data in case of unexpected data loss or damage. From a copy, this is how you can get back to SharePoint.

After making a backup, these six simple steps will bring back SharePoint:

- Open **SharePoint Central Administration** on the computer that was backed up to start.
- Start by going to **Backup and Restore**. Then, click on **Restore from Backup** and find the backup file.
- Pick a repair point and the group of sites you want to bring back.
- Choose which parts of the backup you want to get back, such as permissions, lists, and libraries.
- Pick one of the repair options, like "**overwrite file**" or "**create new sites**."
- Click **OK** to finish.

If you use SharePoint, you should back up your info and any parts that are related to it often. One more thing to think about is making a backup plan for the business. Having an off-site data storage option, double-checking files for accuracy, and backing up and testing emergency recovery plans right away are all part of this type of plan. The only way to be sure that the SharePoint recovery process works is to check and update files often, even on days when nothing much happens. Because it is more open and easier to access, a backup and emergency recovery option that is hosted in the cloud is worth considering. Finally, use normal business security steps to keep the backup data safe from threats like those that come from the internet. Don't forget that there's no place like home, but there is also no place like a current backup if you need to restore SharePoint from a full-farm copy.

Restore from Full Farm Backup

To make sure your data stays safe, follow these four steps to get back to SharePoint from a Full Farm Backup:

- Make sure you have the right accounts and permissions to do what you need to!
- Choose "**Backup and Restore**" from the Central Administration System Settings menu.
- Click "**Restore from Backup**" and look for the file that has a full copy of your farm.
- Choose which parts to bring back, check that the settings are right, and then begin the repair.

Remember that this could take a while, depending on how many things you have. To be ready when you need to be, check and test your saves frequently. Before you try to fix broken data, you should restore it from a backup. The SharePoint documentation says that this method can be used to get a farm back to the way it was before a disaster. Some backups, on the other hand, can bring SharePoint back to life like a zombie bug!

Restore from Granular Backup

There are three steps to recover from Granular Backup for SharePoint:

- ❖ Go to the backup area and find the group of sites.
- ❖ Put the site files back where they belong in SharePoint.
- ❖ Do a full search of where the information came from.

Make sure that item-level fixes won't get rid of features that are already there. Granular saves offer options. They can get back some things and information without messing up the rest. This way, admins can get back lists or papers that were deleted by accident.

Restore via PowerShell

PowerShell can be used to quickly bring back SharePoint from a backup. It's hard to do, but it makes sure that all of your data and settings are found again. What to do:

- Log in as an administrator to the SharePoint Management Shell.
- Type the following: **Restore-SPFarm -Directory <Path to Backup Folder> -RestoreMethod Overwrite -Item** Restore Type'. 'Restore Type' could be an online app, content database, or group of sites.
- Hit **"Enter"** and wait for the repair to finish.

You need enough file room to be able to get to the right place. Each fix has its own needs based on the size of the backup, the amount of free space, and the position of the disk. A top worker once used PowerShell to quickly bring back a database with an important document library. He was happy that nothing had gone wrong and that no data had been lost or damaged after two hours. He is even surer now that PowerShell is a great tool for SharePoint managers. When you need to recover SharePoint from a backup made by someone else, it's like having a superhero on hand. They're great when you need them, but not all the time.

Restore Using Third-Party Backup Solutions

You can use outside tools to bring back SharePoint from a backup. These options give your information an extra layer of safety to help keep it safe. Follow these six steps:

- Pick the best service that isn't made by Microsoft to back up your SharePoint system.
- Check to ensure that you have a copy of the important files and data.
- Read and follow the steps that came with the third-party option to set it up and install it.

- Choose the most recent backup version with the necessary data.
- Start fixing it the way the seller tells you to.
- Check that all of your information is back when you're done and see how the system works.

Note: Each seller may follow a different set of steps. Do what they tell you. When you restore from a file, be careful not to mess up. If you do, it could change how the current user sees the site.

IDC's Worldwide Quarterly Purpose-Built Backup Appliance Tracker shows that Dell Technologies brings in almost a quarter of the world's purpose-built backup market's revenue. When SharePoint is backed up regularly, IT teams stay calm and business data is protected from digital disasters.

CHAPTER 15
CREATING WORKFLOWS WITH MICROSOFT POWER AUTOMATE

Understanding Workflow

A workflow can be used to run either a process that is focused on people or a process that is focused on computers. For example, five people might work on a process, sometimes at the same time and sometimes one after the other. If these five people are in the same room and finish the process at the same time, it wouldn't make much sense to use a workflow to plan their work. People can be spread out in different offices or desks, or the process can go on for a while. A workflow can help organize and keep the process on track. A process may also talk to and work with other computer systems. One example is a method that needs to get information about customers from a Customer Relationship Management (CRM) system. You could also pull information into SharePoint from Twitter and the CRM so that when someone publicly talks about your company on Twitter, a workflow is started. A workflow can include almost anything you can think of.

Introducing Microsoft Power Automate

The new wave of workflow is Microsoft Power Automate. It was built from the ground up to work with Microsoft 365 products as well as third-party products (not made by Microsoft) like Dropbox, Amazon, Twitter, Facebook, and almost every other online service in the world. Employees can set up and organize processes that work across multiple apps. If you think of Microsoft Power Automate, you should picture an online workflow engine that works with all websites, not just Microsoft ones. Microsoft Flow is now called Microsoft Power Automate. Microsoft Flow is often talked about in pieces about workflow in Microsoft 365. Instead, you can think of Power Automate now. The names of things at Microsoft change all the time so don't worry if you see a new name. Likely, the technology isn't new; the name is.

Access Microsoft Power Automate

There are two ways to access Microsoft Power Automate:

- In any Microsoft 365 service, like SharePoint, go to the Apps menu and find the Power Automate icon.
- Go to https://flow.microsoft.com/ to see the Microsoft Power Automate page. Keep in mind that the domain still uses flow, which was the old name for the workflow engine.

Getting familiar with Power Automate

Your web browser can be used as a creation tool by the Microsoft Power Automate service to set up automatic processes known as flows. Here is a picture of the planning setting. Home, Action Items, My Flows, Create, Templates, Connectors, Data, Monitor, AI Builder, Process Advisor, Solutions, and Learn are some of the menu options that are available on the left side of the page.

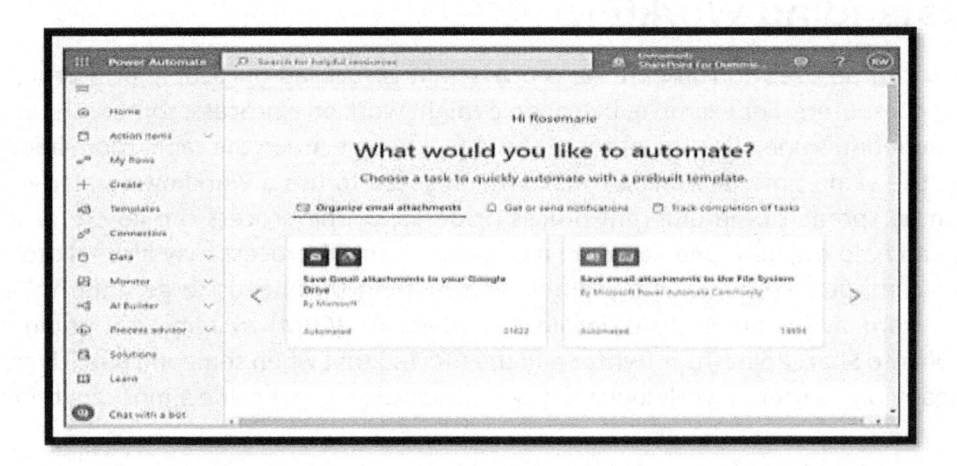

If you ever get lost, the **Home link** will always take you back to the home page. The start page gives you an outline of Power Automate and is a good place to go back to when you need to. Approvals and business process steps can be found on the Action Items page. To see the **Approvals link** and the **Business Process Flows link**, click the Action Items heading in the menu on the left. The Approvals page will show up when you click the Approvals link. If you click on the "**Approvals**" link, you'll be taken to the page shown below. There, you can create a new approval workflow or get or send approvals and act on them. That's right, you can look at the history of decisions right here.

135

My Flows is the most important page in Power Automate. You can see all of your flows and the flows for your team when you click this link. **The tabs will help you organize the flows into groups like Shared with Me, Cloud, Desktop, and Business Process.**

- **Cloud flows** are processes that start immediately, right away, or on a set plan when certain things happen in the cloud.
- **Desktop flows** put together processes for tasks you do over and over on your machine. Like putting your files and documents in order or getting info from the same source every day into an Excel file.
- **Business Process Flows** are made for worker processes, which mean that people always do the same steps. Let's say people want to open a new account. They should always follow the new account workflow.
- The **Shared with Me flows** are flows that others have created and shared with you.

If you go to the Create navigation item, you can begin a new workflow. The Templates link takes you to the Templates library. Templates are flows that are already made and can be changed to fit different situations. Like, you can set a flow to remind you in ten minutes or begin a review process when something new is added to SharePoint or Outlook. There are so many templates to choose from, and new ones are being added all the time. There is a good chance that someone has already made a template for the workflow you want to use. The next item on the menu for getting around is Connectors. Plug-ins are what give Power Automate its power. Well, Power Auto-Mate can join a lot of different services and goods thanks to its connections. You can make processes that work with well-known sites and goods here. Do you remember when we talked about Amazon, Twitter, Facebook, and Dropbox? This is where you can find links to connect those items to almost any other online service or item in the world.

Keep in mind that you may need to pay for a paid account to connect to some services.

- The **Data navigational link** lets you add data to your flows so that it can be looked at and choices can be made in the workflow process. You will spend a lot of time in this area once you know how to use Power Automate.
- The **Monitor option** is where you keep an eye on your flows. Notifications fail, and alerts are some of the things you will see.
- The **AI Builder option** lets you use popular AI models to improve your processes. You could teach a model to, say, look at new bills and pull out important information. As the model learns, it can change to new billing forms without any help from a person. You can use a lot of different AI models with Power Automate.
- **Process Advisor** comes next. You can think of it as an automatic way to see how your processes work. After that, you can look over the images and figure out how to make your processes better.
- Under the **"Solutions"** link, you can group flows into a single block that can be deployed. One item that can be used is called a solution, and you can group flows that work together to make them easier to use and keep up to date. In very big companies with a lot of flows, solutions can be helpful.

- Finally, the **Learn travel link** is where you can find Microsoft's step-by-step instructions on how to learn.

Building your first flow

1. In SharePoint, go to the top left area and click on the Microsoft 365 apps menu. Then, choose Power Automate.
   - ❖ The Microsoft Power Automate page starts when you open a new tab in your web browser.
2. On the left side of the page, click the link that says "Templates."
3. When you type "**SharePoint**" into the search box and press "Enter," the themes that are related to SharePoint will show up.
   - ❖ There is already a template that can do exactly what we want it to do.
4. Select the "**Send approval email when a new item is added**" template, which is the last one in the third row in the picture below.

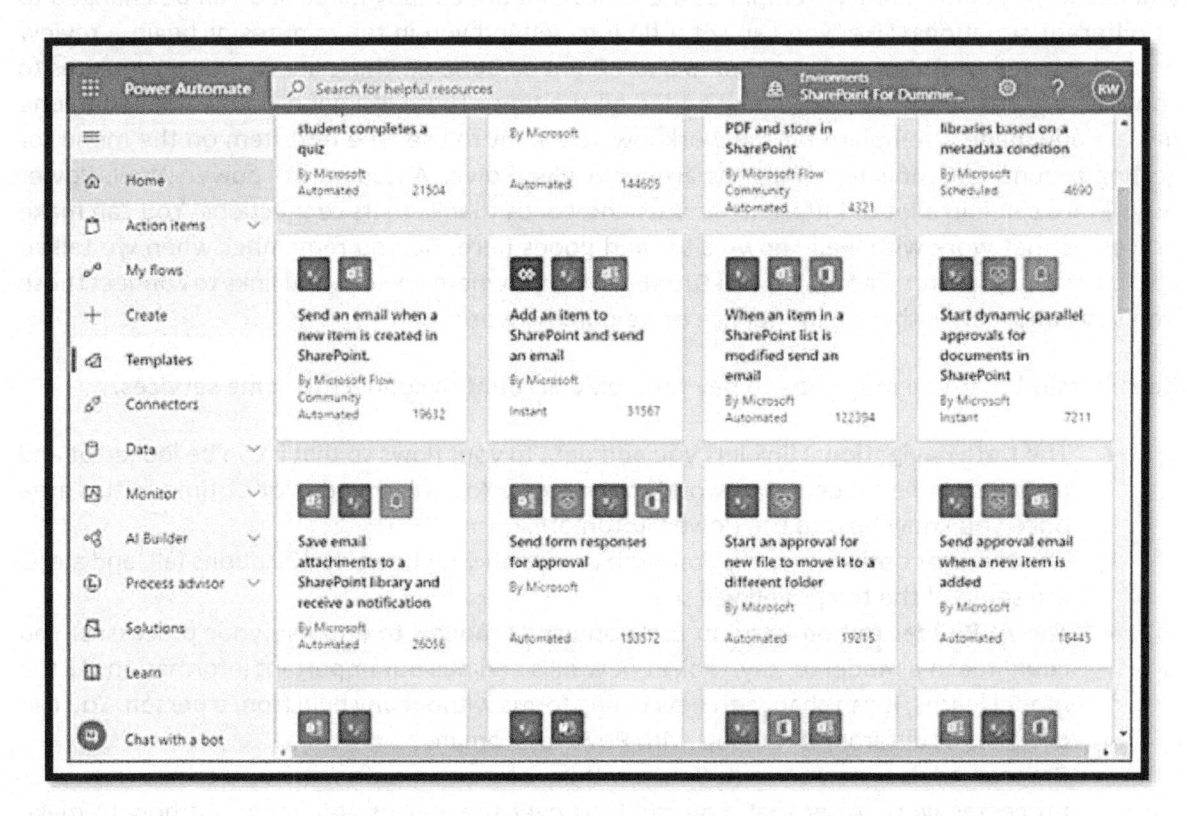

It brings up the page for this template, which shows how the workflow works. (Not a typo.) What you can see below is how the workflow starts in SharePoint and then goes to Microsoft 365 and Office 365 Outlook (email).

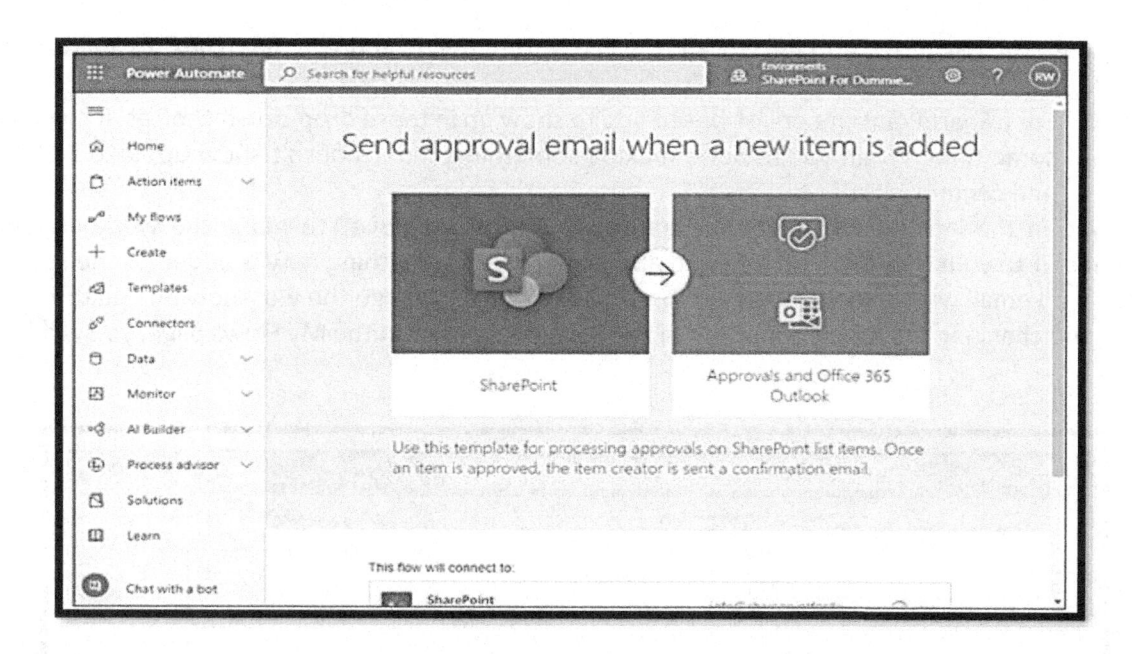

One thing we like about Microsoft services is that they take care of identification for us. You will see that this workflow crosses services if you look at the permissions it needs. We don't need to set up any extra permission for our person because they are already a part of Microsoft 365. After we sign in to each service from within the flow, it "just works."

5. To find your List-based app's SharePoint site, click the drop-down button next to SharePoint Site Address and select it.

138

6. Choose the **List-based app** the workflow will use from the drop-down menu next to **SharePoint List Name**.

> ❖ For a SharePoint site or List-based app to show up in these drop-down choices, it can take some time. When you're done making something and it doesn't show up, take a break and come back later.

7. Type in the information about the approval, then click "**Save**" to make the workflow and connect it to your SharePoint List-based app. Now, when something new is added to the list, an approved email will be sent to let everyone know. You can change the workflow by updating the flow and changing the target email, email message, and time. On the My Flows page, you will find it.

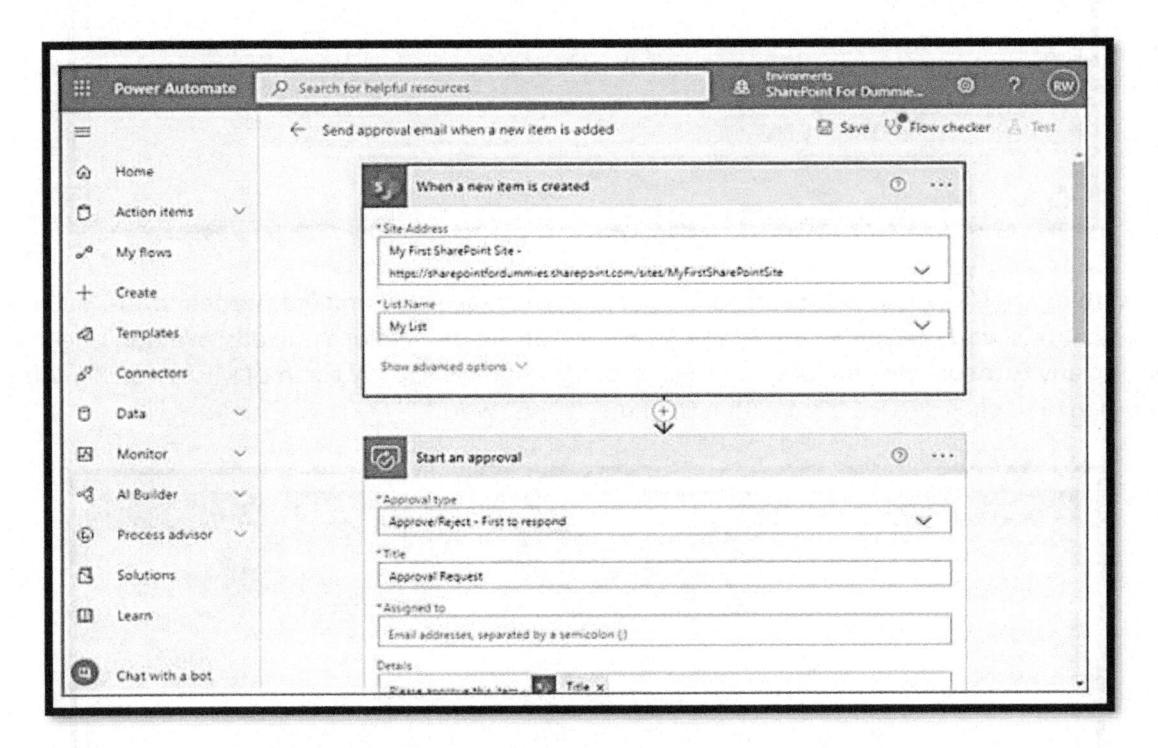

Using the Traditional SharePoint-Only Workflow

For the reason that it throws open the doors of SharePoint and links it to the rest of the world, Microsoft Power Automate is the workflow of the future. Some companies might still want to employ the conventional workflow that SharePoint provides, which keeps all workflows contained inside SharePoint itself. You will learn how to activate the standard SharePoint workflow system in this part so that you can choose if you want to continue using it or whether you are prepared to move on to the next generation of workflow with Power Automate. As a tool, SharePoint Designer was used in the process of constructing the traditional workflows in SharePoint. Power Automate has taken the position of SharePoint Designer, and the former is no longer used after its replacement. There is a possibility that you will still see SharePoint Designer if you are using an earlier version of SharePoint On-Premises. On the other hand, Power Automate is the tool that you should utilize for SharePoint Online and newer versions of SharePoint. People who are acquainted with the out-of-the-box workflows that were provided in earlier versions of SharePoint will be pleased to learn that these workflows are still present in the current version of SharePoint. As of right now, they are included in the site collection function, which is disabled by default. It is necessary to enable the Workflows feature for your site collection to turn them on, as seen in the picture below.

CHAPTER 16
BUILDING BUSINESS APPS WITH POWER APPS

Introducing Power Apps

We felt a sense of excitement when we first began utilizing Power Apps from Microsoft. Initially, it seemed to be a platform that was developed exclusively for SharePoint. On their mobile devices, we made the Power Apps that we developed accessible to as many different kinds of users as possible. People began using SharePoint all of a sudden, and until that point, they were completely unaware that they were using SharePoint. After using an application on their mobile devices, they were aware that it provided a solution to a particular business issue. At first, we considered Power Apps to be a mobile application platform, and we used it nearly entirely in conjunction with SharePoint because of this. Now that we have some experience under our belts, we have realized that Power Apps is more than simply making SharePoint applications available on mobile devices (although this is still the value that we consider to be the most significant). Even while we conceive of Power Apps as mainly a mobile experience, you can also integrate the Power Apps that you design into SharePoint sites. This is something that you can do.

Signing into Power Apps

Clicking on the Microsoft 365 app menu and then choosing Power Apps is the simplest method to access Power Apps. Alternatively, you can access Power Apps by opening your web browser and going straight to the website where they are advertised. On the Microsoft website, the Power Apps website may be found at https://powerapps.microsoft.com. You will use the credentials that you have for Microsoft 365 to log in to the Power Apps website.

Getting familiar with Power Apps

To develop applications, the Microsoft Power Apps service makes use of your web browser as a development tool. The environment for development is shown in the following:

You will find the following navigation options along the left side of the page: **Home, Learn, Apps, Create, Data, Flows, Chatbots, AI Builder, and Solutions**. Take note of these options. If you should get disoriented, the Home navigational link is your buddy since it will always bring you back to the beginning. When it comes to constructing Power Apps, the main page of Power Apps is always an excellent place to begin since it has information that provides an overview of the platform. Next up is the **Learn link**. There is a Power Apps community as well as guided learning and support topics that can be found via the Learn page. When you are initially getting started with Power Apps, it is important to make sure that you spend some time going through the Guided Learning experience that can be located on the Learn page. Spending this time will not only spare you a lot of aggravation and difficulties in the future, but it is also time well spent. You will be sent to a place that displays all of your Power Apps when you click on the Apps link. You will discover the most recent applications that you have produced, apps that have been shared with you, apps that you have permission to change, and apps that are a part of your organization.

The **Create link** can be found that follows the Apps link. You may build a new Power App by clicking on the build option in the Control Panel. During the process of developing your first Power App, you will make use of this in the next section. The Data link comes after the Create link in the list. There are now connections for **Entities, Connections, Custom Connectors, and Gateways** included in the Datalink, which has seen expansion. This is the location where you can manage the data that you are utilizing in your Power Apps as well as build connections of your own. Because data is the most important component of a business application, you will spend a significant amount of time working with it after you have gained experience in developing and personalizing Power Apps. Following the Data connection is the Flows navigational link, which gives you the ability to immediately integrate your Microsoft Power Automate processes into your Power Apps. You can construct virtual agents that reply to conversations by clicking on the Chatbots link available on this page. Consider a chatbot to be an automated response system that individuals can use to interact with one another and conduct discussions that are directed to them. If you expand the menu, you will have access to more options, such as the ability to create a new chatbot and to list all of your existing chatbots.

You can expand your applications using standard AI models by utilizing the AI Builder, which is a more complex functionality. The navigational link for Solutions is located at the very end of the list. Solutions is a feature of Power Apps that has only been around for a short while (Microsoft is always adding new functionality to its products). Solution enables you to encapsulate a group of Power Apps and transfer them all at once to another environment rather than moving them one at a time; this is a significant improvement over the previous method. Imagine a solution for a finance team that is built on Power Apps and contains applications that are used by financial departments. This is the concept that gives rise to Solutions.

Building your first Power App

One of the most straightforward applications of Power Apps is to enable users to interact with a bespoke SharePoint List-based application using their mobile phones or tablets. This is a highly powerful usage of Power Apps. At this point, almost everyone has a smartphone. Developing an application that enables your users to interact with a SharePoint list delivers your intranet to their mobile devices.

Create a Power App for dealing with a SharePoint list by following these steps:

1. Open your web browser and navigate to the SharePoint list.
2. Pick **Integrate** from the drop-down option that appears when you select **ellipsis**, and then pick Create an App from the fly-out menu for Power Apps.
   ❖ There is a dialog box that appears, and you can input a name for the application.

3. **Enter a name and click Create**. When you click on the link, your browser will take you to the Power Apps Studio, which is the development environment for Power Apps.

Although it may have an appealing name, Power Apps Studio is only a web page that has a great deal of functionality to develop applications. When it comes to working with it and building Power Apps, all you need is your usual web browser. Since we began with an already existing SharePoint list, the majority of the laborious tasks involved in developing the Power App were already completed for us.

4. Click the play button, which is located in the upper-right-hand corner of the page, to bring up a preview window for the application.

The preview may be used to get an idea of how the application will seem when it is viewed on a mobile device. It is necessary to establish a list in SharePoint since the list that stores the information for this application does not yet have any items in it.

5. In the upper-right-hand corner of the screen, you will see a plus symbol. Click on it.

There is a form that displays that is a representation of the columns in the SharePoint list.

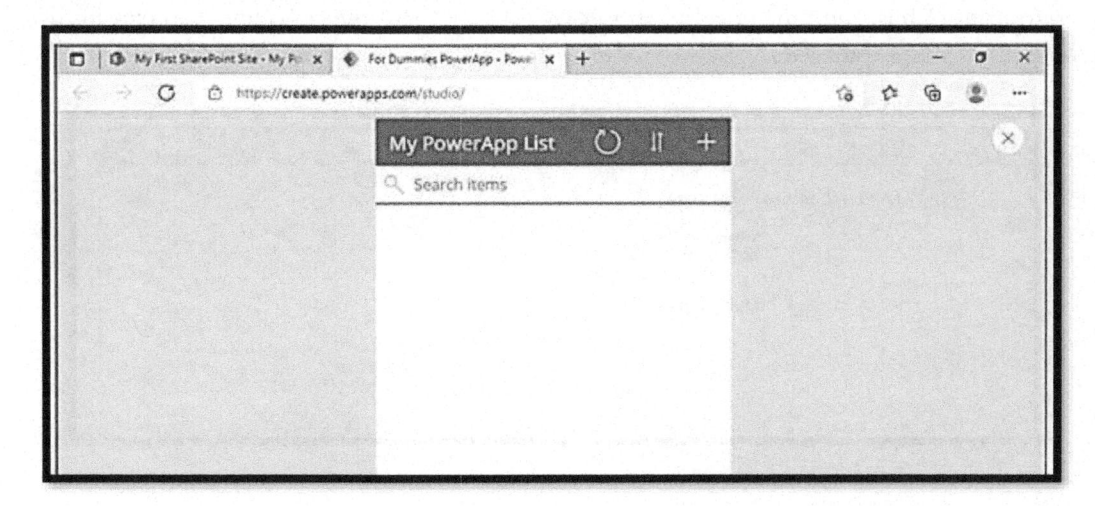

6. If you want to make a new list item, you must first fill out the form with the necessary information, and then you must click the checkmark that is located in the upper-right corner of the application.

The main page of the application will be refreshed once a new list item has been added. To verify that the item was generated, let's go back to our SharePoint list that is shown in our web browser.

7. Open the My Power App list in our browser and verify that the new item has been generated from the Power App.

Note that if you have numerous tabs open in your web browser that are related to Power Apps, then you may need to refresh the page to view any new things that have been added.

Next, let's create a new item in the SharePoint list in our web browser and then confirm it appears in the Power App.

8. To create a new item in the SharePoint list, click the plus sign (+) (which is a new item in the traditional experience or a new button in the new experience). After that, go to the Power App preview and click the refresh icon, which is a circle-shaped symbol.

Our new product has been included in the Power App. Currently; a Power App can be used to interact with a SharePoint list.

With Microsoft Power Automate, Power Apps can be integrated. Through the use of this combination, you can bring SharePoint into the realm of mobile devices while simultaneously incorporating your workflow. From our point of view, this is a significant step forward in the field of technology.

Sharing your Power App

Once your Power App is ready to use, the last thing you need to do is tell other people about it. To give someone a Power App:

- In Power Apps Studio, open the Power App you want to share.
- If you did what was said before, you will already be looking at the app that was made for the SharePoint list. After clicking on the File tab, click on the Share button.
- Add the people you want to be able to use the app by name or email address, and then click Share. The app's access instructions will be sent in an email.

Using Power Apps on your Mobile Device

There aren't many problems with using apps you made in Power Apps Studio. Both the Apple App Store and the Google Play Store will have the Power Apps app, which you will find there. When you're ready to use the Power Apps app, open it and log in with your Microsoft 365 account. All the Power Apps you've made and any that have been shared with you will be shown to you.

Embedding a Power App within a SharePoint Page

The majority of users will access Power Apps via mobile devices. But Microsoft added a feature that lets you put a Power App right into a SharePoint page as well.

Here's how to add a Power App to a SharePoint page:

1. Go to the SharePoint page where you want to add the Power App.
2. In the **Advanced** area, click the **plus sign (+)** to add a Web Part to the page. Then, choose the **Microsoft Power Apps Web Part**.
3. Look at the page about your Power App in Power Apps to find the Web link for it.
    - You will find it by going to Power Apps' Apps menu bar, clicking the radio button next to the app you want to embed, and then clicking Details at the top of the page.
4. Copy the Power App's URL or App ID and put it into the Web Part's configuration zone.
    - The Power App will be added to the Web Part.
5. Click "**Republish**" to make the page public, and then look at how the Power App is built right into the SharePoint page.

The Power App was designed for a mobile device. We would probably want to make it wider if we were making it for a computer browser.

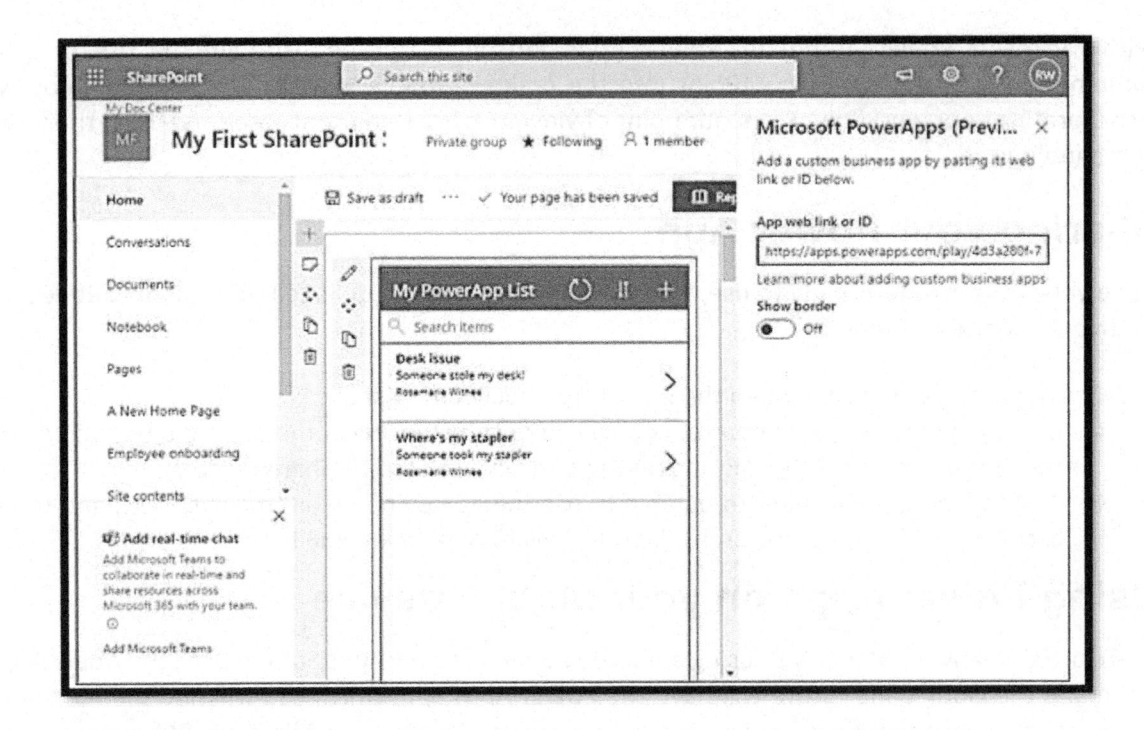

Viewing SharePoint Sites in a Web Browser on a Mobile Device

The best way to work with SharePoint on a mobile device is to use Power Apps. People can still work with SharePoint using the web browser on their mobile devices if they don't want to install the Power Apps app. Depending on the size of the web browser being used, a site will display differently thanks to a SharePoint tool called Mobile Browser View.

When the feature is turned on, mobile devices can see the site in three different ways:

- In classic view, the site is shown with HTML links to the different parts of the menu.
- The modern view shows the site's menu using tiles that you can click on to move around.
- The Full-Screen UI view of SharePoint on a mobile device is the same as the view on a desktop computer.

Creating views for small screens

You can choose if a view of your app data should be available on a mobile device when you make it. You can choose whether the view should be the mobile device's usual view. The app's views can be seen at the bottom of the app settings page, like **List Settings or Library Settings**. There is an area that shows if the view is mobile-friendly and if it is the default view. These sections can be seen on the List Settings page for an app in the picture below.

147

Targeting devices using channels

When someone views your complicated SharePoint site on a mobile device, you may want to change how it looks. In SharePoint, you can use the Device Channels feature to do this. With Device Channels, you can tell certain devices to use certain style sheets and master pages. When someone browses the site on a certain device, like an iPad or Android computer, it looks different on that device. Custom master pages and style sheets are very technical tasks that should only be done by web writers with a lot of experience.

Note: The SharePoint Server Publishing Infrastructure tool is only available for sites that have Device Channels enabled. To make and set up channels, go to the Site Settings page and click on the Look and Feel part. Then, click on the **Device Channels link**. You give a new channel a name, a nickname that can be used in website design code, a description, and rules for inclusion when you make it. Based on the available platforms, a web artist can then change how the SharePoint main page looks. The development of master pages and the use of Device Channels in code are outside the purview of this book, but you should be aware that you have the option when customizing SharePoint. SharePoint now shows up differently on different types of devices because of this.

CHAPTER 17
REALIZING YOU ARE A SHAREPOINT ADMINISTRATOR

Changing Your Site's Basic Information

The site's title, description, and image may be the first things you want to change on a SharePoint site. These small changes will make your site look more professional and unique to your group or team. After that, you can use SharePoint's efficiency tools. In the top left part of SharePoint Team sites is a site icon.

In a Team site, the usual picture is a square with the title of the site written in a few letters. There is a setting in SharePoint that lets you change this picture. You used to have to worry about how big your logo was. SharePoint makes the process a lot easier by having you pick a logo picture from your computer or a Library app on your SharePoint site. Then, SharePoint changes the image's size automatically to make it fit the logo's needs.

To change the general facts about a site:

1. Go to your site's home page, click the gear button that looks like a gear, and then choose **Site Information**.
    - ❖ On the right side of the page, the Site Information box shows up.
2. Click the "**Change**" button to pick a new design.
3. Look for the picture you want to use as your badge on your computer.
    - ❖ When you browse and select an image, SharePoint automatically uploads it to your SharePoint site for you.
4. Change the Site Name to what you want, and in the Site Description text box, write a short description of the site. This is also where you can change the site's privacy settings.
5. To save your changes, click "**Save**." At the top, you can see your new title and image.

Finding Site Settings

It only takes a few clicks of the mouse to get to the Site Settings page. Click on the gear icon that looks like a gear and select Site Contents. Next, click on the button that says Site Settings. As shown in the picture below, when the Site Settings page starts, it shows a list of links that are all grouped into different types. The Site Settings page can be hard to understand and use. But don't worry. Over time, as you manage a SharePoint site, you will learn all about the different settings pages and be an expert in no time.

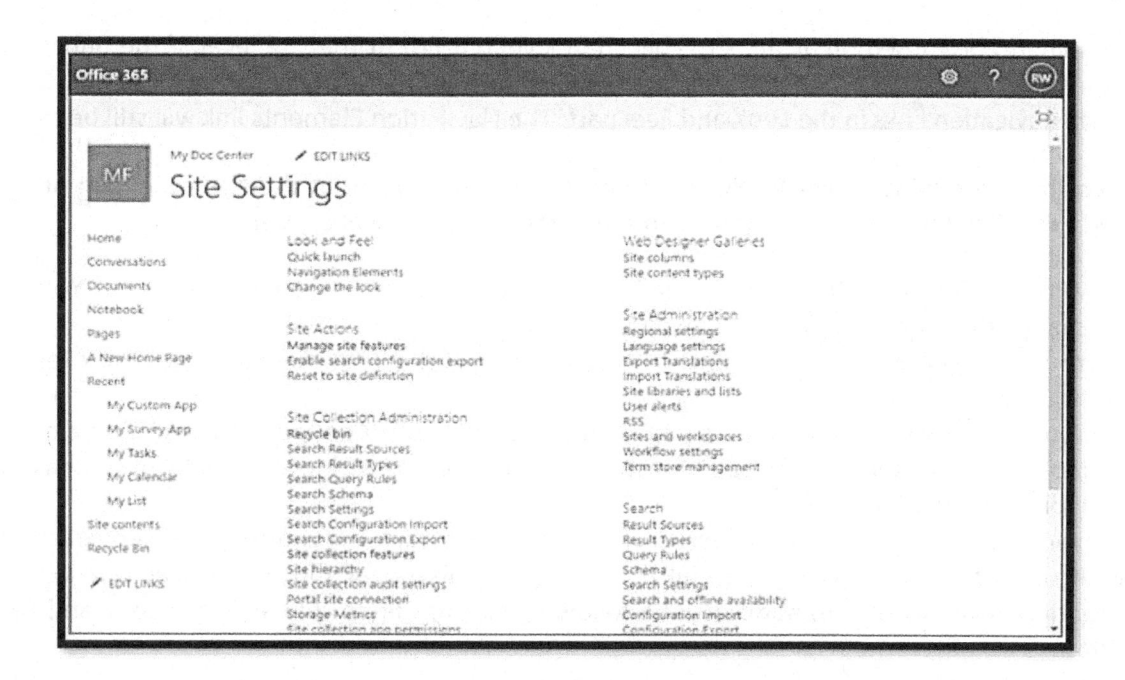

Depending on your permissions and the type of site you are managing, different settings links will show up and go away. For instance, if you are in charge of a site collection, you will see the **Site Collection Administration** part. You won't be able to see the links or even the whole **Site Collection Administration** area if you aren't. If you read about a settings page and can't find it, it's likely that you don't have the right permissions or are on a site that doesn't have that setting. For instance, this can happen whether the posting function is turned on or off. Most of the time, SharePoint moves names and links around based on how the site is set up.

Digging into Site Settings

If your site is built on the Team Site template, the Site Settings page has seven groups of settings: Look and Feel, Site Actions, Site Collection Administration, Microsoft Search, Web Designer Galleries, Site Administration, and Search.

Look and Feel

Site Settings has a section called "*Look and Feel*." This section has links to change the look and feel of the site, the left menu pane (called "Quick Launch"), and other navigation elements. There are a lot of simple things you can change on your site to make it your own. The Look and Feel part of the Site Settings page shows how frustrating SharePoint can be. The links in this part rely on whether the Publishing function for SharePoint Server is turned on or off. You might get frustrated if you don't know this because you might read about a settings link but not be able to find it on your own SharePoint site. There are even more problems: the links are different if SharePoint Server Publishing is turned on at the site collection or site level. It is possible for SharePoint Server

Publishing to be turned on at the site collection level but not at the site level. If the publishing feature was turned off at the site collection level, you will only see the Top Link bar and Quick Launch navigation links in the Look and Feel part. The Navigation Elements link will still be there.

When the SharePoint Server Publishing feature is not turned on at the site collection or site level, the following setting links can be found in the Look and Feel section:

- With **Quick Launch**, you can change how the menu works on the page's left side. You can change the order, add headers, and links.
- You can use **Navigation Elements** to turn on and off the Tree View and the Quick Launch window.
- You can change the site's colors and layout by clicking on "**Change the Look.**" Some of the looks are crazy and fun, like Sea Monster and Immerse. The Composed Looks gallery has the looks you can pick from.

When you activate the SharePoint Server Publishing Infrastructure feature at the site collection and site level, the Tree View and Top Link bar setting links disappear and are replaced with a single Navigation Elements link. **In addition, the following settings links appear in the Look and Feel section:**

- You can make your own SharePoint site designs with **Design Manager**, a web-based tool. The tool has a wizard that helps you upload design files, change page layouts, edit your master page, publish your design, and package it.
- **Device Channels** lets you change how your site looks and works depending on the device being used to view it. The site can be shown in a certain way on a channel that has been optimized for the device. There is a channel that can be set up for smartphones like the iPhone and Android. You could set up a new route for the iPad or Surface computers. And finally, you can set up a route for tablets and desktop browsers.
- You can set the usual behavior for how images and movies appear on the site using **Image Renditions**. For images on a page, you can change how they are shown by setting their width and height.
- The "**Import Design Package**" button lets you bring in a design package made by a third party or an in-house artist.
- **Navigation** lets you change how the navigation works and control the links that go to it. You can change both the world navigation (at the top of the page) and the current navigation (on the left). You can change the order of the main links and show or hide the ribbon on the Navigation settings page.
- Your choice of which master page the site and system use is made on the **Master Page.** Pages that are used by the system, like when you view an app, are on the system master page.
- With **Page Layouts and Site designs**, you can decide which page layouts and site designs to show site visitors. A gallery holds all the page layouts. People who use your site can only use certain page layouts and site themes, which you can control on this settings page.
- **Welcome Page** is the landing page for a publishing site. You can use this settings page to determine which page should be used for the landing page.

- The **Top Link bar** lets you change how the page's navigation works.
- In **Tree View**, you can turn on or off Quick Launch (left navigation) or a special type of navigation on the left that shows a tree of the site's material.

When the SharePoint Server Publishing option is turned on, the Look and Feel area looks like this:

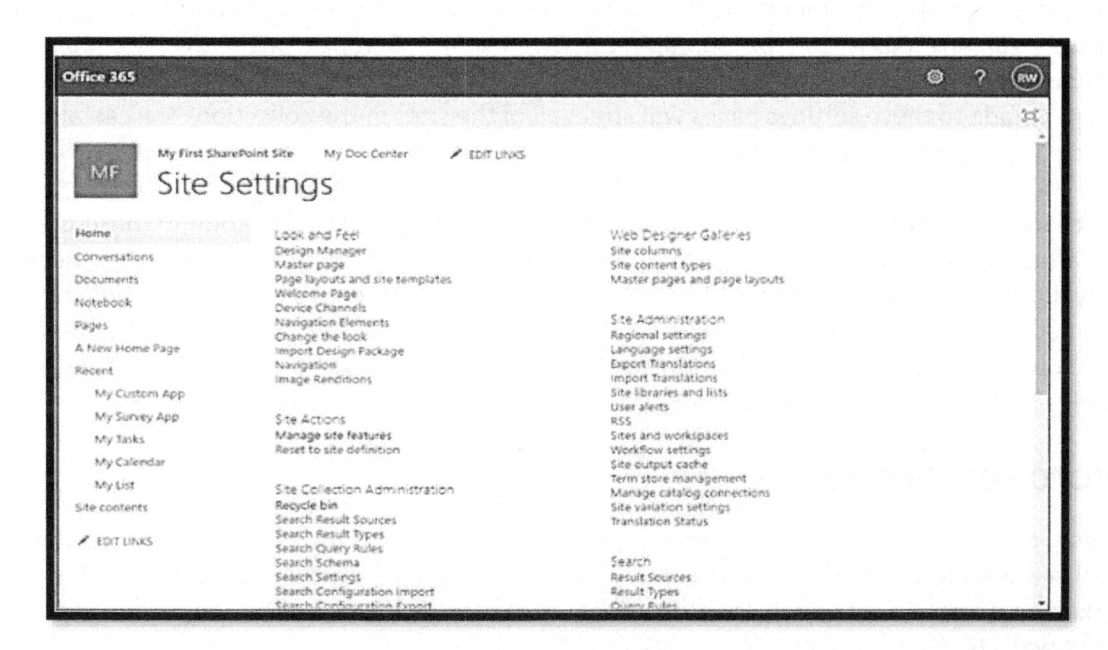

We had to turn on the SharePoint Server Enterprise Site Collection features before we could turn on the SharePoint Server Publishing feature in Site Collection Features. This also added some links to the Site Settings page. This is a great example of how quickly SharePoint can become hard to use once you change how it normally works. If you try to turn on a feature that depends on another, you might get a strange error message, like we did. We only knew to turn on the Enterprise tools first because we had done it before and it worked. That's why we say you never really understand SharePoint. Every day we find out something new about it.

Site Actions

You can change how SharePoint works on a site in the Site Actions part of the Site Settings page. Using the Manage Site Features link, you can turn on or off certain features. This is important because some features will only show up when other features are turned on. For instance, the **Save Site as Template link** and the **Enable Search Configuration Export** option only show up when the SharePoint Server Publishing Feature is turned on. When it is turned off, they go away. Your site can also be returned to its original template meaning, or you can delete it.

Site Collection Administration

A site collection is a group of sites that can be used together. SharePoint lets businesses give out different levels of management. Like, you could be in charge of a group of sites, and each site could have its boss. It is important to delegate tasks so that the work needed to keep a lot of websites running easily can be spread out. On the Site Settings page, the Site Collection Administration area is where you can manage the whole site collection. Because of this, any changes made to these settings pages will affect all of the sites in the collection. You can also turn on or off a feature here to make it work on all the sites in the collection or not work at all. If you are a site collection administrator, you can become a SharePoint farm administrator. If someone is in charge of a SharePoint farm, they use a tool called Central Administration to make changes that affect all site groups in that farm. In the Site Collection Administration section, there are many links to pages with settings. Most of the links work like the ones in the Site Administration part, but they affect all the sites in the collection, not just the one you're on. Remember that links will show up or go away depending on whether a feature is enabled or not. For instance, this settings page changes when the SharePoint Server Publishing Feature is turned on.

Microsoft Search

There is a way to change search settings in the Microsoft Search area. When you click on the link, you'll see a screen called Microsoft Search. This is a new function that still looks like it's being worked on. Things about search, like the number of questions, views, and top keywords are shown on the website.

Web Designer Galleries

The capacity to reuse content is a recurring subject across SharePoint. When you put in the effort to create anything, you want to be able to make use of it in a significant number of different situations. In SharePoint, reusability may be achieved via the use of data containers, templates, layouts, and solutions, among other similar components. To manage all of these reusable components, the Web Designer Galleries area is where you should go. Gallery storage is where the components are kept, and these galleries are intended to retain the components that you use while constructing your websites. Taking all of this into consideration, the term Web Designer Galleries is just ideal. (This is a welcome change from other technologies and acronyms with names that are monstrous, such as XSLT, HTML, and CSS.) The following links may be found in the Web Designer Galleries part of the Site Settings page (it is important to **remember that the things you see may vary depending on whatever features you have selected to be active):**

- ❖ The gallery known as **Site Columns** is comprised of columns that may be used in various parts of the website. An example of this would be the creation of a column on the website titled "Product Name," which could be added to any application on the website. Existing site columns are included in the default installation of SharePoint.
- ❖ **Site Content Types** is a gallery that gives you the ability to employ site content types, which are a collection of columns, across the site. These site content types are stored in

the gallery. Take for instance the scenario in which you want to save all of the information on a product. A product can have a wide variety of data fields, which are referred to as site columns. These data fields may include Product Name, Product Description, Product Bar Code, Product ID, and most likely a great deal more. A content type might be created by first creating a site column for each data field, and then combining all of the data fields into a single content type. You can now just add the content type whenever you wish to deal with a product, and all of the columns will be added along with it. This is a significant improvement over the previous method of adding each data field to each app across the site. SharePoint is pre-installed with a variety of content categories at the time of installation. To facilitate quick referencing, the different sorts of information have been categorized.

- All **Web Parts,** both those that come pre-installed and those that are purchased from third-party vendors are kept in the Web Parts gallery. There are functional components that may be added to pages, and these are called Web Parts.
- The gallery known as **List Templates** is where an application that has been saved as a template is kept. It's a bit of a name mistake that List Templates was given. Considering that all lists and libraries in SharePoint are referred to as apps, this gallery would be more appropriately referred to as App Templates. On the listing settings page, there is a link for every app that is based on a list. You may find the link to Save List as Template in the area that is devoted to Permissions and Management. The List Templates gallery is where you will find the list app that you have saved as a template once you have done so. You may then take the template and post it to this gallery on a separate SharePoint site from where you first uploaded it. After it has been submitted, a new app type will appear on the page that displays your applications, and you will then be able to develop apps based on the template that was uploaded. In situations when you have spent a significant amount of time developing a list app to your specifications and then need to move it to a different place, this comes in useful.
- A gallery that includes all of the master pages and page layouts is referred to as the **Master Pages gallery**. A master page is a page that is similar to a template and its purpose is to ensure that all of the pages on the website have the same look and feel. Just to give you an example, have you noticed that the navigation is located on the left side of every out-of-the-box SharePoint site, the header is located at the top, and the pages are located in the middle? The master page that comes pre-installed with SharePoint is responsible for all of this. () It is preferable to delegate the creation of bespoke master pages for your business to developers. Master pages require a significant amount of effort and have the potential to rapidly become a project that is a nightmare. Additionally, SharePoint necessitates that the master page be comprised of certain elements and operate in a particular manner. A page layout is a notion that is comparable to that of a master page; however, it is intended to serve as a template for a single page only.
- The gallery that contains SharePoint themes is referred to as "**Themes**." One definition of a theme is a collection of typefaces and colors. When you apply a theme to your SharePoint site, the site will transform wonderfully. There are a variety of themes that

come pre-installed with SharePoint, and you also have the option of having a web developer create your unique themes.
- ❖ The **Solutions gallery** is a central location for storing individualized SharePoint solutions. All of the functionality that was created specifically for SharePoint is bundled together to form a SharePoint solution. A Web Solution bundle (WSP) is the name given to the full bundle on its own. Either your in-house developers or a third party might be responsible for the development of a SharePoint solution for your organization. For instance, the business Portal Integrators has produced a variety of SharePoint solutions for customers located in a variety of destinations throughout the globe. When they provide the finished product to a customer, they also deliver the WSP to that customer. The Human Resources department is the focus of one of these potential solutions. If you buy it, you will get a Workspace Provider (WSP) that is equipped with a wide variety of SharePoint features that are tailored to the Human Resources department. When you upload the WSP to this gallery, your Human Resources department will immediately become a fan of SharePoint.
- ❖ **Composed Looks gallery** is concerned with the overall appearance and atmosphere of your website. By extending the concept of themes and including a background picture and a master page, the composed appearance is a relatively new feature that has been introduced in SharePoint. Microsoft SharePoint comes with a variety of different composed styles. To provide you with a sneak peek, SharePoint ships with three different constructed styles that are termed Sea Monster, Breeze, and Immerse. Should you so want, you will be able to look forward to enhancing the appearance of your SharePoint site.

Site Administration

Within the Site Settings page, the Site Administration area is where you will be able to handle the choices that are unique to this particular site. Other sites that are included inside the same site collection container will not be impacted by the modifications that you make in this section. In contrast to the **Web Designer Galleries** area of the Site Settings page, which contains components that are used across the site collection, this section does not include any of such components. In other words, if you submit a solution, it will be accessible to other sites that are part of the site collection. When it comes to determining whose website the Site Administration page impacts, it is simple to get confused. In particular, this is the case if you are in charge of managing many sites or if you are an administrator of a site collection. When dealing with the Site Administration settings, you must ensure that you are on the appropriate site. We are unable to discuss all of the settings that are included under the Site Administration area since there are so many of them included. Explore these settings, we say. **Regional Settings, User Alerts, Workflow Settings, Term Store Management, Popularity Trends, and** even **Translation Status** are some of the settings that can be found in the Site Administration area. However, the Translation Status setting is only accessible when the SharePoint Server Publishing Feature is activated.

Search

Within the **Site Settings** page, the **Search** area is where you will be able to modify all of the search capabilities used by your website. Use of search may be an extremely effective method for increasing productivity. Exploring the potential of SharePoint search is something that should be done since it is worth the time.

Conclusion

SharePoint is an effective platform that provides a broad variety of tools and capabilities to assist teams in collaborating, managing material, and streamlining work processes. Creating a digital workplace that is more effective and well-organized for your team may be accomplished by gaining an awareness of the fundamentals of SharePoint sites, which include their structure, important features such as document libraries and lists, customization possibilities, and the process of adding applications. When you use SharePoint sites, you may think of it as constructing a digital office space in which everyone can collaborate on projects, exchange data, keep track of tasks, and communicate efficiently. It's almost like having a virtual hub where information flows easily and everyone is on the same page at all times. Improved productivity, enhanced collaboration, and simplified processes are all possible outcomes that may be achieved within your business via the use of SharePoint's features. The tools that are necessary for success in the digital work environment of today are made available to you by SharePoint, regardless of whether you are a small team or a huge business. To get the most out of this customizable platform, it is important to remember to explore and experiment with the many capabilities, to personalize your sites so that they meet the requirements of your team, and to continue learning about the latest upgrades and functions that SharePoint has to offer. Through the use of SharePoint, you are not only able to construct websites, but you are also able to establish a digital workplace that enables your team to operate more efficiently and successfully together.

INDEX

"

"sales" NEAR "China", 116
"sales" NEAR(5) "China", 116
"sales" ONEAR(5) "China", 116

2

2. Click the "Change" button to pick a new design., 149

3

3. Look for the picture you want to use as your badge on your computer., 149

A

A business plan, 97
A comparable company analysis, 97
A computer bug can also erase or damage data., 104
A content analysis, 110
A document that lays out compliance standards, 110
A file can be an audio file, 40
A higher probability of individuals producing their collections, 43
A more efficient and simplified procedure of creating lists, 33
A number of complex alterations are required to prepare our Document Library, 50
A pilot wave, 124
A SharePoint List can be created in this way using a template, 34
A SharePoint list is a group of files that your whole organization can access and share, 30
A SharePoint site, 4, 25
A state-of-the-art SharePoint Team site, 20
A Strengths, Weaknesses, Opportunities, and Threats (SWOT) analysis, 97
A Team Effort, 54
A Web Part Page called the Welcome Page, 97
ability to create a PowerApp from a list, 31
ability to share, 90
about Amazon, 136
Access and modification privileges, 60
Access Microsoft Power Automate, 134
Access Requests, 58
Access the "Permission levels" link found in the menu on the Permissions page., 61
access the app's settings, choose "Classic Experience.", 27
access the full-size view on your PC or phone, 15
Access Your Board, 28
accessible on the Dashboard list page, 95
Accessing App Settings, 72
Accessing Files, 20
Accessing SharePoint, 9, 13, 20, 59, 82
accommodate changes within the organization, 44
accommodate various organizational demands for communication, 7
Acquiring the skills to add, 36
Action Items, 135
Activate policy tips and alerts to ensure compliance., 67
Active Directory (AD) Groups, 56
Add a permission policy description, 107
Add an App, 27, 34, 70
Add custom content types, 50
Add from existing site content types, 50
Add Result Block, 120
add Teams to an existing SharePoint site, 25
Add the name of the Document Set, 100
add the new column to the list., 35
adding a description, or choosing a column format., 35
Adding a new field to a list, 34
Adding Apps to Your Site, 70
Adding Attachments to a SharePoint List, 36
Adding Columns to a List, 34
Adding SharePoint Pages, 21
Adding SharePoint Pages and Lists to Teams, 21
additional news, 9
additional options, 14, 56, 59
Add-PSSnapin Microsoft.SharePoint.Powershell, 128
Adjacent to the site creation button, 11
Administrative metadata, 40

Administrator preparations before applying IRM, 105
Administrators can adjust these settings in the Microsoft 365 admin center., 11
ADVANCED DOCUMENT MANAGEMENT, 97
Advanced Options, 70
Advanced settings, 76
Advanced Settings, 50, 77, 78, 122
aforementioned groups, 46
After making your selection, click "**Delete**.", 36
agreed conditions, 44
AI Builder, 135, 136, 142
alert verifying the successful upload of the file., 12
Allow Rules to Send Documents to a Different Site, 102
AllowFilesWithKeepLabelToBeD, 108
A*llowFilesWithKeepLabelToBeDeletedOD*B, 108
allowing users to view previous versions, 2
alphabetical order, 38
Alternatively, drag and drop files into the Teams channel for quick and efficient uploading., 20
An introduction to the services company, 97
An on-premises Active Directory connected to Microsoft 365 is already in place, 56
an option/drop-down menu, 46
analyst can design a scorecard and report items, 95
Analytics purposes, 19
Analyze organizational content, 111
Annual Report, 115
Annual Reports +Marketing, 115
Anonymous Access in SharePoint Online, 65
Another factor that could discourage sharing, 58
any other sort of file, 40
appearance of teams' websites, 126
applicant details, 33
Application Site Creation, 2
Application Site Creation with Reduced Permissions, 2
apply bulk edits, 36
Apply IRM to a list or library, 106
apply your selections, 79
Applying IRM, 105
approval workflow, 135
Approvals, 135
Approvals and business process, 135
Approvals link, 135
Approvers, 63
Artificial intelligence, 44
aspects of the SharePoint start page, 9

Asset Manager Template, 32
assistance from Syntex, 44
assistance of the Data, 95
assistance of the Data Connection library, 95
associated SharePoint site, 25
Audience targeting settings, 80
available for sites, 148
AvePoint, 127
Avoid inventing words only for amusement., 45
Avoid using the default Document Library, 50
Azure account, 59

B

Back up your data, 130
Backing up every month, 129
Backing up your SharePoint config files, 130
backup and emergency recovery option, 131
Backup Folder, 132
Backup SharePoint Configuration, 130
Backup via PowerShell, 128
Backups every three months, six months, or a year, 129
Backups Every Week, 129
Backup-SPConfigurationDatabase, 128
basic content type, 52
beneficial aspect of the tenant, 7
Best Practice, 56
Best practice metadata management, 42
Best Practices for SharePoint Backup, 129
BI Center site, 90
Blank Site, 8
Blog Site, 8
bn2.vortex.data.microsoft.com.akadns.net, 19
branding, 2, 5
Breaking permission inheritance, 56
broad variety of tools and capabilities, 157
Browse tab, 69
Browse user information, 62
Build and Share Reports, 94
build subsites, 4
building a new site, 6
building a site, 5, 50
building a site and adding a Document Library, 50
BUILDING BUSINESS APPS, 141
BUILDING BUSINESS APPS WITH POWER APPS, 141
Building compound search queries, 116

Building compound search queries using Boolean operators, 116
Building your first flow, 137
built on Power Apps, 142
built using Dashboard Designer, 94
business can use IRM safety, 103
Business Intelligence Center, 92, 96
business intelligence solutions, 96
BUSINESS INTELLIGENCE WITH SHAREPOINT, 90
business intranets., 7
business platforms, 16
Business Process Flows, 135, 136
Business Process Flows link, 135
business solution development, 3
business wiki, 126

C

Cadillac of business intelligence at Microsoft, 91
candidate details., 33
Carpool for specific topics like carpooling, 20
central library, 95
Centralized Branding Management, 2
Centralized business intelligence, 90
certain files or parts of files, 129
certain site collections., 7
change column types, 33
Change how members can share, 58
change how your library is set up, 72
change the general facts about a site, 149
Change the view from PC to mobile, 16
Changing site views, 13
Changing the title, 74
Changing Your Site's Basic Information, 149
charge of handling documents, 48
Chatbots, 142
Check the settings, 128
Check-In/Check-Out, 2
check-in/check-out prevents simultaneous editing, 11
Checking the Privacy Statements, 19
Choose "**Backup and Restore**", 131
Choose "**Farm Backup**", 127
Choose "**Farm Backup**" and then click "**Start Backup.**", 127
choose "List settings" from the dropdown menu, 34
Choose **Advanced Settings.**, 50
choose **Browse** to locate the file, 99
Choose how you want to share the site., 87

Choose the "**Format this column**" option., 39
Choose the **app launcher icon**, 10
Choose the different kinds of material, 51
Choose the type of column you want to add, 34
Choose where to save the copy., 128
Classic Experience, 27, 28, 69
ClearPeople's Atlas, 44
click "**Browse**" to find and select the file, 12
Click "**Restore from Backup**", 131
Click on **Request.**, 71
Click on **SharePoint Store** in the menu bar, 71
Click on the "Settings" button, 34
click on the **Device Channels link**, 148
click the "**No**" radio button, 122
Click the Add Promoted Result link., 120
click the Library Settings button., 72
Click the New Query Rule button, 120
Click the **Settings button**, 70
clicking **List Settings**, 122
clicking on the "**Attachments**" button., 37
clicking the "Activate" button, 101
Client, 46, 62, 77, 79
client-side software, 91
Cloud flows are processes that start immediately, 136
CloudAlly, 127
Co-Authoring, 2
Co-authoring on SharePoint Pages and News, 1
collaborate on projects, 24, 157
collaborate with other individuals, 25
collaborating, 2, 3, 157
Collaboration, 20, 24, 31, 126
Collaboration and Co-authoring, 20
COLLABORATION IN SHAREPOINT, 20
Collaborative solutions like Groups, 24
collection and its subsites, 5
collection in SharePoint instead, 6
collection of indications, 94
column values, 104
Columns, 34, 35, 49, 52, 73, 100
commands available, 50
commercial and nonprofit organizations, 2
Common messages received by users, 19
Communication Site, 7
communication sites, 7, 126
Communication Sites, 7, 126
Communication websites, 7
Communications, 73
Community Site, 8

160

Community sites, 8
component of Office Online Server, 90
components that are used across the site collection, 155
Composed Looks gallery, 151, 155
Conclusion, 157
Concurrent editing, 21
Conditional Formatting, 39
Conditional Formatting in List Views, 39
Confirm Activation, 101
Connectors, 135, 136, 142
Consider a chatbot, 142
constructing a digital office space, 157
constructing personalized forms, 11
contemporary experience was introduced in 2016, 5
Content Approval, 75
content editing phase, 44
Content list, 95
Content managers, 111
Content Organizer, 98, 100, 101, 102, 103
Content Scheduler Template, 32
content type., 52, 97, 98, 154
Content Types, 48, 50, 51, 52, 73, 76, 78, 99, 153
Content-Type settings, 48
continue learning about the latest upgrades and functions that SharePoint has to offer, 157
continuous updates, 1
controlled metadata, 44
Copying content information, 104
core components, 94
corporate network, 18
correct Office Graph settings., 11
corresponding custom information, 48
create a folder, 95
create a Group, 25
Create a Microsoft Team from a SharePoint team site, 25
Create a new Business Intelligence Site, 96
create a new chatbot, 142
create a new item in the SharePoint list, 145
create a new team from an existing Microsoft 365 group, 25
Create a permission policy title, 107
create a site, 4, 5, 6
Create a subsite from your web browser, 87
Create an App from the fly-out menu for Power Apps, 143
create and manage SharePoint teams, 25

Create Dashboards, 94
create global content kinds later., 47
Create Major and Minor (Draft) Versions, 75
Create major versions, 50
create new sites, 131
create user-friendly websites, 1
Create your metadata columns, 46
Create your own SharePoint group, 56
creates a new team and links, 25
Creating a digital workplace that is more effective and well-organized for your team, 157
Creating a List, 31
Creating a SharePoint List from a Template, 32
Creating a SharePoint List or an Excel table using data, 33
Creating a SharePoint List or an Excel table using data from an Excel file is a practical option, 33
Creating a SharePoint Site, 87
Creating and Customizing Lists, 31
Creating and Managing SharePoint Teams, 25
Creating and Using Content Types, 45
creating any site collections, 6
Creating Custom Views, 38
Creating DLP Policies, 67
creating or configuring new Document Set, 98
creating **private sites**., 1
Creating views for small screens, 147
CREATING WORKFLOWS WITH MICROSOFT POWER AUTOMATE, 134
CSS, 13, 153
current standard for making a site, 4
Custom group, 48
Custom Send to Destination, 77
Custom views and conditional formatting, 39
customizable nature, 11
customizable platform, 157
customization possibilities, 157
Customize a Welcome Page, 97
Customize SharePoint List Views, 37
customize the presentation of a list, 38
customized view, 38
Customizing SharePoint lists to meet your company's unique, 34
CUSTOMIZING SHAREPOINT WITH APPS, 69

D

Daily Back-Ups, 129

161

Dashboard Designer, 94, 95
Dashboard Library, 94
dashboard material, 94
dashboards, 90, 92, 94
data about data", 40
Data Connection library., 95
Data Connections library, 95
data integrity, 11
Data Loss Prevention (DLP) in SharePoint, 66
Data Sources, 95
data-centric platform, 39
Date Paid, 46
Date Received, 46
declare connections to data sources, 95
Default Experience options, 69
default installation of SharePoint., 153
Define metadata for each of the categories above, 46
Deleting Columns in a SharePoint List, 35
Deletion of items, 108
departmental portals, 7
describe your files, 31
Description, 46, 73, 88, 99, 120, 149, 154
Design, 61, 99, 111, 151
Designed for monitoring and tracking the progress of work tasks, 33
Desktop flows, 136
Determine Backup Frequency, 129
Determine the types of documents you want to store in your SharePoint DMS, 45
develop applications, 141, 144
Develop retention schedules, 111
development environment for Power Apps., 143
development tool, 141
Device Channels, 148, 151
Dialogs, 77, 79
Different Methods to Protect Your SharePoint Data, 127
different types of sites, 126
Differential Backup, 127
digital work environment of today are made available, 157
DISASTER RECOVERY, 127
DISASTER RECOVERY AND BACKUP STRATEGIES, 127
Discover content with the SharePoint start page, 9
Discovering SharePoint, 20
discuss all of the settings, 155
diverse audiences, 1

Document Approval Workflows, 3
Document Center, 8, 88
document classification and organization, 11
Document Collaboration, 2
document libraries, 7, 8, 12, 31, 82, 84, 104, 105, 107, 157
Document Libraries, 2, 11, 82, 105
Document Management, 2, 13, 45, 50, 53
Document Management and Collaboration, 2
Document Metadata, 2
document processes, 11
Document Retention, 107
Document Search, 3
Document Set content, 97, 98, 99, 100
Document Set Content Types, 99
Document Set format, 97
Document Set is created, 98
Document Sets, 97, 98, 99, 100
document sharing, 2
Document Template, 76, 78
document work product, 97
Document workflows, 11
Documents and lists are stored in apps, 14
Documents can be opened, 3
Documents Library, 95
Documents that list the costs incurred for the products, 46
Dropbox, 134, 136
Drop-Off Library acts, 101
Drop-Off Library., 102
Duplicate Submissions, 102

E

each metadata property, 46
Editing Files, 20
Editing Items, 36
effective management of SharePoint, 39
efficiently exhibit content, 7
Employee, 46, 75, 119, 121
Enable Classic Experience, 27
Enable Search Configuration Export, 152
encourage participation and teamwork, 8
Engage in Discussions, 28
enhanced collaboration, 157
enhancing your collaborative efforts and productivity, 9
Ensure Permissions, 102

Ensure Prerequisites, 101
Ensuring the security of your company's sensitive information, 39
Enter a name and click Create, 143
Enter the URL for SharePoint Online into the address bar, 14
Enter the URL of your SharePoint site in the address bar and press Enter., 9
enter your login information to log in to SharePoint, 9
Enter your SharePoint site's URL in the address bar, 9
entering a URL every time, 16
Enterprise Metadata and Keywords, 73
Enterprise Wiki, 8
establish a digital workplace, 157
Establish a Document Library, 50
Establish Content Types, 47
establishment of control procedures and rules, 43
Estimates, 45
Evaluate and improve document management practices, 111
evaluate the data, 90
Event Itinerary Template, 32
Every business needs to back up SharePoint, 127
examine the functionality of SharePoint Online, 13
Excel Data, 91
Excel Reports, 95
Excel Services, 90, 92, 94
Exchange, 66
exchanging information, 8
existing chatbots, 142
Existing guests, 55
existing site collection, 5, 6
expedite procedures, 11
explore and experiment with the many capabilities, 157
Exploring the potential of SharePoint search, 156
Exploring the SharePoint Home Page, 10
Extra information about the content of a file is called metadata, 40
extremely effective method, 156

F

facilitate better teamwork and communication., 24
facilitate the digitization of business operations and communication, 1
Facilitating frictionless communication,, 4
fast links, 7

faster performance, 13
feature on a site, 101
Featured Links, 11
Figures out what kinds of data fit in the "records" group., 110
file storage system, 1
Files are sorted and described using metadata, 40
files saved in OneDrive can be readily shared and viewed from SharePoint., 4
filtering, 11, 38
Filtering, 34, 38
Filtering offers the capability to view items, 38
Find **"Discussion Board"** in the Classic Experience's app list and choose it, 28
Find the Survey app, 70
Finding terms in proximity, 116
FINDING WHAT YOU NEED WITH SEARCH, 114
Finding your way around, 84
flexibility of SharePoint, 124
folder crazy, 77
Folder Partitioning, 102
Folder Permissions, 60
Folders, 43, 77, 78, 100
folders for storing files, 2
Form settings, 81
Form Settings option, 81
Frequently Visited Sites, 11
friendly websites and extranets, 1
Full Backup, 127
Full Control, 39, 60, 61
Full Farm Backup, 127, 128, 131
fundamental structure, 94

G

gaining an awareness of the fundamentals of SharePoint sites, 157
Gateways, 142
Gather records from the record center site, 112
gear icon, 34, 40, 69, 85, 86, 87, 102, 119, 122, 149
General Settings, 73, 74, 122
Get a group of reps, 124
get extra information, 92
Get rid of at least one fake set., 130
Get the stuff you lost back from the full copy., 130
Getting familiar with Power Apps, 141
Getting familiar with Power Automate, 135
Getting Rid of Items, 36

GETTING STARTED WITH SHAREPOINT, 9
Give the column a name that accurately describes its purpose or content., 34
Give your Content-Type a name on the next screen, 48
glancing at the name of the view at the top of the page, 14
Go to the backup area and find the group of sites., 132
Go to the list where you want to add the column., 34
Go to the list's column settings., 39
Go to the Microsoft 365 Portal., 27
Go to the Site Collection's root, 47
Go to the **Start menu** and click on **Administrative Tools**, 130
good record-keeping, 111
Google Chrome, 9
Granting and Revoking SharePoint List Permissions, 40
Granular Backup, 127, 128, 132
Granular backup is needed for SharePoint to work, 128
Group allows you to consolidate individuals, 24
group your Content Types, 48
Grouping, 38, 89
Groups and SharePoint, 24
Group's operations, 25

H

Handle Duplicate Submissions, 101
Header, 84
Helps in tracking and managing issues, 32
Hierarchy Managers, 63
hiring statuses., 33
history of decisions, 135
home button, 4
Home navigational link, 142
How are SharePoint Lists and Libraries Different?, 31
How Do I Manage SharePoint Online Permissions?, 62
How IRM can help protect content, 103
How IRM cannot help protect content, 104
How to check user Permissions in SharePoint Online?, 64
How to configure the record center archiving mechanism in SharePoint Online?, 112
How to make applying metadata easier for everyone, 43

How to switch between mobile and full-screen view, 15
how to use various browsers to access SharePoint, 9
How you did this in the past, 123
HTML, 69, 147, 153
HTML standards, 69

I

Identify records management roles, 111
Important, 16
important business intelligence, 92
important features such as document libraries and lists, 157
Importing dashboards, 94
improve team collaboration, 24
Improved productivity, 157
improved teamwork, 2
Improvements to the Document Library Version History, 1
improving SharePoint's features,, 2
In what way do these services work together?, 24
include "metadata" before adding site content kinds., 50
include features like grouping, 11
Includes sections for job positions, 33
Includes sections for task details, 33
includes SharePoint Online, 16
Including and excluding terms, 115
including other components, 95
including SQL Server, 90
including the kind, 45
including the metadata, 5
incoming documents, 101
Inconsistent metadata and non-organizational language at a site level leads, 43
Incorporating SharePoint data and features, 3
Increased probability of data silos and file duplication, 43
Increased probability of needing assistance, 43
increasing productivity, 156
Incremental Backup, 127
in-depth study of the situation, 91
Individual Permissions, 62
individuals and companies, 1
information about information, 40
information about the library documents, 77
information flows easily, 157

Information handling, 43
information panels, 93
Information Rights Management, 103, 105, 107
Information Rights Management (IRM), 103, 105
Information Type provide information about a file, 40
initiate sorting, 38
input a name for the application, 143
Inserting Items, 35
Inserting, editing, and deleting items in a SharePoint list, 35
inside the Documents library, 95
installed applications, 12
Instead of requiring your staff to tag files, 45
instruments for performance monitoring, 93
Integrate your Information Architecture, 44
integration of Copilot AI, 2
Integration with External Systems, 3
Integration with Microsoft 365 Apps, 3
Integration with Microsoft Office, 3
intelligence (BI) reporting, 92
Internet Explorer, 9
interview schedules, 33
Intranet Management, 126
Introducing Microsoft Power Automate, 134
Introducing Power Apps, 141
Introducing SharePoint Apps, 69
introduction of SQL, 92
Introduction to Metadata in SharePoint, 40
INTRODUCTION TO SHAREPOINT, 1
Invite people menu, 57
Invoice, 46
Invoices, 45, 46
IRM cannot protect restricted content, 104
IRM helps protect material that isn't open to everyone, 103
IRM-enable SharePoint document, 104
Is this network traffic from the SharePoint mobile app?, 19
Issues Tracker Template, 32
It shows the Library Settings or List Settings page., 72
IT staff set up the right tools, 111
Item Permissions, 60

J

job applications, 33

K

keep in contact with your colleagues and the office, 13
Keep things simple at first, and then as you go, make adjustments., 45
keep track of paperwork, 16
keep track of tasks, 157
Keep Up Audit Records, 101
keeping track of chores, 11
Key Features and Capabilities, 1
Key Performance Indicators, 91, 94, 95
keystroke hackers, 104
KPIs, 91, 95

L

Latest Site News, 11
Launch a Microsoft SharePoint website, 14
Learning about the Core Features, 90
libraries in SharePoint Online, 13
Library app, 72, 74, 75, 76, 77, 78, 79, 84, 149
Library apps only, 75
Library Settings page, 50, 72
Library Settings., 106, 122, 147
Limit external sharing by domain, 55
link Filter Web Parts, 96
List Information, 73
list item, 37, 40, 60, 79, 145
List Permissions, 60
List Settings page, 72, 75, 77, 80
Lists and libraries in SharePoint, 30
locate the "**Upload**" option, 12
Log in as an administrator to the SharePoint Management Shell., 132
Log in using your work or school account, 14, 15
Log in using your work or school account credentials., 14
Login Screen and News Feed Interface, 17
Look and Feel, 148, 150, 151, 152

M

machine learning tools, 44
main online browsers, 9
maintaining clarity between the two entities, 50
maintaining inventory information, 11

Make a copy of the real setting and put it in the test case., 130
make a DLP policy in SharePoint, 67
Make a file plan, 111
make a file plan report, 73
Make a full copy of the test site., 130
Make 'New Folder', 50
making a personalized list template a priority, 33
Making copies with screen-capture programs from outside sources, 104
making new views according to your requirements, 38
Making Search Your Users' Best Friend, 118
making the desired changes, 36
Manage Duplicate Submissions, 102
Manage Folder Size, 101
manage tasks associated with SharePoint documents, 4
managed information, 44
Management and Permissions, 107
managers link a Microsoft 365 group, 63
managing documents, 2, 3, 8, 74, 131
Managing documents, 8
managing many sites, 155
managing material, 157
Managing Permissions in SharePoint Online, 62
Managing SharePoint List Permissions, 39
Managing SharePoint Online Security, 54
Marketing app, 114
Master Pages gallery, 154
Members, 39, 55, 56, 61, 63
messaging and collaboration app, 25
Metadata and Content Types, 40
Metadata such as **Location**, 40
metadata tagging, 11
MFA, 59
Microsoft 365 ecosystem, 24
Microsoft 365 ecosystem has three key components, 24
Microsoft 365 Group connection, 56
Microsoft cloud, 1
Microsoft Flow, 3, 134
Microsoft Lists's Forms Experience, 1
Microsoft made an app for SharePoint, 69
Microsoft Office Integration, 3
Microsoft Office Online, 4, 20
Microsoft OneDrive for Business, 3, 13
Microsoft Planner, 4

Microsoft Power Apps Web Part., 146
Microsoft Power BI, 91
Microsoft Power Platform, 3
Microsoft Purview Data Loss Prevention, 66
Microsoft Purview has rules to keep you from losing data, 66
Microsoft Search, 150, 153
Microsoft SharePoint Syntex and Viva Topics, 44
Microsoft Teams, 3, 20, 21, 25, 26, 42
Microsoft website, 141
Microsoft Word, 13, 84, 85, 99
Microsoft's continuous dedication, 2
Microsoft's SharePoint is a strong platform with excellent features, 2
Mobile Accessibility, 3
mobile app has **Enterprise Search**,, 18
mobile application, 13, 141
mobile browser, 13
Mobile Device, 147
mobile device running iOS or Android, 18
Mobile Devices, 13
Monitor Key Performance, 93
Monitor the upload progress, 12
monitoring and applying your established information architecture to each and every file., 44
more advanced SharePoint Designer, 34
More external sharing settings, 55
More time spent looking for anything, 43
More time to get new hires up to speed, 43
Mozilla Firefox, 9
MS Teams site, 42
Multi-Factor Authentication (MFA), 59
Multiple accounts, 16
Multiple files, 42
Multiple team members, 21
My Flows is the most important page in Power Automate, 136
My initial thought is multi-factor authentication, 59
mydock365.sharepoint.com, 15

N

navigate across groups, 42
Navigate through folders and subfolders within the SharePoint document, 21
Navigate to a group-linked team site that you own., 25

Navigate to the "**SharePoint**" section of your Microsoft 365 account., 27
Navigate to the file list and choose "**Attach File**.", 37
Navigate to the SharePoint center for management., 67
Navigate to the SharePoint website and choose **Settings**, 16
navigation, 5, 12, 14, 40, 74, 84, 87, 89, 136, 142, 150, 151, 152, 154
Navigation, 13, 21, 53, 73, 151
necessary information, 145
New and existing guests, 55
New and Existing Guests", 55
new Channels, 25
new Document Set, 97, 98, 99
new employee, 119, 120, 121
New Experience, 69
news from websites, 9
Next steps, 105
Norway, 114
Noteworthy, 70
number of complex alterations, 50
number of different groups have engaged in a substantial amount of conversation, 91

O

Office Data Connection, 95
Office programs, 84, 105
On the "**Permission Levels**" page, 61
On the Library Settings, 75, 77
One of the task management tools in Microsoft 365, 4
One or more end-user waves, 124
OneDrive for Business, 3, 15, 20, 21, 54
OneDrive have a scale that is equal to "**Anyone**", 54
Only people in your organization, 55
Only Users Who Can Edit Items, 75
Open Microsoft 365 and log in., 10
Open Mozilla Firefox., 9
Open **SharePoint Central Administration**, 131
Open the internet browser on your phone., 14
open the OneNote notebook for a site, 15
Open the web browser on your application, 15
Open your web browser, 82, 85, 87, 143
Opening Non-Office Files in Desktop Apps, 2
Opening Non-Office Files in Desktop Apps via OneDrive and SharePoint, 2
operate more efficiently and successfully, 157

Optimize SharePoint DMS for a 5,000 Item Limit, 53
option in SharePoint's settings, 27
option of publishing the Excel data, 90
organizational demands for communication and collaboration, 7
organizational structure, 42, 90
organization's vision, 91
organizing contacts, 11
original SharePoint Store experience, 71
Other examples include dashboards, 92
Other Security Features To Consider, 59
other types of analytical tools, 93
Outlook Integration, 3
overview of numerous news posts,, 11
Overview of records management planning, 111
Overview of SharePoint, 1, 112
overwrite file, 131
Owners, 39, 55, 56, 59, 96

P

Page content, 84
Page Layouts and Site designs, 151
Part of M365, 125
part of O365, 125
partnerships with GitHub, 2
People create a collection of documents that are linked together for a variety of different kinds of undertakings, 97
performance monitoring and analysis, 93
PerformancePoint, 90, 92, 93, 94, 95
PerformancePoint Services dashboards, 94
PerformancePoint Services., 94
Permission Level, 61, 62, 64
Permissions and Access Control, 3
Permissions and Management, 40, 73, 154
PERMISSIONS AND SECURITY, 54
PERMISSIONS AND SECURITY IN SHAREPOINT, 54
Personal web parts, 62
personalization, 11
personalize dashboards, 95
personalize your sites, 157
personally identifiable information (PII)., 66
Pick a repair point and the group of sites you want to bring back., 131
Pick out the tab's pages and list., 22
picture carousels, 7
Plan compliance for social content, 112

Plan compliance reporting and documentation, 112
Plan email integration, 111
Plan how content turns into records, 111
planning setting, 135
platform for managing content, 1
PO #, 46
PO Date, 46
PO number, 49
Point your browser to the SharePoint List that you want to add files to., 37
Policy Tips, 67, 68
Policy Tips and Alerts, 67
Popularity Trends, 155
possibility of constructing a new dashboard, 94
possible outcomes, 157
Post Creation Capability, 11
Post to the channel about this tab, 22
potential customer, 97
Power App, 142, 143, 144, 145, 146
Power Apps community, 142
PowerPivot, 91
precise information, 92
pre-configured structures, 7
pre-configured structures and features, 7
prefer Forms-based authentication, 19
preferable choice in certain cases., 6
Prepare the Document Library, 50
Prepare the Document Library for Custom Content Types and Custom Metadata, 50
presentations, 8, 97
Preservation Hold library, 107, 108, 109
Preserving Context, 103
Press the "**Create link**" button., 48
previously taught and learned patterns, 44
primary objective, 1, 45
procedure for adding files to a SharePoint list, 37
Process Advisor, 135, 136
process automation,, 3
process map, 40
produce Web Part pages, 94
products or services, 45
progress updates, 33
project announcements, 7
Project groups or teams may collaborate on team sites, 7
project or organization, 32
Project Site, 8
project sites, 8, 126

proof of financial transactions., 46
protect private data in Microsoft 365 services like OneDrive, 66
Provide Board Details, 28
provide organizations and businesses, 1
provide your login credentials, 9
Purchase Order, 46, 48
purchase order date, 46
purchase order number, 46
Purchase Orders, 45
put the Marketing app at the top of the search records, 114
Put the site files back where they belong in SharePoint., 132

Q

Quarter, 115
Quarterly, 115, 133
Quick Launch, 74, 93, 150, 151, 152
Quick Property Editing, 77, 79
Quotes, 45

R

Rating settings, 80
REALIZING YOU ARE A SHAREPOINT ADMINISTRATOR, 149
real-time chat, 26
rearranging columns, 38
Receipt, 46
Receipts, 45, 46
recommended websites, 9
Record Centers, 112
Records attesting to the receipt of money, 46
Records management, 108
RECORDS MANAGEMENT, 110
RECORDS MANAGEMENT AND ARCHIVING, 110
Records management settings, 108
records management solution, 111
records management system, 110, 111
Recruitment Tracker Template, 33
Regional Settings, 155
Reindex and index non-default views Document Library, 77
Remote interfaces, 62
remove any material from the list, 39

Removing Content from Search Results, 122
reorganize on-premises document storage solutions, 1
reports are the elements, 90
Request an app from the SharePoint Store, 71
requirements of your team, 157
Resource-Specific Consent, 2
restore older versions, 2
Restore via PowerShell, 132
RestoreMethod Overwrite -Item Restore Type', 132
Restore-SPFarm -Directory, 132
Restoring SharePoint from Backup, 131
restrict external sharing, 7
Retention labels, 108
Ribbon commands that are located on the Dashboard list page, 95
root site, 4, 5
Route Documents to Different Libraries, 100
Rule Managers, 103
Rule Name text box, 120
Run button on Dashboard Designer, 94

S

safeguarding data privacy, 39
Same meaning, different terms, 117
save and share data, 4
Save Changes, 36
Save the policy rule to enforce data protection measures., 67
save the settings, 122
Scorecards, 90, 92, 94
seamless integration, 20, 52
Search, 17, 18, 21, 31, 77, 79, 101, 114, 115, 116, 117, 118, 119, 120, 121, 122, 150, 152, 153, 156
Search area, 119, 153, 156
search bar, 21, 71
Search box, 114, 115, 116, 117, 118, 121, 122
Search results, 31
Searching for a string using quotation marks, 115
Searching for Content, 114
section titled "**Permissions**,", 88
Security and Compliance, 59, 66
security groups, 5, 6, 56, 61, 63, 64, 123
Security groups should be introduced to SharePoint groups, 56
see the **Approvals link**, 135
see the file on your website, 15
see the Microsoft 365 start page for SharePoint, 10
Select "**Add new item**" from the control, 36
Select "**Backup and Restore**.", 127
Select "**Mobile view**" from the option under **Tools**, 16
Select "Policies" from the left-hand menu., 67
Select "**Subsite**" from the drop-down menu, 87
Select "**Switch to PC view**.", 15
Select "Discussion Board", 28
Select a Draft Item Security choice button in the Draft Item Security area, 75
Select columns from, 49
Select **Document Set settings**, 99
Select Local SharePoint Results (System) from the Result Source drop-down list., 119
Select OneDrive from the tile list., 15
Select **Subsite** from the menu, 89
select the column title representing the desired sorting criterion and click on it., 38
Select the Content Organizer function, 101
Select the desired kind of list to be created., 32
Select the file on your device that you would want to attach, and then click "**OK**.", 37
Select the unwanted column in the list's settings, 35
selecting **Add members to group**, 57
Send approval email when a new item is added, 137
sensitive information, 39, 59, 66
Sensitive Information in SharePoint, 66
Set "**Allow management of content types**" to "**Yes**" to integrate designated types of site information, 50
set up a process or use Power Automate to do it., 112
set your own permission level if necessary, 56
setting column validation, 35
Setting Up Discussion Boards, 27
Setting Up Discussion Boards for Team Communication, 27
Settings page, 73, 75, 78, 80, 119, 122, 149
several methods that can be mixed and matched, 44
several parts to the Library, 73
several possibilities for maintaining accurate company records, 36
share documents or make apps, 74
Share files from OneDrive and collaborate, 21
Share your site from your web browser, 85
SharePoint Admin Center, 54, 89
SharePoint and Data Loss Prevention, 66
SharePoint and Microsoft Teams work hand in hand, 3

SharePoint and OneDrive for Business work hand in hand to provide customers with a private cloud storage area, 3
SharePoint automatically tracks versions of documents, 2
SharePoint contains a library called Dashboards, 94
SharePoint design, 9
SharePoint DLP Policies, 66
SharePoint DMS is fantastic, 53
SharePoint enables you to manage this from a single location, 41
SharePoint files, 3, 20, 25, 26, 31
SHAREPOINT FOR ENTERPRISE SOLUTIONS, 123
SharePoint form, 81
SharePoint Groups, 55
SharePoint has emerged as a top choice among current technologies, 1
SharePoint home page in Microsoft 365., 10
SharePoint in Microsoft 365, 9
SharePoint interfaces, 4
SharePoint Intranet Development, 125
SharePoint Intranet for Enterprise, 126
SharePoint Intranet On-Premises Solution, 125
SharePoint is a versatile platform, 1
SharePoint is an effective platform, 157
SharePoint is an effective platform that provides a broad variety of tools and capabilities to assist teams, 157
SharePoint is one of the key tools in the Microsoft 365 suite, 1
SharePoint isn't comparable to other systems like WordPress or Umbraco, 1
SharePoint libraries, 3, 31, 104
SharePoint list by using pre-existing samples, 33
SharePoint List Management, 34
SharePoint lists, 31, 34, 35, 36, 39, 95, 104
SharePoint Lists' customization options, 33
SharePoint Lists,, 31, 36
SHAREPOINT MOBILE ACCESS, 13
SharePoint mobile app, 18, 19
SharePoint Mobile App, 16, 17, 18, 87, 89
SharePoint Mobile App Interface, 16
SharePoint mobile app's data, 19
SharePoint Mobile Browser Interface, 13
SharePoint Online Admin Center, 59
SharePoint On-Premises, 114, 140
SharePoint Page, 146
SharePoint Permission Levels, 60
SharePoint Permissions, 60
SharePoint recovery process, 131
SharePoint search tool, 114
SharePoint Server 2016, 19
SharePoint Server Enterprise Site Collection features, 152
SharePoint Server Publishing option, 152
SharePoint site collection, 4
SharePoint Site Templates, 7
SharePoint start page, 9, 10
SharePoint status indicators, 94
SharePoint Term Store - term set Department example, 41
SharePoint will be covered extensively here., 30
SharePoint's document management and collaboration functions, 2
SharePoint's tool,, 127
Sharing settings, 54
Sharing your Team site, 85
Signing into Power Apps, 141
simplified processes, 157
Single line of text, 34
Site Actions, 99, 101, 150, 152
Site Actions menu, 99
Site Administration, 102, 113, 150, 153, 155
Site Administration area, 155
Site Administration settings, 155
Site Collection Administration, 98, 119, 150, 153
Site Collections vs. Sites, 4
Site Columns, 47, 48, 49, 153
Site Content Type information page, 99
Site Content types., 48
Site Contents, 11, 70, 71, 72, 87, 89, 119, 122, 149
Site Contents in SharePoint, 11
site or library, 15
Site Permissions, 60, 61, 85, 86
Site settings, 55, 64, 101, 102
Site Settings, 47, 48, 64, 98, 99, 101, 102, 119, 148, 149, 150, 152, 153, 155, 156
Site Sharing, 56
Sites *connected* to Microsoft 365 groups, 57
Sites *not connected* to Microsoft 365 groups, 56
sites vs. site collections, 5
Sites with Hub Sites, 89
Sites.create.All, 2
slideshow, 40
small team or a huge business, 157
Solutions, 135, 136, 142, 155

some of the settings that can be found in the Site Administration area, 155
Some third-party tools, 127
some types of software can send, 104
Sort, filter, and group files quickly., 42
Sorting and Filtering, 38
Sorting items, 38
Sorting items through sorting allows for organizing a list based on distinct criteria like date, 38
sorting to effectively organize and analyze data., 11
specialized and well-organized platform, 96
specific Drop-Off Library, 101
Specific email, 59
specifications, 92, 154
Specify allowed content types, 98
Specify default content, 98
Specify shared metadata, 98
specifying a default value,, 35
spreadsheet, 40, 92
spreadsheets, 93, 95, 97
SQL Server Reporting Services, 91
SQL Server Reporting Services (SSRS), 91
SSRS, 91
Stand-alone, 125
standard SharePoint Document Library, 42
Start a Discussion, 28
Start by going to **Backup and Restore**, 131
starting from scratch, 33
Status Lists for tracking, 95
Step-by-step instructions for adding items to a SharePoint list, 35
Store Backups Securely, 130
streamlining work processes, 157
structure of the website, 8
Structured data, 11
Submission Points, 103
subsite level, 60
Successful Intranet Portal with SharePoint, 124
Suggested Sites for You, 11
Suitable for tracking recruitment processes, 33
Supporting the SharePoint mobile apps online and on-premises, 18
system's strong functioning, 52

T

'Tabs for your team', 21

Taking pictures of what's on a screen, either on film or digitally, 104
Targeting devices using channels, 148
task assignments, 33
Taxonomy ontology tools, 44
Team Site, 7, 83, 150
team sites, 7, 16, 126
Team Sites, 7, 16, 62, 125
Teams and Groups, 25
Teams and SharePoint, 20, 25
Teams can greatly enhance your team's efficiency, 24
Teams creates a new folder, 25
Teams is a chat-based collaboration solution, 24
Template Selection, 88
templates, 5, 7, 8, 32, 33, 34, 77, 78, 87, 88, 136, 153
Templates, 135, 136, 137, 154
Tenant settings, 54
term set management options, 42
term set options, 41
Term Store, 41, 42, 43, 155
Term Store - term set options for managing terms, 41
Term Store Management, 41, 155
terrific notion, 91
Test Backup and Restore Processes, 130
text documents, 95
Thank goodness everything is in place now, 53
the "**Backup Options**" page, 131
the "**Site contents**" page., 4
The "**Sites You're Following**" section, 11
the acquisition of Datazen respectively., 92
The **Add Promoted Result** dialog box, 120
The Add Query Rule page is displayed., 120
The app is incompatible with the SharePoint Server's unverified SSL certificate, 19
The built-in groups should not be altered or removed, 56
The center panel, 93
The center panel – examples and links to helpful information, 93
The **Create link**, 142
The **Data navigational link**, 136
The degree of customization, 96
the **Document Library** app, 69, 78
the **Document Set's Welcome Page**, 100
the Document Version History area, 75

the drop-down menu, 53, 64, 65, 69, 89, 101, 102, 139
The environment for development, 141
The **FAST** technology, 114
The flexibility to add or remove columns, 33
The Full-Screen UI view of SharePoint, 147
the Grid view, 36
the **Home link**, 135
The **ID, Created, and Modified** columns, 36
The last stage in a document's lifecycle is the record stage, 112
the **Learn link**, 142
the **Learn travel link**, 137
the List Settings page, 34, 72, 147
the menu options, 135
The Microsoft Office 97–2003 file types, 105
the Microsoft Power Apps service, 141
The Microsoft Power Automate page, 137
The **Microsoft Power Platform,,** 3
The **Monitor option**, 136
The new wave of workflow is Microsoft Power Automate, 134
The objective is to provide organizations and businesses with the necessary tools, 1
The owners, 63
The Permissions pane opens., 85
the PO date, 49
the process of adding applications, 157
The sales figures for China are excellent, 116
The **search functionality**, 10
The Search interface in the SharePoint App, 17
The **Shared with Me flows**, 136
The SharePoint platform, 25
the SharePoint Server Publishing Feature is activated., 155
The SharePoint Server Publishing Infrastructure tool, 148
the **Site Collection Administration** part, 150
The **site creation feature**, 10
the **Site Settings** page, 101, 119, 148, 149, 150, 152, 153, 155, 156
the **Sites I'm following or Promoted sites** on the Sites page, 14
the standard method of constructing a site is more like creating a site collection,, 5
the use of SharePoint, 157
There are two broad categories into which metadata can be divided, 40

Third-Party Backup Solutions, 129, 132
third-party screen grab software, 104
three organizations, 24
timelines, 33
To test, make fake data., 130
Toggle between the PC and mobile views., 15
Top Link bar, 151, 152
Translation Status, 155
Translation Status setting, 155
Tree View, 151, 152
Trojan horses, 104
turn on IRM, 104, 107
Turn on IRM service using the SharePoint admin center, 104
Two of SharePoint's most popular features are lists and libraries, 30
Type a formula into the Formula box to make a confirmation formula, 80
Type in the person's email address that you want to share the site with, 86
Type the description of the result block into the description text box, 121
Type the URL of your SharePoint site into the address bar and press Enter., 9

U

UDC, 95
Understanding How SharePoint Search Works, 114
Understanding SharePoint Backup, 127
Understanding SharePoint Library, 31
Understanding SharePoint list, 30
Understanding SharePoint List Permission Levels, 39
UNDERSTANDING SHAREPOINT SITES, 82
Understanding SharePoint Sites and Hierarchy, 4
Universal Data Connection, 95
unusual data, 19
up and running, 104, 123
Upload Documents to a Drop-Off Library, 101
Upload some documents, 53
Uploading and Managing Documents, 12
Uploading documents, 85
Uploading Files, 20
upper-right-hand corner of the screen, 87, 144
usability of the Business Intelligence Center, 96
Use a phased roll-out plan and telemetry, 124
use information rights management (IRM),, 103

Use the IRM service that was set up in your setup, 104
User Alerts, 155
User Who Can Read Items, 75
user-made applications, 3
username and password, 9
Users and Permissions, 64
Users can arrange their files in more practical and aesthetically pleasing ways, 42
Users can use Planner boards to create and manage tasks, 4
users working on intranet sites, 18
using Dashboard Designer, 94
using **Image Renditions**, 151
using IRM tools with SharePoint Online, 104
using lists in SharePoint, 11
using Microsoft SharePoint Online., 13
Using Power Apps on your Mobile Device, 146
using PowerApps, 81
using PowerApps" radio button, 81
Using **SharePoint**, 24
Using the Traditional SharePoint-Only, 139
utilize a different version of the file, 101
utilize SharePoint metadata, 44
Utilize the data obtained, 47
Utilize the information for your company across all of your websites in one location., 45
Utilize the search bar within Teams to search for specific files, 21
Utilize your tablet or mobile device, 13

V

Validation settings, 79
valuable documents and information, 1
various data kinds, 11
various options prompting, 10
various types of dashboards, 92
Veeam, 127, 129
Vendor, 46
version control, 2, 11, 25
Version control, 11
Version Control, 2
Version History and Comments, 21
version of SharePoint on-premises, 81
Versioning, 31, 50, 73, 74, 75
view of contemporary lists, 35
View Only, 61

Viewing and Refining Search Results, 117
virtual hub, 157
Visio models, 97
Visio Services, 91
Visit the Central Administration website, 127
Visit the **site's settings** page, 113
Visitors, 39, 55, 56, 63

W

web browser, 13, 15, 87, 88, 89, 135, 137, 141, 144, 145, 147
Web Browser, 9, 147
Web Designer Galleries, 47, 150, 153, 155
Web Designer Galleries area of the Site Settings page, 155
Web Interface, 9
Web Interface and Desktop Applications, 9
Web Part page by using the Ribbon commands, 95
Web Parts, 80, 82, 85, 96, 154
web-based tool, 151
Welcome Page, 97, 100, 151
Welcome Page's appearance, 100
What can you do with a Document Set?, 97
What is managed metadata?, 40
What is the difference between site collections and sites?, 5
What not to do, 123
whole Document Set, 98
Why manage metadata?, 43
Why should companies adopt a SharePoint Intranet Portal?, 125
Why use metadata instead of folders, 42
wide range of use cases., 8
Wikis for businesses allow for collaborative editing and content production., 8
Wildcard searches, 115
Windows program, 84
Word documents, 97
WORDS(CA, California), 117
work of a large dataset, 91
Work Progress Tracker Template, 33
work with SharePoint Lists, 34
Workflow, 73, 134, 139, 155
Workflow Settings,, 155
WORKING WITH LISTS AND LIBRARIES, 30
Working with SharePoint Teams and Groups, 24

173

Writing down or copying things that are on a screen, 104

X

XML, 90, 105
XSLT, 153

Y

Yammer, 4
You belong to a large organization with numerous departments and multiple business units, 6
You can access the "Next Steps" panel, 26
You can access your intranet with the press of a button, 16
You can add a reason for your wish if you want to. After that, click **Send request**., 72
you can add details about the file,, 12
You can add the app to your site once it's been accepted., 72
you can choose a theme from Microsoft's list, 30
you can configure additional settings for the column, 35
You can control who can access and interact, 39
You can find specific links that provide information, 94
You create documents and information that are hundreds of gigabytes in size, 6
you create on the website, 95
You must collaborate with other parties by sharing content, 7
you'll receive a confirmation message, 12
Your business needs an active Office 365 subscription, 16
Your Recent Sites, 11
your site's sharing features will vary, 56

Made in the USA
Coppell, TX
10 September 2024